"A Healing"

James Woods

A.K.A.

Jimmie Joe

Jim

"A Healing," by James Woods. ISBN 1-58939-806-8 (softcover); 1-58939-807-6 (hardcover).

Library of Congress Control Number on file with publisher.

Published 2006 by Virtualbookworm.com Publishing Inc., P.O. Box 9949, College Station, TX 77842, US. ©2006, James Woods. All rights reserved. No part of this publication may be reproduced, stored in a retrieval system, or transmitted in any form or by any means, electronic, mechanical, recording or otherwise, without the prior written permission of James Woods.

Manufactured in the United States of America

Dedicated to our Commander in Chief;
George Walker Bush
and our
"Grunts in the Sand".

In my appreciation for the wisdom and political courage *President George W.* demonstrated in recognizing, than acting upon, the danger from extreme Islamic fundamentalists to our way of life, our freedoms and our future generations survival.

The most radical Sect of Islam, the "Wahhabis" operate nearly all Islamic Madras's (schools) worldwide, teaching their young students insidious hatred directed toward the long-term annihilation of infidels including all Islamite's who live in peace with Infidels. Madras's have, in affect, been training imminent "little terrorists" for several generations. The future consequences of these madras's *will* be a depraved hypnotic despot emerging as leader who will be granted this abundant supply of activist indoctrinated young males who, whether they are aware or not, are awaiting the call to "Allah's tenet". They will answer.

Their belief in self-destruction while engaged in warfare against the infidel as a one-way ticket direct to heaven assures they will be formidable enemies. With our failure to accept and confront this danger the "Wahhabis" will begin achieving their goal of world domination for Allah and with this domination will be coerced conversion to the Wahhabis sect of Islam, if conversion is refused, death by slitting ones throat or beheading will be the Infidels reward.

Their ingrained religiously fanatical drive combined with visceral brutality will easily overcome the less fixated, more peaceful oil producing Persians and Arab countries from within. We will be allowing the "Wahhabis" control over most of the world's crude oil, thus an unlimited source of income with the accompanying power money purchases. This will not only wreak havoc on the worlds economy, it will in time most assuredly give "Wahhabis terrorists" access to various atomic weaponry and the Armament systems for delivery of their warheads to any coordinates points on Earth.

With the "Wahhabis" zealous dedication, tunneled vision to their cause, viciousness with a total lack of human compassion for "Unbelievers", does anyone actually believe they will not use atomic weapons in achieving their "covenant with Allah"? They believe "Allah" demands their view of Islam and under the pains of Hell "Allah" will be obeyed. Their mass deaths in an atomic holocaust has the blessing of instant deliverance straight to heaven and the incalculable number of infidel dead is a "Glory to Allah" much more satisfactory to their demented egos than a vehicle filled with a few tons of explosives. This obedience of "Allah's" wishes as interpreted by the "Wahhabis" have no time constraints, one, ten, or a hundred years makes no difference, so my friends at what stage do we prevent the "atomic holocaust?

Prevention of the "Wahhabis" or any terrorist groups' threat or attempt to gain control of the Middle East crude oil supply will require a procession of outstanding Western leaders far into the future; my reverent prayer is we continue finding such men.

Every new leader must have a through understanding of a "Wahhabis type" enemy and the religious convictions behind their reasoning for the conquest of our Human race. The "Wahhabis Sect" will attempt to dictate Allah's objectives using their definition of Islamic teachings.

Every new leader put forth by the West must also have a spine as stiff and an ideology as true as the one George Walker Bush and Tony Charles Lynton Blair share with freedoms cause.

Terrorists are <u>not Soldiers,</u> they have no identification, no rules, no compassion for the innocent and they melt into the civilian populace after doing their deed. A Soldier has no way of recognizing Terrorists as the enemy so he must either; catch Terrorists in the act, catch Terrorists with terrorists supplies, or depend on intelligence from the local populace before he can kill or capture Terrorists. A new method of warfare *"but we will learn"* and we will defeat this scourge on mankind.

Please George W. don't let America fold again!!
James Woods

In fond remembrance:

Norma Jean Zentmyer
Helen L. Ritter
June Weaver

With due credits;

Any single poem of this publication may be reproduced, transmitted, transcribed or translated into any language in any form without the written permission from the author, an amount more than one poem must have written permission.

Certain facts are gleaned from the Internets military history section.

http://about.delphi.com/n/main.asp?=abusmilitary&nav=messages&msg=2092.1

http://www.cfcsc.dnd.ca/links/milhist/korea.html

http://www.kimsoft.com/korea/kr-warv.htm

http://www.koreanwar-educator.org/Home.htm

www.thehistorynet.com/MilitaryHistory/articles/2000/0400_text.html

http://www.geocities.com/Pentagon/1953/

http://www.thehistorynet.com/MilitaryHistory/articles/0496_cover.htm

"Korea the First Year" By;--James F. Schnabel"

Jimmie Joes 'e-mail

alaska1960@yahoo.com

---

*This book contains some prose and poetry of
my first two Books below.*

"Love, War and Little Children" [ISBN # 0-75961-203-x]

"A Boy and His Journey" [ISBN # 0-7596-5966-4]

TEXT OF THE KOREAN WAR ARMISTICE AGREEMENT
Signed, July 27, 1953
Article III Relating to Prisoners of War (Page 272)

Wayne A. " Johnnie" Johnson's' List
1931-2005

Containing four hundred ninety-six names of those who died on the nearly four hundred mile "Death March North" from the Taejon area of South Korea northerly to the Yalu River including three years of incarceration in North Korean and Chinese Prisoners-of-War "Camps".

Death thru execution, dysentery and other medical neglect was a daily occurrence and "Johnnie" for three years duly recorded those names along with the date of deaths and the outfit they belonged to on his two hidden forbidden "lists. (Page 246)

Johnnie was not a one shot hero, he risked his life with every name recorded on the duel lists he kept, nearly a thousand times he risked detection in the course of three years. Johnnie Johnson was a "long term hero" and should be considered for the "Congressional Medal of Honour", plus the Silver Star he was awarded!

Jimmie Joe

Bear with me friends

In the beginning my writings were neither written as/nor intended to be a book, chronologically you will find time-lines overlap, possibly several times. You may find the examination of a particular ghost ("demon") could be repeated thru overlapping of time as my *search* approaches from a different direction causing an altered emotional response to be examined on paper white with pain in black, this book is about discovering and curing pains location, it is about "A Healing".

I began writing thru a *desperate need* for survival without conscious direction or objective and I admit absolutely none of my prose came close to meeting that *desperate need*. The non-expressive confused prose writings morphed into poetry; I do not understand it but after several hundred pages of discarded typed prose and many published pages of poetry on the web I was able to write prose giving expression to emotions that made sense, for reasons unknown I needed to create the poetry first.

Many of these writings are a series of distraught emotions unwrapped from time, they fell out quite well mixed in their own right, some words just seemed to drop from my mind onto the paper without thought, rhyme, nor reason.

I was never adept in English class, most of the time I was skipping school and going fishing with my dog "Old Gent". Between skipping all that school, hunting, fishing for those fine "bluegills" and joining the Army at the end of two years spent in the tenth grade, it's a bit amazing I can read or write at all. I ask your patience with that which I attempt.

The latter half of this book is a Partial compilation of articles written by James Woods over a span of several years as he sought to sort out and face the "leftovers of his war-zone".

This is the third and final book of my "healing time" and hopefully it will assist some of my fellow Veterans, who may be troubled by their war, find the path leading to a first step toward a healing.

Jimmie Joe

About this book

Autobiography of "A Healing"

This book is an attempt to give thoughtful insight into this combat infantryman's personal chronicle concerning "leftovers of a war-zone" inadvertently carried to civilian life from distant battle grounds, these leftovers shall here-fore-to be referred to in a very personal and uncomplimentary manner as "demons".

Said "demons" first appeared shortly after I arrived stateside from Korea in 1951, thru the next five decades a fluctuating solitary battle of coping was taking place inside my head and I wasn't winning. No one would know of these "demons" or the extent of this turmoil until I finally faced and partially defeated them during my poetic writings as I constructed my web pages in 1998/99. Later during the writing of my first two books from 2000 to 2003 I was able to delve more deeply into pain as my courage began to exert itself and I faced "two Small Children".

I unwittingly won "my solitary war" in 2004 and sometime during 2005 this winning crystallized in my conscious mind; I must note this unconditional winning may have been *enhanced or delayed* by my near death experience on February 11th 2004, which irrevocably changed my thoughts and understanding of death. I found death wasn't necessarily a "bad" experience; therefore I cannot be sure what caused the healing to be absolute.

I know I am very grateful for my mind being rendered all encompassing as it applies to freedom from the randomly recurring distress I had carried in my head for nearly a lifetime.

I realized in 2005 this book would be the closing chapter of my life therefore I needed to disclose all, pass this narrative on to my children, my friends from the past and the future.

I've tried my best to be candid with the recalling of emotions at different junctions of my life, I've tried to be honest with my memories but many years have passed and some memories could be clouded with time, I don't think so but they could be.

The memories of unidentifiable pain stored in the "dark compartment of my brain" were never clouded, were never very far from conscious reality and are the reasons writing became a desperate need for my survival, a need that has been fulfilled.

This saga covers *my lack of courage to face wars "demons,"* Nineteen Fifty-one began the "demons" first decade; this was a decade of adjusting to living with the turmoil of "demons".

The second and third decades were my acceptance of the painful turmoil caused by the "demons", I learned to shove them into their compartment where, if I kept my mind occupied, they stayed and when they "flashed out" I became much better at getting them back into their box, relative speaking life was good.

In the early part of the fourth decade the last of my children left home, I retired from work and for the first time in my life I was alone with my "demons". Being alone was quite detrimental to my mind, as I began the downhill slide I continued into a near capitulation to the "demons" in a virtually fatal battle and as I approached the latter half of the fourth decade life was no longer good, it was almost as bad as life gets.

I continue on to the fifth decade where I won the confrontation, a confrontation I should have fought years earlier. I must admit *I didn't even try* as there was no concept within my mind I could change any "leftovers from the battle-grounds". I had a haunting fear I might be a "section-eight" case, apparently I wasn't but it did bother me enough to cause concern and for me to question myself about it.

I seemed to have been oblivious, probably ashamed of an *admitted need,* or was merely incapable of locating any method I could have used at the time; I was convinced it was "just I"

Sadly, thru ignorance mixed with unidentifiable fear of the unknown, I forced any traumatic thoughts back into a hidden arena in some dark corner of my brain, as long as I kept thoughts and emotions there I would be safe from *societies threat of ridicule, from their knowing I just didn't measure up to their concept of how a "man" should believe and behave.

I would not however be safe from the traumatic pain the images always arrived with nor from the times I had to refuse to break down and cry like a baby when the long dead children appeared, they lived inside my head off and on for five decades.

I found myself with no choice except to live those years in the midst of fluctuating mental anguish with its accompanying painful turmoil and *that damn stiff upper lip* American society decreed us to wa!k around with in those days.

*Societies only threat was my perceived belief they would think less of me for not living up to their idea of what a "man" should be. Hell, I was already bothered by that; inside I wasn't living up to what I thought I should be but society wasn't aware of it. We were dumb as moose turds in those days; there is just no other for to word it!

When we were discharged we no longer had the "Squad of Brothers" support, we basically lost them as soon as we rotated out of the war zone, and we were mentally alone. We were discarded into a culture that professed being totally civilized from which a *small but vital part of our emotions* would continue to be isolated; an unknown number of us were left in a reality we could not absorb. This reality was like a movie film which soaked up and recorded the pains of war and held off the showing for a future time, then when we saw what we and others had done, the pain we had seen and inflicted would become our own, deserved or not it was ours; to adjust to, come to terms with or defeat.

The carefree world of the nineteen-year old "Boy" was not, and would never again be, the world of the twenty-year old Veteran, the Veteran "home" from the trials and tribulations one suffers with exposure to any war zone, in any war.

The resulting healing is the criteria, neither the methods I used to find my way, the conflicts I investigated nor the stumbling route I seemed obligated to travel in my search are important. I bounced off many walls while walking countless paths-of-pain before finding the place in my mind where ease prevailed and war had no corner left in which to hide. --- I was "home".

James Woods/aka/ *Jimmie Joe*

"A Healing"

The type of urban warfare we are fighting in Iraq has unavoidably caused thousands of deaths among civilians; men, women and children have been killed or gravely wounded. Our Warriors who view this will have these images seared somewhere in their minds blended in with the wounding and deaths of their Buddies. These disturbingly tragic images will be carried home from the war zone and for some painfully interrupting their lives as civilians. An unknown number will need special understanding with counseling, to not only mollify the recurrent images ("demons") with the resulting painful turmoil they carry, but more importantly to help their minds accept what has happened in "their war" can not be changed and must be faced before there is any chance "A Healing" will take place.

For most of us the "guilt and pain" we carried home from war was never earned nor was it deserved, it seems to be a natural by-product of war that affects different people with varying degrees of intensity regardless of whether they had short or long term exposure to a war zone or actual combat on the ground.

Until we absolve ourselves of "guilt and pain" we will never quite make it "home", so my friend as you read on please realize the path I walked in suppressed pain for years has been or is being walked by unknown numbers of; Veterans of World War Two, Korean War Veterans, Vietnam Veterans and will be trod by Iraqi Veterans in numbers that will remain unknown. This path is not pleasant to walk nor is it pleasant for those we love to live near, *there are exits along the pathway and **if you are made aware** you can find yours, when you do the painful memories will be replaced with an acceptable sadness.* That may not sound like much but it's a whole new world and life takes on more joyous meaning with the "demons" gone.

The two Korean Children left my conscious mind soon after we'd departed the crossroads in October of 1950 and didn't appear inside my head for over three years. They first appeared

A Healing

in dreams after the Korean War ended in Nineteen-fifty-three, the dreams went away but visions of the two small children, exactly as they appeared huddled together by the ditch in Nineteen-fifty, would spontaneously materialize clearly in my mind for over five decades. I wouldn't be thinking about them, they'd just flash in, that happened with other memories but the Children were by far the most pain producing.

The vision of their broken bodies slowly faded with time leaving only four pain filled haunting "eyes", those accusing eyes silently pleading for help I could not give were what I battled, a recurring battle I could not win.

Fifty years ago there was little knowledge regarding the effects on a mind of "post traumatic stress disorder" (PTSD), there was no combining of those four words or the initials, I was unaware of any counselors or counseling, there was a section 8 (the psycho ward), always referred to with extreme negativism.

We now know more concerning a minds adjusting after the battles have ended but I don't believe we're quite there.

I question the science of the discipline of psychotherapy as it is used to treat PTSD, in the past they have used too damn many drugs and fried to damn many brains, I do not forgive the VA for their mistreatment of those Veterans entrusted to their care.

I am hopeful the VA has evolved in its treatment of injured minds so Veterans of the Iraqi War with wounded minds will be made whole and welcomed "Home" in a shortened span of time.

All my writings have been directed to the pathways concerning my long-term inability to find my "time for peace" after my "time of war". I was a good Soldier in the war zone, as a civilian in the peace I was a lost bewildered Veteran with a hidden war living inside where none would know or see.

What were accepted everyday happenings in times of war, in times of peace became ghostly "demons" trapped inside some part of my mind, erupting in spontaneous mental images off and

James Woods

on for decades during waking hours and for the first several years filling some nights with a realism of repeating dreams in battles that never took place. These were battles where I was always alone, fighting a platoon of Chinese in a vee formation with bayonets fixed, taking place on gray shell pocked landscapes with the trees blasted into snags and stumps. I would feel fear in this dream but it wasn't all encompassing, it was easy to deal with.

I never won those battles, nor did I ever lose. I was without a weapon but I needed to stop them, so as I ran I would stop, pick up a dead enemies rifle, turn, go down on my right knee, aim and fire at the lead Chinese. The bullet would go about twenty or thirty feet out barrel and drop to the ground, I would swear, try to rack in another round but it would jam. I would be off and running again and the whole process would be repeated again and again, at times this battle seemed to last all night.

This repeating dream was one in which I would get hit by a artillery round and my body would completely disappear in the explosion, all that was left were my distorted shriek shaped lips mutely screaming into a soundless totally black void, it was a dream that filled me with uncontrolled terror in my sleep. This was the only dream that caused me to scream, it was the only dream causing me to awaken setting bolt upright in bed sweating and shaking as if I had malaria. The first couple times I blubbered unexpected tears before regaining composure, in later times I still awoke with a scream but there were no tears.

I don't know how many times I had this dream, probably less times then I seem to recall, the vividness and lucidity is starkly with me today after about fifty years. The long term "imprint on a Mind" from a year in a war zone and the varying unfavorable reactions from different minds is an enigma I accept.

My repeating dreams did not occur every night, they did however occur to often, for a while they were a son-of-a-bitch to live with and nights at times were looked forward to with a certain amount of apprehension.

A Healing

I thought only I was the one with these "demons", I was convinced my inability to cope was of my causing, my weakness, my lacking the strength or resolve to make them stop.

The Nineteen-Fifties and Sixties were still a time of "keeping a stiff upper lip", society's false profile of a "real man" damaged unknown numbers of young Veterans leaving many of us with compartmentalized minds filled with distressful turmoil, trapping, confining and then, in silent torment we suppressed the flashing purgatorial images of "our" war zone from the world outside, a world we quickly learned, which would never understand.

To our detriment we carried out the task of maintaining our perception regarding societies norm, we accommodated societies expectations of what a Warrior/Veteran/Man should be, we would have been ashamed not to. A crack in our armor, a momentary breaking down, a few sudden tears gushing out before we could stop them were not acceptable, it was not the way a "man" should act. Those around us felt that way and I must confess we felt that way ourselves, it was a demand fostered by society in those days, without a doubt we have echo's from those times still with us in this day and age.

We carried wars hidden garbage for decades and allowed none to see inside where a "Boy" struggled with his pain, fear and isolation, hidden away from any chance of healing were wounds of war that left no visible battle scars.

I was wrong all those years about myself, I wasn't alone with emotions of inadequacy due to my inability to control the memories of war or stop the hurt. I measure up quite acceptably with other Veterans of combat, we all have varying amounts of "shit" in our "honey-buckets" with no parleyed instructions, no given opportunity of locating a decent time or place to dump it.

As the bucket became full we were obligated to continue carrying it, we had no alternative as it was part of who we were and who we are, we could only attempt to conceal it from the world outside our heads.

Unknown numbers of Veterans suffered this burden to varying degrees, some for a lifetime, never knowing how or where to dump their garbage. Most of us never admitted we had a bucket until one day it became too heavy to ignore and the bill of laden for all that "shit" from our past came due, the weight of life at this time seemed unbearable and regrettably some of us turned down the wrong path in dealing with --------------

Death, at that instant in time, becomes the "Buddy we need" and sadly "life is surrendered to our heads fatal demand from a temporary despondency", this despondency traced back to our unidentified long-term depression, to unknown, untreated PTSD.

These Warriors at the end were sure suicide was their only recourse for neutralizing the "demons" living inside their head, their only chance for peace and atonement and *most of them don't even become a statistic of their own war, may they find the peace we could not give them as God Holds Them and Blesses them.*

Jimmie Joe

A Healing

My daughter Cynthia with my grandchildren, Christopher and Jessica left my home in 1985 and as my retirement progressed I slowly lost what I *seemed* to have been all my life, an adjusted, sober parent who had raised "up to seven" children from 1967 thru 1981 without a helpmate.

This section I did not want to divulge as my family will see it, I say to them "I love you" and please don't let it bother you too much as it is a families normal reaction to a father who has turned into a slightly weird drunk and they have no idea why he changed, he's not pleasant to be around so they stay away.

Beginning about 1986 thru 1989 I slowly spiraled downward toward the impatient "demons" waiting with their deadly demand and a fateful night in October 1989. During this period of my life I basically felt shunned by my children, the ones in Alaska and the ones living outside. A couple would visit a few times but I guess it was not too pleasurable, I didn't know I needed someone to understand what was taking place in my head, that I needed help. I continued on in ignorance, without help, down a pathway guiding me to a rendezvous with my own mortality.

Beginning with the latter half of 1986 in the course of a few years time I became what *I would have described* as a weak-willed person who capitulated to buried PTSD and booze, now I would just say I was sick, it's okay to be sick. I started drinking being well aware booze could cause me to become an alcoholic but apparently I was at some stage of depression and naively felt the tradeoff worth the risk. I am very thankful I didn't become addicted to the booze, however I was the "Fishhook Bars" calculatedly dedicated drunk for a few years.

*By 1988 I was on **my** bar stool at the "Fishhook Bar" twelve to sixteen hours a day, I dreaded going home each night after the bar closed and facing my increasingly hostile "demons" in one-sided battles that seemed to ensue more and more frequently, it was a struggle I always lost. I never stood a prayer.*

James Woods

As I went into the summer of 1989 dedicated drinking became a cause without joy and the booze no longer seemed to mollify the "demons" from my cabin at night. One fall night in October 1989 the ramparts I had built thru all those years crumbled and I was left without any defense against a foe it seemed I could neither recognize nor defeat. I was incapable of even defining this foe who demanded such a high price.

I couldn't then and still can't delineate any logic to the painful turmoil those "demons" caused inside my head; why all this "shit" should have taken place, why it took so many years for me to realize my honey-bucket had been filled decades ago, why psychologically at this point in time had that damned bucket seemed too heavy to carry or endure, and why had I weakened and caved so thoroughly to a foe existing only in my head.

His forty-one mag he took to bed,
silently told his friends good-bye.
Cocked it and pressed it to his head
about an inch behind right eye.

This is the night I believe hopelessness was all my brain exuded, I didn't even attempt to think of a reason for living in a world that had closed in upon me with such painful fury, I was tired, extremely tired. I was living in a world that for the past few years had battered my defenses, building the confusion with pain to the point it was unbearable and I didn't even know why. I still don't know why the confusion, I still don't know why the pain thru all those years, all I knew at the time was I had to stop it.

I cocked my forty-one mag, raised it to my temple, took the slack up from the trigger, and told my children and friends goodbye.

I was hollow inside, without hope or even the desire to want to hope, *I didn't pray to God or think of the affect this would have on my children or friends,* that would come later, thank God it did.

A Healing

I slowly squeezed the trigger engaging the seer, the hammer would ride part way over it, I never knew how close I was to busting a cap, I would go so far then slack off, then start again. How many times I rolled the seer partially up the hammer I don't know but I am so very thankful I never tripped the hammer.

This was *my time of extreme hopelessness and is one of life's most defining moments in my mind, more so chronologically it's a clearly defining moment in my life's time-span.*

As chilling as it is for me to admit, for all purposes except pure blind luck, I committed suicide that night, my brain went thru all the necessary steps and I met all the garbage that leads one to the act of suicide.

Somewhere, imbedded thru all the confusing desolation inside my brain, the simple thought of who would find my body, my Daughter? or a Friend?, burst thru and connected, I slowly turned the gun away, lowered the hammer and in total exhaustion proceeded to sob like a weakened baby, Amen jimmie joe, Amen.

I am eternally grateful to whatever or whoever stayed my finger from adding that extra bit of pressure on the trigger thus keeping the hammer from dropping. I've thanked "God" many times for this life I still have, I've thanked everyone and everything possibly contributing to my life being spared.

Jimmie Joe

The book *"Suicide Wall"*, by Alexander Paul is a must for Veterans, anyone for that matter and all who care for those with suicidal tendencies or those who have already committed the act.

http://www.suicidewall.com/SWStats.html

While doing research for his novel, Suicide Wall, Alexander Paul contacted Point Man International and was given the name of a retired VA doctor, and conducted a phone interview with him. In that interview, the doctor related that his estimate of the number of Vietnam Veteran suicides was 200,000 men, and that the reason the official suicide statistics were so much lower was that in many cases the suicides were documented as accidents, primarily single-car drunk driving accidents and self inflicted gunshot wounds that were not accompanied by a suicide note or statement.
According to the doctor, the under reporting of suicides was primarily an act of kindness to the surviving relatives.

There is no diligent agency tracking suicides by Vietnam veterans so the estimates are all over the place, from a low of 20,000 to a high of 200,000 as of 1998. I found no record of suicides by WWII or Korean War Veterans.

I now know I was very long way from being alone with this hidden affliction, mine was not debilitating nor did it keep me from working and most of the time enjoying life.

Suppressing wars memories was a struggle with varying degrees of turmoil thru the years as those memories were imprinted quite deep, always there, always appearing unbidden and always causing the mind some detriment with pain, why the pain I do not know. I observed literally hundreds of dead in the combat zone and was only bothered in a peripheral way, those two small children for reasons unknown to me were a torture to my Soul for five decades.

A Healing

In the beginning I had no thoughts or concept of writing for its therapeutic affects, but my friend writing has preformed something close to a small miracle of enhanced tranquility in my mental outlook and has made these later years of life much more pleasant. It has been well worth the fear, pain and tears shed during my writings to have achieved the serenity these lines seem to have produced within me.

Healing was a gradual drawn-out process, not noticeable in the beginning with the writings for my web page in Nineteen Ninety-eight and Ninety-nine. A small amount of healing occurred thru the first book, quite a bit more thru the second book. With my writings thru this book mending seems to continue and as my writings approached the end of this book I feel I must be nearing the optimum as I feel very close to being at complete peace with my past.

I don't know when the "darkened compartment" with its pain, guilt and fear left my mind, however for the last several years' serenity has blessed me more and more and if an event flashes my mind back to the remembrances of the war zone, the emotional pain that use to accommodate certain mental images is now only a twinge of sadness.

My life was not ruined by wars memories, uncomfortable at times but worth the living most of the years. I've had a wife, held my child and caught those fish in places wild, overall it's been more than a good life.

James Woods

James Woods

"A Healing"

With my research beyond the Eisenhower Papers it became necessary to know events of the pre, during and post Korean War period. I learned, due to lack of funding, malfeasance, or simply lacking any wisdom whatsoever congress left us intentionally unprepared for war, including WWI, WWII, Korea and Vietnam.

This lacking caused thousands to die due to the absence of a standing well trained military being formed during the years America was at peace. When we knew a few years in advance we would be at war, as with WWI and WWII, we did not prepare due to Congresses unwillingness to fund the cost of *adequate preparedness*.

In *peacetime prior to President Reagan's tenure*, America held her military in low esteem, not worth the dollars a well-trained, well-equipped military would cost. We paid dearly with the lives of our young men and many times over in the cost-plus expense of quickly building the military to proficiency.

Koreas' first few months were fought with an under-trained army of occupation forces in poor physical condition using worn-out WWII arms and ordinance. Throughout most of the Twentieth Century Congress in peacetime refused to fund either adequate personnel, oversight of sufficient training, or research and development of armaments and communications required by our military to not only survive, but to win a war, to win with the least loss in lives of our young men who do the fighting.

We learned operational combat methods via on-the-job-training and many young boys would pay with their lives for our politicians' previous malfeasance. I believe the main *lacking those first months of the Korean War* and most responsible for men dying needlessly were communications, miles of WWII como wire with hidden breaks and pathetic old WWII radios having batteries that wouldn't hold a charge. Distressingly tied for first place would be the inability of small units, surrounded or cut off, to fight a defensive battle *as a team* or fight their way out of any tight places, again and always *as a team*.

A Healing

Inadequate training in peacetime gets us killed in war and lets the enemy live. This need to send under-trained troops into battle reflect directly on the politicians who have held the purse strings, the unnecessary deaths of these young men was a betrayal by the same politicians.

In the first hectic months of the "Korean Police Action" communicating between units was, in many cases, not possible, leaving units cut off and trapped with no way to convey their need for relief. An unacceptable number of confusing situations and deaths resulted from units lacking the ability to simply talk with each other.

How ignorant I was of the politics of a limited war, of any war for that matter. The politics of war begin years before the start of a war; they begin with the politician's attitude regarding oversight with constant updating preparedness for the military. Politicians must have ingrained honour and respect for our military's sacrifices in the past and those which will be demanded in the future. They also begin with funding to train and retain professional military cadre who will train draftees when needed and with enough *trained units* to repel or slow the enemy down long enough for the cadre to train the draftees.

From the Gulf War in 1991 to present our military has been well trained, exceptionally efficient and well equipped!!

I arrived home from Korea about August of 1951 and my civilian peers barely recognize our country as being in a state of war. It was as if I had entered the "Twilight Zone" and only I was in the real world, of course the opposite is true my world had become disoriented. I had a good deal of trouble accepting the fact they did not care about the "Boy's" dying overseas, of course they would never word it that way.

While a few million innocent Koreans; old men, women and children died in protracted pain and horror ... *my homeland yawned, partied and rightfully worried about the draft.*

James Woods

Most subjects I cover in my writings by necessity are unpleasant, not what my life's been about. The years nineteen-fifty/fifty-one spent as a Combat Infantryman in Korea were only a background, a place with events I labored to keep out of my conscious mind. They were always there, always crowding my Soul a bit and I was always feeling the confused distress about the *unidentifiable emotional pain* that seemed to accompany certain spontaneous war memories. My Soul at times seemed to exist close to purgatory, this Soul in distress I refer to as "Boy".

This was a reality I kept hidden, this place where "Boy" was in turmoil with his war, a war long over for me the "Man" but a realism that would not leave the "Boy". This hidden reality built to desperation in the foreground one fall night in 1989 (38 years after I'd left the battle-ground) and thankfully my *"unseen ones"* (Angels?) bestowed the courage to still the hand of "Boy" and let me live to realize an old Warriors' needed atonement with the added future gift of my "time of peace".

It would take about nine additional years to begin my writings and six years later this, my third and last book, to accomplish my final mending. The amazing education (for myself) is the books were basically the same, in the second book I had not been absent from my "demons" long enough to express my analysis of life with nearly all my "demons" gone, *hopefully enough time has passed and I am far enough from the emotional adjustment to record accurate philosophies of what seems missing in the first two books. I felt clarity, in many cases was lacking, and it should have been for the enigma of my thoughts had not yet been solved.*

I don't know why it took over fifty years to come full circle, I fought my way thru alone, I wrote alone and except for one time I cried alone. At some point I found I could not release "Boy's" reality, I seemed trapped in the need to finish this chore.

A Healing

Most of my writings were required before the courage came and I was able to expose, segregate, then isolate my semi-veiled "demons", it was then I could face them. I may have rambled and babbled a little but it's only because I didn't know what path to take, where it would lead and at times, *why I was writing.*

I thought something was wrong with me,
a weakness I must hide.
The hurting, flitting pain I'd see,
I must hold back deep inside.

My friends;

The resulting healing is the criteria, neither the methods I used to find my way, the conflicts I investigated nor the stumbling route I seemed obligated to travel in my search are important. I bounced off many walls while walking countless paths-of-pain before finding the place in my mind where ease prevailed and war had no corner left in which to hide. --- I was "home".

James Woods/aka/ *Jimmie Joe*

James Woods

"A Healing"

"An Accepted betrayal?"

"EISENHOWER'S PRESIDENTIAL PAPERS" REGARDING HIS knowledge of the nine hundred and ten Prisoners of War abandoned in North Korea in Nineteen Fifty-three, which I read in Nineteen Ninety-seven, were the distressing stimuli I needed to get on track to launch my writings. I was so full of pain, disbelief, and rage with my country I needed an outlet. Disbelief and rage are gone, the disappointment about that time in our history will probably remain until my ashes are scattered over several favorite fishing areas of *my Alaska.*

My rage subsided long before I finished writing; there is however deep anger when I think of those "Boy's" lives after their betrayal. I still can't believe our government would commit such a reprehensible act; they did and it is not a rare occurrence, they carried it out several times in the twentieth century. Our obligation forward is to take steps to assure we never again abandon our P.O.W.s to the enemy.

I am no longer naïve about our government's willingness to sacrifice her *"little Tin Soldiers"* for political expediency. They feel safe with their "secret files" not to be opened for forty years, sadly, I am convinced they believed these sacrifices worth this "betrayal" of our men so as not to rock the boat after achieving the long sought Korean armistice.

Many lives were saved by not resuming the war to obtain those POWs release, however I cannot weigh their decision in favor of lives saved at the cost of Honour with the sacrifice of our POWs lives, to death or possibly worse, to years of torture.

A Healing

Eisenhower knew POWs remained in Korea
September, 16,1996
Credit: Correspondent Carl Rochelle

Newly disclosed documents suggest that as many as 900 U.S. servicemen were left behind in North Korea after the United States and North Korea exchanged prisoners following the Korean War. The Dwight D. Eisenhower Presidential Library released the declassified papers. *The public didn't know about those abandoned by our government, but it is clear that Eisenhower did. Five months after the war, in a document dated December 22, 1953, Army Secretary Robert Stevens met with President Eisenhower and told him the Defense Department had the names of 610 Army people and over 300 Air Force prisoners still held by the North Koreans.*

Continued on URL
http://www.cnn.com/US/9609/17/korea.pows

Credit:
National Alliance Of Families

In 1996, during Congressional hearings, Col. Philip Corso, former Military Advisor to President Dwight Eisenhower provided testimony that leaves no doubt that many hundreds of American POW's were abandoned at the end of the Korean War.
In his testimony, Col. Corso stated: "*In the past I have tried to tell Congress the fact that in 1953, 500 sick and wounded American Prisoners were within 10 miles of the prisoner exchange point at Panmunjon and were never exchanged.*" Col. Corso's testimony was backed

up by a declassified document showing that the Pentagon knew, in 1953, more than 900 POWs were held but not released by North Korea. *A Dec. 22, 1953 memo states that the Army was inquiring about the disappearance, from a camp of 610 Army and 300 Air Force POWS, before the POW exchange.*

This information seems to back up ColCorso.

http://nationalalliance.org/korea/korea.htm

http://nationalalliance.org/korea/k-alfond.htm

Credit:
Coalition of Families of Korean & cold war pow/mias
Background of Korean War POW/MIA Issue

The Korean War ended on July 27, 1953. The Chinese had controlled U.N. prisoners and were primarily responsible for accounting for them. POWs were returned throughout that summer during Operations Little and Big Switch. In the end, there were 8,217 Americans who did not come home and who were not accounted for. The U.S. government ("USG") was indignant at the time, citing various sources of information that indicated a grossly insufficient accounting by the Communists.

http://www.coalitionoffamilies.org/korean_issue.html

A Healing

Credit;
James Brooke
New York Times, 1996

Numbering in the thousands, the list of Americans sent to Soviet labor camps is long and varied. They include left-wing Americans who emigrated to the Soviet Union in the 1930s only to be arrested as spies during Stalin's xenophobic sweeps; hundreds of dual nationals sent to Siberian labor camps after Stalin annexed Latvia, Lithuania, and Estonia in 1940; about 500 American military prisoners kept after World War II by Stalin as bargaining chips; about 30 F-86 pilots and crewmen captured during the Korean War and transferred to the Soviet Union in a secret aircraft industry intelligence operation; and as many as 100 American airmen who survived downing of spy planes over Soviet territory during the Cold War.

Continued on URL
"http://www.kimsoft.com/korea/mia-russ.htm"

James Woods

"A Healing"

IN EVERY MAJOR WAR OF THE 20TH CENTURY, WITH THE
EXCEPTION OF WWI IN 1918 and the Gulf War in 1991, we have
knowingly left some of our captured Warriors in the prison camps of
our enemy, *they would never be repatriated.* I.e.: WWII (*abandoned
to Russia our **Ally** in WWII*), Korea (abandoned to North Korea,
China, and Russia), Vietnam (abandoned to North Vietnam, China,
and Russia?) and the Cold War (abandoned to Russia).

These were traitorous acts of dishounor practiced by
supposedly Honourable politicians, recorded in their *"secret
memos", stored and protected in government "secret" vaults for
forty years or more as political convenience dictated.*
In reality I knew our Warriors were expendable in wartime
combat but after the war has ended not a single Warrior should be
abandoned. If it is necessary to continue a war or go to war to
acquire their release then so it shall be. *All captured Warriors
must be returned home at the cessation of hostilities, any less a
demand by our politicians is devoid of all justice, all honour.*

While this betrayal, uncovered by the release of
Eisenhower's Presidential Papers, prompted my need to initiate
writing, I continued writing for a much deeper, more personal
purpose. This reason, unknown to me at the time, was a narrative
I had been mentally writing, scribbling, erasing, dodging and
hiding from for nearly fifty years. I had neither the wisdom nor
the courage to record my mental battle on paper until it was
virtually too late; I put off these *final writings in this book* until
after a visit from my own mortality on February 11th, 2004.

I write of wars small children dying
and the "Boy's" we left across the sea.
I write of an old man who's been trying
to cleanse his war, his long past war,
as he walks his mind where there's no peace,
thru times of inhumanity.

A Healing

"A Healing"

I naively began writing without thoughts as to why writing had become such a necessity, or why I *now* had this demand to recognize *ghosts* I had been able to *not quite deny* for years. I had known of these "demons" for decades but refused to admit acceptance of their existence. I disparaged myself for the weakness of being powerless to overcome the demonic harassing of my conscience. I would push the thoughts; the memories back, continually attempting to bury them ever deeper, thrusting them back to a place where they would finally stop. They never did.

I was ashamed of being unable to feel normal inside, I carried fear others would discover my lacking, discover how I suppressed tears when certain subjects came up, how my stomach muscles twisted tight anytime a person would try to discuss war or how during certain films with refugees or little children, I would have to leave and be alone. This part of me was always alone, intentionally isolated from family and friends, occasionally living in beleaguered exile off and on for decades due to my ignorance and inability to find my way thru the labyrinth of pathways twisting always away from the exit doors of wars indelible imprints on a mind.

My lack of courage to face the fear of *unidentifiable emotional pain* was possibly the reason I was oblivious to the healing I needed, a healing to eradicate the hidden guilt and angst of a Soul battered from war with bruises that would not heal. I denied those bruises, even to myself, all the while having to live with the same pained turmoil whose existence I denied. The perceived shame and *social stigma of the times* were probably a strong collaborator in my denial, *I wouldn't fit society's concept of a Warrior, and every bit as bad, it did not allow me to fit mine.*

Somehow putting tens of thousands of words on paper white with pain in black I seemed to have unconsciously accomplished a healing leading to atonement for my war, a banishment of hidden "demons", and guidance along a route where I would, after five decades, achieve "my time of peace", my time of ease with what I was and what I am.

James Woods

I was okay, I approached the normality of many Veterans of combat whose honey-bucket became a bit full and no one told them of a decent time or place to dump it.

He'll learn to play pool games quite well,
as slowly he drinks more.
While wannabe's brag of their hell
he keeps his own in store.

My Veteran friends on the bar stools who won't shut up, society is not interested in your honey-bucket or the "shit you" carry in it, some will accept you dumping it once or twice, if you continue dumping where it shouldn't be empted they will draw away and quite soon will avoid you where possible.

There is nothing therapeutic about constantly dumping your honey-bucket on everyone you bump into. Keep it out of sight until you are at least sober, bring it out with a trusted friend but not over and over. There comes a time when it's your "shit" and yours alone, it's never been the whole worlds and they owe you nothing.

This book is my dumping ground; I can dump everything right here, actually it took three books and several years to dump it all out of my system. *Do you know anyone who would want to listen to someone's "shit" for that long, drunk or sober?* I know I've had my fill from some drunk on a bar-stool a few times and unless you're dumping on a combat veteran *no one is going to know how you feel, why you feel or what the hell you're talking about and most will not care!* There are more wanna-bee's in bars then those who have "been there, done that" and chances are the wanna-bee will be the one bragging while the one with the tormented Soul will be silently sipping his Jack Daniels.

Sorry about those last two paragraphs but if you need to get over mental trauma from "Your War" you need to understand that *untold numbers of us have fought or are fighting the same*

A Healing

psychological battles for Peace-of-mind as you. **I know of none who have accomplished a healing leading to their "Time of Peace" living the lifestyle of a drunk or in the public forum.** I'll share a shot of Jack Daniels with you but lets talk fishing.

This healing of a tormented soul, a soul at times existing within some periphery of purgatory, this soul in turmoil I shall refer to as **"Boy"**. Thru lack of knowledge I inadvertently abandoned "Boy" to wander alone on distant battlegrounds, a lost "Boy" frequently drifting in and out among wars dead, suffering and dying, drifting in and out for far to many years.

"My front" denied this "Boy's" existence to the world; my fear and unintended ignorance denied him healing. Ultimately my writings stumbled onto a breach so as to turn my thought process to a pathway leading to a type of courage to take the first honest step in facing and examining the children dying. For five decades when they appeared in my head I'd force them always back into that safe darkened compartment of my mind. The courage to finally examine *"our pain"* was the first step leading to atonement and in time showed the way to my conscious atonement. With this conscious atonement "Boy" was salvaged from his untenable exile and I was well on my way to acceptance of the trials and tribulations of this young Warrior with tears denied for so many years.

As I welcomed "Boy" home thru these writings my time of peace became my living reality, my memories of war were now lived within the bounds of *comfortable sadness.* I was no longer beleaguered by secreted unwarranted guilt or painful recollections appearing unbidden inside my head and nearly destroying any fleeting hope for "my time of peace."

I won the most critical battle of my life thru these writings, I was as I *appeared,* always alone whether thinking or writing. *I am convinced others were there, unseen,* patiently guiding when the pain became to much, allowing capacious tears to wet my shirt, helping with the words I would need for healing and staying my finger, not allowing that tragic bit of extra pressure on the trigger one fall night in nineteen eighty-nine.

James Woods

I did not write alone as I feel I was enabled by the "unseen ones", I do not write only for myself and I don't know whom to thank for my deliverance from spontaneously recalling a place filled with the ancient gray wasteland of wars traumatic scenes to these fields of Green with running laughing Children. I am very thankful.

I truly did not believe "Boy's" retrieval possible and I am astounded this healing of my essence was accomplished without knowledge of, or consciously being capable of self-therapy, nor why I now feel whole.

James Woods /aka/ *Jimmie Joe*

A Healing

"A Healing"

Local Vietnam Veterans and some Korean Vets I met thru the Internet after 1998 talked me into publishing my poems on the "web" as they seemed to strike a healing of sorts in some. The e-mails I received thanked me, a few "God blessed me" for my writings, especially some Mothers and Daughters, as they saw their Warrior in a more understanding light. The number of Vets who thought they were alone with their Ghosts of War surprised me; I found I was not unique in that which I had carried silently and alone for nearly a lifetime.

Mon, 21 Apr 2003 16:20:06 –0400
"A Boy and His Journey" -<u>E-mail review</u>

Hi Jim;
I ordered your book from Amazon about two weeks ago. My husband read it in two settings. I read it in four. I can't tell you how much we both enjoyed it. My husband was in Korea in 1959. He spent a year there. He cannot quit talking about your book. My husbands younger brother (Charles Chapman) was killed in Vietnam on October 31,1967 he was only 19 years old. He also has a brother Michial, who went to Vietnam two times. He was seventeen when he joined the Army. Of course his Mom and Dad had to sign for him.
He has been going to counseling for some years now. When I read your book I knew I had to get your book to him. We took it to him one evening and at 5:30 the next morning he was knocking at our door. I let him in and he wrapped his arms around my husband, crying, and said "Brother I need to talk to someone". He said "I have been up all night and I am only on page 51" and have read some of it over and over. He also said he wants to meet the man who wrote this book.

He said one of his councilors in Gaylord is not counseling anymore and he wants to get your book to him to read. I talk to Mick almost every day and I know it is helping him, but he has a long way to go. Almost forgot, Mick has an army buddy who lives near him who can't read very well so he is going to set and read this book to him, after he gets through reading it.

Pat (Van Zant) Chapman,
Onaway, Michigan

Wars **seeming** not to measure up to approval by the majority of Americans are considered not quite "real wars" and as they continue on year after year they become ho-hum wars as viewed by America. The country gets tired of wars **seeming** to have become a war without a cause, the public is not aroused and the wars **appear** unjustified. The young people end up in the streets hating not only the war but hating and blaming the Warriors who are doing the fighting. One hell-of-a lot of those protesters were in the streets for the simple reason it was "*the IN thing to do*" and some were there because the draft scared the hell out of them.

After such a war many Veterans ability to adjust and cope is negatively magnified several times over, they carry undeserved guilt mingled with abject pain, regretfully some percentage of Veterans will live with, and feel, a torment of the damned.

Korean Warriors were ignored by America as they rotated home one by one, there was absolutely no welcome home, no recognition by the general public of an *actual war* such as World War Two. *There was a war, a bloody damn civil war that cost far too many innocent lives, the civilian dead numbered between two and six million.*

Hard numbers are not possible to come by as North Korea will not release its figures and the North's cities were basically bombed back into the Stone Age; the starvation age may be a more correct wording, if honesty is required.

A Healing

Vietnam was such a war as would try men's souls, the Warriors treatment at home was unforgivably cruel and the hate spewed by misguided "Flower Children" pierced the Warriors already wounded minds. Unfortunately many retreated back within themselves, the joy of being alive and home turned into a curse of degradation. Far too many Vietnam Warriors were denied their homecoming, their hope for adjustment, and their "time for healing" by vast numbers of America's young people (Flower Children) whom I shall hereafter refer to as *"Simple Asses"*.

Vietnam was America's first TV war, their first view of the vivid horrors of war and America folded. I will not debate the righteousness of Vietnam. I will debate the *"Simples Asses"* that denied young men like "Michial" their "time for healing".

They now have political power and our *politicians public ranting* against the Iraqi war will produce, as in Vietnam, tens of thousands of "Michial's" and it's all done in the name of peace. Moose CRAP! *For far too many it's still the IN thing to do, done in the name of a non-political climate? They reek dishonesty.*

How much more difficult will Iraqi Veterans adjustment be with the daily TV's *"fanatical public ranting"* against the war by politicians? We didn't have as much public "ranting" by politicians on or off T.V. during Vietnam; "Simple Asses" alone did the irredeemable damage to the *critical time of Warriors finding his way home, his way to adjustment. Forty years later many Vietnam Vets are still struggling with their orientation process, the finding of a comfort zone in their mind where they can call, and feel at "home".*

The more unacceptable a war by our country's peoples, the more war will try a Warriors soul. The more war tries a Warriors soul, the more difficult a Warriors adjustment. The more difficult a Warriors adjustment, *the more likely at some future time a pistol is raised to a Warriors temple.*

Jimmie Joe

James Woods

How do we cope with unjust politicians?

Politicians were giving aid and comfort to our enemies early on in the Iraqi War; long before the time of the Democratic primary in March 2004 the enemy had been monitoring our politician's coverage on all media sources. About Mid-March 2004 to Mid-March 2005, the number of car bombs, IEDs and combat deaths doubled over the year preceding Mid-March 2004.

Beginning in March 2004 the ten Democratic Presidential hopefuls concentrated on disparaging President Bush and the Iraq War. They did not debate each other's qualifications or discuss why they were qualified to be president, ninety percent of their discussions rancorously involved the Iraq war and President Bush. Eight of the ten presidential hopefuls were mean spirited with forked tongues of vipers maliciously attacking the moral righteousness of the Iraqi War and the moral competency of our President George W. Bush. These attacks were/are detrimental to America's war on terrorism; they encourage our enemies in upping the pace of killing our troops and innocent Iraqi civilians.

These attacks on the Iraqi War and President Bush have been continued by many high placed politicians thru the election period, they have now been going on for nearly two years unabated. They continue but are even more deceitful, venomous, and obdurate in showering their rabid abhorrence on President Bush then during the campaign. *They hate him, he's stuck in their craw and they can't spit him out.*

America "folds" quite easily when the liberals get on their platform and preach peace at any cost. Historically this peace has come at the incalculable loss in lives of those we came to help; many liberals are in reality insensitive uncaring bastards whose thought process barely extends past their only real goal, the next election. You know who they are, you've seen them on TV, you've seen their red faces distorted in fury as they degrade our President, you've seen their fists banging down on the podium all directed toward the Iraqi War and our Commander and Chief.

A Healing

The terrorists know every speech a politician delivers, he has nearly instant access to every media, and he uses this access for judging where America stands in relation to Americas' resolve to continuing the Iraqi War or pulling out.

http://icasualties.org/oif/

March 20th. 2003- May 1st. 2003 Major combat ended, we suffered 140 Warriors Killed In Action.

---

*May 1st. 2003- March 1st 2004 KIA 444 =45/month. The **45 a month killed in action** were all prior to the ten Democratic presidential hopefuls debates.*

---

*March 1st., 2004 -Dec. 1st. 20005 KIA 1611= 77/month. The **77 a month killed in action** all occurred during and after the ten Democratic presidential hopefuls' debates.*

Terrorists increased their use of EIDs, vehicle bombs and small scale automatic weapons attacks to kill more Americans as they observed our politicians public reaction to the war and the vicious degrading of our Commander-in-Chief, President Bush.

Their method of operation is based on killing, killing, killing and they are not selective; Americans, Brits, including all members of the coalition and their own countrymen; Shiites, Sunnis and Kurds; men, women or children none are important, it's the killing that will be forcing World and especially American public opinion further against the war. Our politicians' rabid public dissention has encouraged the enemy, caused an upsurge in car bombs and IEDs attacks contributing vastly to the dead and wounded of Coalition Forces and Iraqi civilians.

The enemy truly believes, from historical fact, if they can kill enough Americans, America will fold. We must not abandon these Iraqis who have suffered thru thirty-plus years of Hussein's despotic rule and the price they have paid so far in this war for their freedom so long denied.

James Woods

Many Warriors will return home with our politician's detrimental words echoing, ricocheting, then trapped in their conscience, now questioning their war, questioning all the death and misery they had lived with and observed. They will begin to feel guilt that isn't really theirs to carry, guilt mixed with pain they do not deserve.

I am sorry my friend, that is a burden Combat Infantry carry home from war, there is no need for a Warrior to commit the act of killing in order to carry the guilt. Witnessing a few or many dead bodies of the enemy or innocent civilians strewn about after a battle or massacre will, with the passage of time, give many a nagging sense of liability, a fleeting touch of guilt.

All this ranting in public by many of our "liberal politicians" will, somewhere down the line, be a large part of the blame when today's future Veteran raises a pistol to his temple and squeezes the trigger. A death that should not have taken place will become a tragic reality.

This breeding of ""demons" of Grief" with the ""demons" of Guilt" will produce a monster-demon that is difficult to live with under the best conditions. This monsters size will be greatly magnified by the *constant negative ranting of politicians* against the war. A percentage of Veterans will become victims of these politicians-distended-monsters, it may take six months, it may take forty years but the monster-"demons" will collect their payment, their charge for war. We all know whom the unfeeling bastards are who furnish nourishment to create such monsters.

James Woods

A Healing

"Memorial Day"
24th. Inf. Div., 34th. /21st., Inf. Reg. --- 1950/51

I THANK MY FALLEN COMRADES AND IT MATTERS NOT IF THEY FELL at Valley Forge, the North or South in our Civil War, nor any War, be it as large as World War II or as small as peacekeeping in the Balkans. It matters not if they fell in a War some of our Countrymen believe was wrong, or a War "I" believe not just and it matters not if they fell in a training accident.

It matters not if a Cross-, a Star of David, a Crescent Moon, or any other inscription carved in stone identifies their mound of earth, and it matters not the Race of the one who rests below.

These have nothing to do with the honour I bestow on our men and women who die in harms way and they have nothing to do with how I feel on a Day such as this. Memorial Day brings back sadness with a bit of pain, reminding me there is infinitely more pain carried for a lifetime by the Moms, Dads, Wives, Children and all who love their Warrior dead.

One hour of one-day a year set aside for remembrance is minuscule, enjoy your long weekend but please take a moment for a prayer of thanks.

I honour you my Warrior Brothers,
I'll join you in a while.
Will you welcome me as Comrade brave?
or will there be no smile?

Have I upheld your sacrifice and death
as I lived time you never had?
Is our Homeland as Free as when you left?
By "Gods own truth" your answer is -----------?
Your answer friend ---------- is mine.

Although our Warriors were young men, in my olden mind we were "Boy's", with much honour and respect I shall refer to them as such.

Jimmie Joe, fishhook junction, Alaska

James Woods

"A Healing"

1997 --- MY WRITING BEGAN IN LONG HAND ABOARD MY CABIN cruiser, "Old White Guy", while at Peaceful Halibut Cove, Alaska.

Why? We can only be healed from within, expressing feelings to ones self *with the painful honesty required.*

> Several years ago I tried to talk,
> it did not do any good.
> My children grown? They kind of balked,
> they never understood.
>
> That was all right, I should have known,
> no way they could understand.
> Even tho my kids were fully grown,
> I never tried to talk again.

Fall, 1989

In the early fall of nineteen eighty-nine I was in the last stages of a downward spiral, my world was fast coming apart and I nearly was not here to be writing what has turned out to be these books. I now know I'm not unique but at the time I was lost in the confusion of my inability to cope with a thirty-nine year old war, a war I no longer had the capacity or desire to continue living with and in the confusion of the lost I became my nemesis as the spiraling "demons" pulled me closer and closer to the abyss.

About four months later, in January of Nineteen-ninety, I attempted talking with a few of my children, Denise, Tom and Cathie, adults in their thirties and tried to explain the tormented time my soul was going thru, it didn't work. In retrospect I fail to see how I could have accomplished anything as I had no concept about what I needed to reveal, I simply blubbered virtually incoherent about it being the war.

A Healing

I feel they thought their dad was weak,
grown daddies should be strong.
My crying when I tried to speak,
I felt they thought me wrong.

I never did get to the part
that pained my soul, that tore my heart.
I'd kept wounds masked nearly forty years
before disclosure made me cry.

They asked "why now", my ignorance of the "why now", along with the confused distress of my mind probably left them scratching their heads and wondering about their Dad.

I remained near the void from which my Angel had saved me four months earlier and was desperate for someone to help me. I didn't know who to ask, I didn't know how to ask and I didn't want to expose my perceived weakness with a person I didn't have a great deal of trust in.

I remained a bit lost for eight more years before, thru painful fury with the revelations in Eisenhower's Papers, the courage came. My writings began in anger in nineteen ninety-seven, became an outpouring tide I seemed unable to stem, and they ended several years later with the healing of "fluctuating distress" I had carried for nearly fifty years.

I retired in 1984 and the last of my Children left home in 1985, my home increasingly became an empty, lonely place. Grandchildren's house filling laughter was replaced by echoing "demons" in the silence of night. These "demons", I had kept leashed for nearly forty years, snapped their leash and had their moment.

I was in mounting despair and adrift without a tangible clue something was deeply wrong and, as it turned out, I no longer knew how to placate the "demons" that finally demanded their payment, their charge for war. My once peaceful cabin on the banks of the Little Susitna River in Alaska nearly became my Armageddon, the Fishhook Bar became my refuge, and my writings, without question, became my emancipation.

James Woods

It'll take about four years or so,
clock ticks slowly at the first.
He'll begin frequenting the Fishhook Bar
and the cause will not be thirst

After those many years to die due to a minds long term
unresolved conflict seems irrational now, thru research I found it
is not rare for Veterans of combat, ghosts of past battle zones are
and remain imprinted rather well. I needed someone quite badly.
No one was there. No one knew. I would continue to hide the
shame of this weakness, this weakness of not being "man
enough" to cope with his war long after the last battle. The shame
of the countless times I had suppressed tears through the years
did not make logical sense, I'd survived the battles, made it home
safely, had a fairly good life, have Children and Friends I love, I
should have been euphoric with life throughout life. ---- *I wasn't.*
Inside I had memories of my war, some of those memories,
conscious or subliminal I inadvertently carried home from war,
they were always there, almost in the back of my mind, waiting,
patiently waiting. With my retirement in nineteen eighty-four
their patience began to ebb and slowly the "demons" became
more demanding. By nineteen eighty-nine they were stronger
than the ramparts I had built thru those many years, one night the
ramparts crumbled and with their failure the darkness closed in, I
could no longer survive with my past nor see a light in my future.
I don't know why I lost my ability to cope and became horribly
disoriented; it's chilling when I think of what very nearly came to
pass. There was not one cell of my brain that said, "Hey "Boy"
come on, get help somewhere". What is disconcerting prior to the
final crescendo of that hellish night is my mind held only one
deadly answer; it was as if I had on blinders with only one
direction, one path to atonement and peace.

His forty-one mag he took to bed,
silently told his friends good-bye.
Cocked it and pressed it to his head
about an inch behind right eye.

A Healing

I told some Children of this in 1999, some will not know until they read this. No one would have known had I not written my books. In the end visions of a Friend or Daughter finding my body overcame the fates and in darkness of my desolation I cried out for God, my Angel *("silent one")* arrived and my *"silent one"* answered, giving me time. Even tho I was not aware of this gift for years, I am now tremendously thankful.

The next day my Daughter Cynthia and my Grandchildren, Christopher and Jessica, stopped by to visit, Lord, what I nearly caused in their life's memory banks is something I don't like to contemplate.

I endured, even tho I would neither be aware of (nor admit to), nor consciously seek, my pressing need of healing for another eight years. The "Boy" who went to war remained behind the grief filled walls where he had been suppressed since he came home from war in Nineteen-fifty-one. Nearly fifty years would pass before my courage came and I set "Boy" free. I am astonished and grateful for what "Boy's" freedom has bestowed.

I forced a nineteen-year-old Soldier "Boy" cringing in the darkened safety of "my minds hiding place" into the light where I could see him. I'd fight him and he'd beg, I'd beg him and he'd burst into tears, tears wrapped in my fearful ignorance and stored out of view for nearly fifty years, stored along with the undeserved guilt and the perceived shame to cry. Finally that nineteen-year-old Soldier "Boy" demanded relief from his anguished journey or, by "Boy's" hand, "I" would die; I opted to live.

I'm to old for battle, a battle which had been untenable at the beginning, became skirmishes most of the years and raged as all out war at the end; I gave up the fight and, with what had to be Gods help, I won our freedom. I released "Boy's" pain with tear filled writings and I was able to say and feel, "Welcome Home Son", it's all right now, it's over.

James Woods

I gave up, I fought no more

> Damn it God won't you help me,
> I don't want to die alone.
> I am lost in pains direction.
> The roads been long,
> please God, *please help.*

> His demon fates had nearly taken him
> to that land beyond the sky.
> His Angel touched him just in time:

> *jimmie joe,* **Hey !** *jimmie joe.*
> Come on "Boy" it's time to cry.

All those years I guess I assumed "Boy" departed because he wanted to stay in "his safe place". I was wrong, "Boy" wanted out, I forced "Boy" to stay veiled; it was "my safe place". I somehow created walls when I was the "Boy" and, as the Man, my misguided place of refuge became "Boy's" prison.

In reality I didn't think in the black and white of those terms, I was a normal nineteen year old when I left for war; I was far from being a normal twenty year old when I came home from war.

I did not have a pleasant thirty-day furlough; *it seemed not quite right to leave your Buddies on the battleground, come "home" and be surrounded by people who don't give a DAMN.* I guess that was normal as we were only five years from the end of "the Big One".

Back at camp I felt at home, not a stranger, not alone. There is still a great deal of ignorance on a "Boy's" adjusting after his battles are over.

"Arriving Home"

> Family and friends were near like strangers,
> Something was not as it should be.
> Home was the same as when I left.
> *The stranger friend was me.*

A Healing

Back then we knew naught about posttraumatic stress, there was no such name, *let alone the varying degrees of it.* We lived with it or we died from it, our life would seem normal to everyone except ourselves and overall mine was excluding the revelations this book is about. They were not debilitating but they were, at times, quite difficult to deal with. The conscious gaining of knowledge by the subconscious long search for adjustment, and muddling through, were unpleasant periods of my life.

Unbidden visions from "Boy's" war frequently flashed inside my head, coping became a way of life. I made it through and survived as well as most. Why the eventual crisis came so late in life is an enigma I doubt if I will ever unravel, possibly the last of my Children leaving home and my retirement within the same year left me vulnerable to an internal conflict I had carried for, at the time, about forty years.

1951 thru 1997,

I thought something was wrong with me,
a weakness I must hide.
The hurting, flitting pain I'd see,
I must hold back deep inside.

October 1950

Southern North Korea, two small Children

I do know they slept, if we hastened their death with too much morphine I just don't know. I had no idea back then I would carry those four pained and haunting eyes mirrored in my head for most of my life, my secret pain and hidden sorrow. I pray they didn't awaken except to Gods caring arms in heaven.

"My Healing"

Two small Children crumpled by the crossroads
with no one else around.
Two casualties of grown-ups war,
soon little bodies in the ground.

James Woods

1998 a time to cry

> Tears gushed from the old Warriors eyes
> but they were not old Warriors tears,
> the tears were from a Soldier "Boy"
> who's age was nineteen years.

Atonement?

> Their eyes no longer dulled by pain,
> a sparkle's what now shows.
> They walk while holding hands with me,
> we walk in summers sunshine
> and we play in winters snows.

> Of course it's all within my mind,
> to my soul it is quite real.
> My lines absolved near fifty years
> we shared that dying field.

These two small Children were and are the _main_ reason for my writings, they are why I sometimes rambled and repeated a bit as I typed and searched, typed and searched some more.

I didn't know where or how to begin, I only knew there was an essential demand to write something. God alone knows how many one-fingered pages I've typed and discarded as I wrote in circles around subjects the anguish of my subconscious mind knew was there but refused to liberate, all the while not knowing the direction I was going and not even quite sure why my journey had began.

It became matter of courage. Courage to face the "Boy's" anguishes, courage to face the Children, _especially the Children_, courage to face my Comrades-in-arms and my Foe. The courage to express my deep sorrow, courage to admit they once lived, courage to say I will remember and courage to feel I care they had died.

I hid my grief of past reality, I fooled the world, I could not fool "Boy's" torment living inside where none could see, _I knew_, _I felt_, others at times may have suspected but they never knew.

A Healing

We had to leave them to die alone,
they died alone in sleep.
I knew no way could I atone,
for years my Soul would weep.

I observed many conditions where gore, pain and many varieties of suffering were as appalling as these two small Children's' dying. I'll never understand why this one piece of time so overwhelmed all other unpleasant trials and tribulations, or why I have taken all these years to acquire the courage to find my way home to "Boy's" time of healing.

"Ticking Clocks"

It took 'til old age, all those years,
for me to get things right.
Now old Man cries a young "Boy's" tears.
He'll cry alone, adjust, atone,
as he frees subconscious from it's night.

I started these writings from my raging fury and pain with Eisenhower's revelations (of our prisoners of war never freed) released after forty-some years in secret files. I ended my writings loving two small Korean Children I'd known less than an hour. These Children have stayed with me, first thru nearly fifty years of emotional torment, and finally thru an emotional bond with acceptance of Love. Is it Gods hand? I do not know, I do know it is a great, unexpected, relief.

I am now at peace with time served in the Land of the Morning Calm. My dead rest where they belong and two small Korean Children's eyes have closed, and they, my Kim and my Leaha, rest a well-deserved rest, I've kept them up a very long time.

Jimmie Joe

fishhook junction, Alaska

James Woods

"A Healing"

About January 1990

> I'd kept wounds masked nearly forty years
> before disclosure made me cry.
> It didn't work with my family.
> Must there be pain 'til I die?
>
> No, seven years has passed,
> alone this time I'll try.
> Alone I'll cry.

1997 – 2002:

I did try, I tried alone, I cried alone, and I wrote page after page of prose, which I discarded again and again as they lacked clarity of meaning. Writing in prose I could not express the turmoil of emotions I had kept bottled up for years, feelings that had become a very real danger to my survival.

I turned to poetry for putting forth deeply held emotions. The results were passable and finally my writings began to delve into emotions I had concealed and had been incapable of expressing for five decades. I ended up with a web page on A.O.L. from which I was encouraged to share my lines of poetry with other Veterans of combat and those who love them.

I wrote these wandering, later therapeutic poems from a series of inter-related distressing and sorrowful journeys of my mind back thru time. I wrote alone and it seemed an absolute necessity I write only when no one could observe me, it was a struggle I could not share. As the size of my web page grew many Veterans and some Veterans wives, and daughters urged me to record my poems in a book.

I didn't finish high school, didn't know sentence structure, couldn't type, spell, use a computer or see very well, how in hell was I suppose to write a book!!

A Healing

Well I did! Even tho they may not be contenders for the Pulitzer nor the Nobel Prize in Literature, *they are mine*. They express my fears, my loves, and my sadness for the "Boy's" who never made it home. My sorrow for the vast numbers of old men, women and children caught in the incalculable misery and torturous pain of a civil war with millions of premature deaths under agonizing conditions. Finally the enemy dead, most as young as myself, their lives just beginning, hundreds of thousands dead along with all the joys of a life never tasted.

Two small Children crumpled by a crossroads
with no one else around.
Two casualties of grown-ups War,
soon little bodies in the ground.

The soul wrenching dying of two small Korean children are especially mine, I've had them with me for over fifty years and always when they appeared inside my head they brought with them a gift of pain. I couldn't adjust to that type of pain for nearly five decades and I've never been able to analyze why a pain so unidentifiable is capable of hurting with such intensity, nor why the intensity does not lessen as years go by. I had a son, "Jimmie Joe jr." who died at two months of age in nineteen fifty-four, it was quite painful to deal with but the acceptance and much of the healing occurred within a time span of months, why is there a lifetime's difference in the minds "grappling hold" on certain occurrences of death and dying? Why the minds inability to cope with the death of two small children for nearly fifty years?

Gave them morphine, could not do more,
I held their little hands.
Gave them morphine 'til they slept,
We played their God in warring land.

We had to leave them to die alone,
they died alone in sleep.

James Woods

I knew no way could I atone
for years my soul would weep.

"Kim" and "Leaha" lived inside my mind for decades, always when they appeared they arrived with a gift of torrential pain. *Sometime during or after my second book, within the last several years,* the pain miraculously but slowly turned around and they were no longer broken bloodied little children with pain filled eyes. Within my mind they became eight or nine year olds and the fields were a peaceful soothing green. *The children are laughing as we hold hands and play together, running and skipping thru peaceful fields of green. There is no war. There is no dying. There is peace.* They appeared with the greatest gift of all; a gift granting my mind forgiveness, a gift of love absolving my decades long burden; they are my children, my "Kim and my Leaha". I know it's all within my head but it's crazy in a good way, I'll keep the way it is now.

Their eyes no longer dulled by pain,
a sparkle's what now shows.
They walk while holding hands with me,
we walk in summers sunshine
and we play in winter's snows.

They are now my little Children
and I'm not a Warrior man.
We walk thru peaceful fields of green,
laughing Children hold my hands.

With the enormous emotional pain of finally gathering the courage to face wars memories of my two small Korean children, I found the pathway to my deliverance, I found the pathway to peace of mind and I may have found my pathway to God.

A Healing

So my friend I wrote the first book and I wept, *I wept as the trauma-afflicted essence of a broken old mans soul was revealed approaching the gates of hell, his back twisted and bent from the years of hidden emotive pain, along with unforgiving guilt and the hopelessness of the damned. I wept soundless streaming tears that left my shirt front soaked, tears making my eyes so I couldn't type. I had to stop several times and each time I would begin typing again the tears flowed like little rivers.*

I seem to have removed the pain from my system thru tears but why did it seem necessary in my mind to carry hidden trauma for fifty years before I could find my way to relief.

I carried PTSD so long because I didn't know what to do with it and I carried the damn stuff right up until it killed me, but it didn't.

I wrote the second book, utilizing some pain from the first, and I wept as the relief of a soul pardoned from the tortures of hell yet not quite believing. I wrote this third book, utilizing some pain from the second, and weeping was reduced to a few trickling tears without the pain of purgatory but with deep sadness.

During book number three I managed to write thru the pain, thru the guilt and typed my way out of the black compartment within my brain where hopelessness lived in destructive defiance to the time of my imprinted war.

I still sniff a bit and my eyes do get a little watery but the tears no longer fall. Amen, my friend, I thank our Father for whatever amount of Peace is now mine to share thru the time we have left.

James Woods
Jimmie Joe

James Woods

A Song of David

THE LORD IS MY SHEPARD, I SHALL NOT WANT, HIS PRAYER BEGAN as the artillery barrage increased, he makes me lie down in. the first piece of hot jagged shrapnel begins its journey thru the young Warriors arm entering his rib cage. green pastures, he restores my soul. the second piece of shrapnel enters just below the aorta and above the liver. Ma' Ma. thru the valley. shadow of death.

The prayer was finished across the Veil in Heaven; Gods caring arms now enfolded our Friend, our Comrade, our dead.

The Warrior who wanted and tried to believe was, by the very act of trying, accepted into Heaven by our Loving God. The Warrior like millions before him and after, friend or foe, will not spend eternity in hell. *God would not create Humans only to cast most into the pains of hell, what pray tell would be the purpose of such creation?*

This I must believe- jimmie joe

The wars dead are and have been in a safe peaceful place.

That I do believe as of February 11, 2004!!!

See next page.

In fairness I don't expect most to believe the testament below. (I would not have had it not happened to me.)

A Healing

"The Path Beyond the Veil"

A testament for my Children, my friends, all whom I love, and those I may not know:

ON FEB. THE 11, 2004 AT AGE SEVENTY-THREE I WENT INTO cardiac arrest and died for a while, (I did not get to the light you may have read about), I seemed to be a bluish semi-shapeless form floating at the inside top of the ambulance and was totally unconcerned with the person the EMT was bent over, *my emotions in this (spirit form?) were totally neutral.* In the past I severely questioned this sort of happening and did not quite believe such a thing could be.

From the inside top of the ambulance I observed the EMT working on me, lean around the ½ partition, say something to the driver and sensed the ambulance suddenly pick up speed swerving in and out of traffic, going over the curbs with sirens and horn blaring (I could hear the siren and horn loud and clear).

I looked out the back window to see what kind of disorder this was causing in the traffic, the sight picture that stayed *clearly* in my mind was a tan chevy type older car that had run over the curb and up on a lawn (a white-haired lady driver was the only occupant). I did not consciously recall or organize these events until several days after I had been resuscitated but upon resuscitation I *immediately sensed a serenity* that somehow had been imposed within my mind.

I feel compelled to send this testament of the "Event" to family, friends and those who may be suffering the loss of a loved one, in the past, recently or in the future, or those who may be approaching death with fear. *Please my friends do not be afraid*, for those who are dying, have gone before or for your own demise.

There is a happening after this life and, although I do not know what it's about, I do know there is serenity with peace awaiting a soul, a spirit, or whatever we become after dying time.

Our new residency on the other side of the veil will be quite different from traditional teachings of our grannies or the preachers.

I do not remember leaving my body, how long I was gone or how I re-entered my physical self (all this could have been a trick of my mind), but this is *my* important learning; *I felt only serenity with peaceful detachment prior to and after several incursions into my heart during the next seven months I was in and out of hospitals.*

I felt an absence of fear and had *absolutely no apprehension* about death or dying. That feeling about death and dying still holds, (I use to be quite fearful about dying because of childhood teachings; i.e. the uncertainty of Hell, eternity etc.) The worse part about dying is the pain or extreme discomfort of getting to the veil, once you're at the veil only peace remains with one step more and the miraculous continuance of existence.

This experience has been a blessing for me and I do thank our Father in heaven most humbly. I am not overly religious and have questioned my ability to truly believe in an after-life or a God throughout most of my adult life. *I do not KNOW there is a God but I now KNOW there is an afterlife and now FEEL there is a God.* I am sure the pathways to our God, our after-life, must be many, quite varied and, most importantly, uncomplicated.

I seem to find myself anticipating peaceful tranquility in an existence I know nothing about, an existence I brushed against for an in instant in time and in the process lost my fear of death, my fear of hell and my fear of the black eternal void. Strange how one "Event" can have such a profound effect after more then eighteen months. While this "Event" is a blessing for my dying time, it is mostly a "calming blessing" in "this" my living time.

I felt a need to share this "Event", whether you personally choose to believe my narrative is unimportant, (I, for one, would not have), but it will help some of you, when the time comes, to experience less fear and emotional pain and more hope that lays beyond in his or her life.

Jimmie Joe

A Healing

A glimpse of maladjustment

IN KOREA ABOUT A WEEK BEFORE OUR ROTATION DATE WE WOULD be pulled off the front line to the comparative safety of Co. Hq., I remember that, I don't remember saying goodbye to my Buddies. I remember going to Japan, stripping naked, going thru the delousing shed and having my body sprayed with DDT to kill the white body lice. We could have any food we desired; I had steak and milk, milk, milk. The Red Cross gave us cigarettes, donuts and whatever else they had. I've heard some say the Red Cross charged the GI's; there was never any charge I had seen.

We sailed to Frisco, rode a bus to Fort Ord and I caught a plane to Chicago the same night. The departure of the plane was held up for us and as I boarded I overheard a civilian complain about holding up the flight for a bunch of "damn GI's", these were the first words I heard from a fellow American. This was my introduction to how some Americans felt about the Korean War veterans. I could care less at the time, I had survived and I was home. I could now live out my life in peace. I was wrong, it would be nearly fifty years before my last battle ended and peace took hold.

I remember flying over the Rocky Mountains and having the euphoria of being alive and going home. Something happened between there and Chicago, I lost my remembrance. I don't remember landing in Chicago, how I traveled from Chicago to Lansing, Michigan or if anyone met me. I don't remember meeting my family, friends or much else on my thirty-day furlough. I remember being at Ft. Jackson, South Carolina but not how I traveled there. I know I felt at home when I arrived at camp after my thirty-day furlough. For some reason my mind had/has blocked nearly all memory of my furlough out, I've tried and tried to remember but I cannot.

October 1951, Ft. Jackson, South Carolina,
about two months after my return from Korea.

Spent time in Army hospital there,
the world twisted not quite real.

James Woods

I'd developed tunnel vision,
was a scary way to feel.
Sights and sounds were far away.
Quite confused in bed I lay.

After a short rest the symptoms disappeared and I was released, the Doctors couldn't find the cause. Our recognition of posttraumatic stress would not evolve for decades. I thought it was just I, thru the next forty-seven years I would be adjusting to my non-adjustment. The years 1951 to 1956 were the most difficult, thru the years that followed I managed to slowly placate and veil most of that which distressed my mind. Thru all this time, in my ignorance, I thought I alone carried ghosts of war, I alone was not quite man enough to cope, I alone held back tears, and I alone went into hiding. I was not alone in being so wrong.

My memory is fine through the time I spent training my platoon at Ft. Jackson, South Carolina, while on maneuvers in Texas and my discharge June 10th, 1952 from Camp Atterbury, Indiana. It was only during my furlough and time at home where memory mostly failed me.

I don't remember asking a Lady to marry me and only vaguely remember the wedding ceremony on December Twenty-ninth, nineteen fifty-one. I do remember consummating the marriage; amazingly my memory of forward time remained excellent thereafter, altho I still have the voids in memory of my time on furlough.

There were many insensitive, ignorant civilian asses wanting to know what it was like to kill a man and other kinds of stupid questions, my stomach muscles always twisted tight, I didn't like it. After while I would either not respond or tell them I worked running a PX, that didn't impress them much and they left me alone. I have Grandkids who, 'til my book, never knew I was in the Army let alone in combat.

I learned well how to hide and keep my thoughts from the questioning world outside my head but I couldn't escape the pop-up "demons" stored inside. I coped by neither talking about nor discussing the "demons" lurking just below the surface, and in

A Healing

truth in those years my family and friends would have had even less reaction than my family did when I tried to talk about it in January of nineteen-ninety.

The Veterans Administration in early years had no concept of the pain their Veterans *may* have carried unless we became so severely dysfunctional we had to be put away, and once they got you I'm not sure they did any more than drug the hell out of you to keep you manageable. I was able to work, raise my family and function quite well but there were always pop-up background snapshots in my head, keeping me on guard and depriving my mind of lasting peace. I left "Boy" abandoned on his distant battleground, imprisoned by me and exiled to the dark arena of a Warriors mind where Friends and Loved ones may not trespass. This arena of desolation is where "Boy" must live so the outside world will never know he is not a real Warrior, he's just a little "Boy" who needs to cry.

Moving to Alaska was almost like going back to the freedom of my childhood. My "demons", while still there, became muted a bit and were nowhere near as demanding and constant. Alaska was to a large degree like coming home, I had peace when working in the "Bush" and while hunting, catching fish in places wild and the pure joy my heart absorbed when my Children were young.

My "demons" were very nearly anesthetized my first twenty-five years in Alaska, they put few demands on me until about a year after I retired and the last of my Children left home in 1985. Increasingly, thru the next five years, I became my vengeance, without awareness I was in a life or death struggle, with deepening awareness I was lost.

Jimmie Joe
fishhook junction, Alaska

James Woods

An old Dogface Sarge Wonders

Two Koreas and a civil war

LET ME BEGIN BY STATING IRREVOCABLY; I WAS/AM FOR OUR intervention into South Korea, we needed to stop aggression by the North Korean Army.

Our pushing to the Chinese border I now deplore, as it is apparent from declassified papers our leaders knew we were running high risk of war with China. Let me also state, true or not, I believe Mac Arthur coveted said war to free Asia from communism. In total millions of civilians died from massacres, disease, and starvation and with three years of our intensive bombing in North Korea, sadly the starvation continues to this day as the result of a totalitarian government that will not bend.

China entering the war in late 1950 prevented our victory without an all out war with China and that would have been a political blunder none were willing to test. We had politics at the start, politics in the waging and politics at the end. Politics of wars prevention should be politician's obligation; the politics of peace will be the prize.

An Infantryman will never be an expert about the war he is involved in fighting, his area of expertise will be confined to his immediate front, left and right, all else will be rumors of unfounded information, some true and some totally false. I've done my best to write as I remember but with the passage of time I may have retained some rumor as my truth. My deeper poems will reflect my truth.

I have studied the history of the Korean War and formed opinions teeming with questions of truth about some Generals, Politicians and Americas peoples after WW II and well past the Vietnam War. Some opinions are carved in stone some are not. They are my opinions as I try to understand my homelands peoples, be we at peace or war; this has now become a small but vital need in my mind. Our past freedoms rest with our Veterans and our war dead, our future freedoms rest with us the living. We have an obligation to uphold those freedoms for which men died.

A Healing

Korea was the first war we didn't win; Vietnam was the first war we lost. It was not the Grunts who tied or lost, our Buddies, our blood and our nightmares of carnage are spread throughout those bloody lands, from the frozen mountains of North Korea to the steaming jungles of Vietnam we paid the price of wars our countrymen couldn't care less about. Our politicians sent us to battle and with disdain denied us our victory. Our countrymen denied us our welcome home. Our WWII Brothers denied us accomplishment and our homeland denied us our healing, we walked quite alone with only the silence of our dead for decades. Korean Veterans were totally ignored as they trickled home thru rotation, there would be few bands to meet the troop ships, few parades at home and very few would even recognize us as having been at war, coming home, for some, became " a bridge to far".

Our Korean War prisoners of war released in 1953 were treated with disdain at best because a few succumbed to Red Chinese brainwashing. Our own military and politicians would hint of disgrace on all POWs because of those few, a sad commentary on Americas understanding, caring or loyalty to those who defended her and a sad commentary on this Veteran who came home and hid from war.

Four percent of Americans taken prisoner by the Germans died in captivity, twenty-six percent of Americans in Japanese P.O.W. camps died and a minimum of forty-nine percent of American POWs in Korea died in the camps. The percentage nears an abominable eighty percent if there were any way to obtain numbers executed just after their capture or not reported as Prisoners of War, this would take in most of the 8200 MIAs in Korea, a huge number considering the area of Korea and it's terrain.

Vietnam Veterans were treated with hate by many of our countrymen, mainly by the young people. We force young men to go to war then we shower them with hate! Vietnam was the only War this country put up with the dishonor some gave our returning Warriors.

In the end I must leave that to my Vietnam Brothers, I will touch on Vietnam occasionally due to the respect I give the

50

James Woods

Grunts who fought that bloody war and the anger I retain at our governments and the flower children's treatment of them.

Army troops occupying Japan lacked training in close air support, none in guerrilla warfare, and little training in tactics. We need constant training and a well equipped modern military in a world at peace, if not America will have thousands of extra body bags in Flag draped coffins showing up during the first few months of future wars.

Peacetime is when Congress should have been backing us up with the best of unit cohesiveness training and arms. To back us only after we're in a conflict has been/will be Congresses donation to the death of thousands. Incompetent political leaders have caused the filling of far too many body bags and amazingly no one has ever held them responsible.

In the first few months of the Korean War our outnumbered, outgunned, ill equipped and under-trained occupation troops were sent into combat to slow down and stop a modern, Soviet equipped and disciplined North Korean Red Army. They had the best of training, tanks and equipment. Their cadre had fought the Japanese and helped win China for the Communists, they were battle-hardened troops and had the cause of "their Civil War". American Troops had no defined cause, no saving our homeland from a tangible enemy. Honour, Duty? We went, we died and the Gold Stars in Moms windows at home were made of tarnished tin, not by the "Boy's" who died but by an America that didn't care.

Equip an ill-trained Army with out-dated, worn-out equipment, pathetic communications and for a while you will end up with chaos. Men tried and died trying, so many lives lost because the Generals, starting from Mac Arthur on down, were complacent after World War Two, duty was an eight to five job, then home to your shack-up. Life was easy, times were good. DAMN but we were so young and those Japanese GIRLS were so great!

President Truman and Congress would not allocate funds for modern, well-equipped and well-trained armed forces. Our leaders and politicians, who should have known better, shirked their duty to our country and the men they ask to defend her. They did more

A Healing

than shirk their duty; they betrayed those men they sent to battle with overly worn radios who's batteries would not hold a charge making communications between many units nearly impossible, armaments leftover from World War II and an ammo reserve of about a month. There was no excuse for the lack of equipment and proper cohesive training in unit tactics or physical conditioning they signed a death warrant for many young GI Joes.

With the lead-time prior to WWII troops at Pearl Harbor and the Philippines were ill prepared. In Korea nothing changed, again men died needlessly, we didn't learn. We saved a few dollars in exchange for the lives of our young inexperienced servicemen. These men should not have died because of overly zealous budget cuts put in by congress, they should not have died because the Generals did not demand they be well equipped and trained and they should not have died because of poor intelligence.

If we must send young "Boy's" to war let it be in a well-equipped, well-trained cohesive fighting unit, fighting for a cause that is "Just". Anything less is a betrayal, not only by our politicians and Generals but also by the American peoples. They elected the damn liberal politicians who disdain the military vocally and monetarily until disdain becomes need, need becomes death, death becomes clay, clay becomes grass and a Mother kneels and cries for a Son who, with training, may have lived.

Where the OSS/CIA was and what they were doing I have no idea. They certainly had not been doing their job else they would have known about the massive buildup of North Korean troops prior to June 25th. 1950. Sadly I'm not too sure some didn't know.

Young American "Boy's" now paid the price for politicians and Generals who rested on their laurels after winning the BIG ONE and did nothing to assure our winning the future "little wars". They did us, who must defend America, a great disservice and were the cause of death for thousands of young "Boy's". On the job training for combat is not what our Armed Forces should be about.

We learned but it was quite gory. We had the North Koreans pushed to near the Yalu River (Chinas border with North Korea) in November 1950. We'd won! Home for Christmas! Home to my Helen! Home to my dog "Old Gent"! Not quite! First us Grunts must deal with the results of an insubordinate General, a President who catered to him until it was to late and a Congress that had no balls to live up to their Constitutional duties. *Hell I doubt if most in Congress ever read our Constitution, our Bill of Rights or listened to their own oath of office.*

> *Us Grunts are those who pay the price*
> *when Politicians do not try.*
> *Us Grunts who don't amount to much.*
> *Us Grunts; The ones who die.*

There were prior warnings from our men to Mac Arthur of Chinese troops among the dead, which he ignored. The Chinese warned our State Department not to put our Army on her border, another warning ignored. There seemed to have been no attempt by Congress or President Truman to reign in Mac Arthur before we reached Chinas border. There was total failure by all politicians up to and including President Truman, a series of fatal decisions that would cost the lives of several million more humans, including thousands of young Americans.

The "home by Christmas" promise was not to be as we were rather busy with hoards of Red Chinese regulars. Mac Arthur's ego and politicians' malfeasance extended the war another thirty-two months. All of Korea and our troops paid heavily for our "trusted" politician's gross blunders. At the best our Generals and Politicians egotistically misjudged China's paranoia of a foreign power at her border, at its worse it was to test the mettle of Communism.

Mac Arthur knew the Oriental mindset better than any Caucasian alive; I feel he knew damn well China would respond to our troops at her border. His last great campaign would be to free China from the communists. His military mind dictated he could and should save Asia from Communism; any of his assurances to Truman that China would not enter were blatantly false.

A Healing

Chinese Regulars attacked the Marines and units of the 7th. Division in northeast Korea in October of 1950 than withdrew for no discernable reason except possibly to show they were serious about us staying back from her borders. At this time diplomacy should have taken over, the war would have ended with well over 3,000.000 lives mostly civilians, saved.

The political decision to battle for the complete reunification of the two Koreas came at a cost in lives only politicians would be willing for others to pay, a cost borne mostly by the Korean civilian populace.

You're right we didn't win. We tied and came home to a country's total indifference, all those dead young "Boy's" and so damn few cared. America gave us no acceptance; no have a beer Buddy, no job well done and no rationale for the acceptance in our minds of the carnage one faces in war. Some "Forgotten Warriors" felt no justification for the taking of life in "Your Forgotten War". Look to yourselves America for ignoring men you send to war, ignoring a reality that will never be yours.

Our next war went beyond the country's indifference to our Korean sacrifice, some bastards harassed and spat on our returning battle weary troops. Very few had the courage to risk jail by spitting on our politicians who approved our intervention into Vietnam's "civil war".

Politicians had no concept whatsoever of the "cause" of the Viet Cong and the Vietminh and committed the vast numbers of ground Troops to do what no army had been able to do for God knows how long. The Vietminh had fought the French prior to WWII, the Japanese during, the French again after WWII and now they were fighting us. The ignorant mind-set of this cold war period could not comprehend there was a vast difference between a war of nationalistic unification and Communism's world threat. We sent men to die for all the wrong reasons plus no support at home. Again we never stood a prayer of victory because of politics at the start, politics during and politics at the end.

Politician's get real stupid as they beat the drums of war, when they finally figure out the cause is wrong they still continue a damn shame. I give you President Johnson's lie; the 1964 Gulf of Tonkin incident was his Big Lie, a collaboration of our top brass and President Johnson. A set up for submission to Congress so approval could be obtained for the huge build-up of ground troops, a boost for Johnson's ego as the war wasn't going well. Again a few million more Humans would die including many thousands of young Americans.

The Tet offensive caused Johnson not to seek re-election in 1968; he didn't want to go down in history as the first President to lose a war. I mention Politicians quite frequently in my writings, always in anger despairingly spun from history. Something has been quite wrong when presidents so easily commit us to wars and Congress rubber-stamps its okay in the name of backing us up, and then does not follow through and allow us the home support to win

Like most wars the final endings in Korea and Vietnam were political decisions. We have three choices of ending a war, total victory, compromise, or just get the hell out. Politically the latter takes the most courage. Human lives and "saving face" do not equate. Some of our Politicians and Generals egos are pure bullshit, war to some is a game played out thru pawns that must protect the Kings image at all costs.

Nearly every Infantryman exposed to enough combat time, with shifting battle lines, carries one or two Ghosts of dead or dying Little Children and/or dead Buddies, Ghosts that will not leave. The effects or degree of pain will vary but it's there, for some a lifetime. Writing these lines was necessary for me; now they are for all that carry visions of a war that somehow never quite seemed important to America, wars that bloodied our souls a bit, wars we carried in the silence and pain of limbo for far too many years.

Young people may learn cold hard facts in history books, they will not learn of war. Only those who lived thru them can attempt to describe wars, the men who fought or the Civilians caught with their homeland at war and there is no other valid picture. Historians and politicians will do the painting but they are colorblind to the uselessness, pain and reality of war. They may or may not add the true facts building up to, causing and ending a war; their ineptitudes are historic classics. These lines

A Healing

are not for the bastard politicians who have betrayed our Warriors, a not uncommon occurrence; they merely stamp their betrayal "secret" for fifty years. Political expediency at its best is sealed in our nation archives, those "secret" files not to be opened for forty or fifty years.

As for you loudmouths on your barstools, those who say "hell man that's war" to cover any incident, those who brag of their killing and those who have never cared, I ask that you please not read my writings, to such as you they will mean nothing.

I now to speak to our Christian Brothers, since our revolution we have sent young "Boy's" into battle, first to earn and than retain our Freedoms. If our Lord had not yet sought them out, or they had not heard, or did not answer, is their fate eternal Hell as they die in battle? There have been over one million who have died in our wars; we demanded the lives of these young men in the name of Freedoms we retain. Was the price many paid their lives plus eternity in Hell? Their sacrifice is not of great significance to most of us, it was vital to those who died, those who died defending our Freedoms.

How do you/we justify sending young "Boy's" into this hellish aspect of dying? The chance of our hearing "Gods Call" exponentially rises as we age, our young Warrior dead do not age. You who send our young to war before the Holy Ghost has touched their Hearts and Soul, you whose words would condemn to Hell those Warriors not "Saved" or "Born Again", yet you accept their deaths as your right. Nay, you have and will demand the sacrifice of their lives/souls as protectors of your Freedoms.

You who are so sure of your place in Gods Love leave some seekers adrift in fear. I believe the bridge you lay out between man and God is exceedingly narrow. God would not build a path so few could find or trod. God's path will hold all seekers of His light.

Your narrow path is a torture of Man and a disservice to our Gods Love, Wisdom and Compassion. I, as a seeker, believe you wrong us, below in my mind proves you wronged us.

A shortened version from page 49

"The Path Beyond the Veil

A testament to my Children, my friends, all whom I love and those I may not know:

ON FEB. THE 11, 2004 AT AGE SEVENTY-THREE I WENT INTO cardiac arrest and died for a while, (I did not get to the light you may have read about), I seemed to be a bluish semi-shapeless form floating at the inside top of the ambulance and was totally unconcerned with the person the EMT was bent over, *my emotions in this (spirit form?) were totally neutral.* In the past I severely questioned this sort of happening and did not quite believe such a thing could be.

From the inside top of the ambulance I observed the EMT working on me, lean around the ½ partition, say something to the driver and sensed the ambulance suddenly pick up speed swerving in and out of traffic, going over the curbs with sirens and horn blaring (I could hear the siren and horn loud and clear).

I feel compelled to send this testament of the "Event" to family, friends and those who may be suffering the loss of a loved one, in the past, recently or in the future, or those who may be approaching death with fear. *Please my friends do not be afraid*, for those who are dying, have gone before or for your own demise.

There is a happening after this life and, although I do not know what it's about, I do know there is serenity with peace awaiting a soul, a spirit, or whatever we become after dying time.

I do not remember leaving my body, how long I was gone or how I re-entered my physical self (all this could have been a trick of

A Healing

my mind), but this is *my* important learning; *I felt only serenity with peaceful detachment prior to and after several incursions into my heart during the next seven months I was in and out of hospitals.*

I felt an absence of fear and had *absolutely no apprehension* about death or dying. That feeling about death and dying still holds, (I use to be quite fearful about dying because of childhood teachings; i.e. the uncertainty of Hell, eternity etc.) The worse part about dying is the pain or extreme discomfort of getting to the veil, once you're at the veil only peace remains with one step more and the miraculous continuance of existence.

I do not KNOW there is a God but I now KNOW there is an afterlife and now FEEL there is a God. I am sure the pathways to our God, our after-life, must be many, quite varied and, most importantly, uncomplicated.

I seem to find myself anticipating peaceful tranquility in an existence I know nothing about, an existence I brushed against for an in instant in time and in the process lost my fear of death, my fear of hell and my fear of the black eternal void. Strange how one "Event" can have such a profound effect after more then eighteen months. While this "Event" is a blessing for my dying time, it is mostly a "calming blessing" in "this" my living time.

I felt a need to share this "Event", whether you personally choose to believe my narrative is unimportant, (I, for one, would not have), *but it will help some of you*, when the time comes, to experience less fear and emotional pain and more hope that lays beyond in his or her life.

Jimmie Joe
fishhook junction, Alaska

James Woods

We still fought on

I know one thing I'd like to feel,
that God and Heaven both are real.
But saying I believe won't do.
Why did our God answer you?

We seek the calm of sureness,
a knowing of our Lord.
We're at fault if we don't find Him
fore we die by bloody sword?

Are we to lacking to be worthy?
Why can't we feel God in our heart?
I prayed for God but could not find;
I just couldn't find the start.

Chaplains didn't have my answer,
I must put finding God on hold.
A young Warrior in Gods wilderness,
fights on thru stench of summers death
and frozen dead in winters cold.

Fights on with death around him.
No thoughts of Heaven nor of hell.
Fights on with mind in limbo.
Where will my soul now dwell?

In pain and mire our life runs out,
you gave us death before our time.
We'll never know what God's about?
Our soul now burns? You share this crime.

Jimmie Joe
fishhook junction, Alaska

"War is hell only if you care"

A Healing

"A Healing"

Us who now live please do forgive,
we've let freedoms slip asunder.
We need you friends, dead Warrior friends,
unleash your cannons' thunder.

Bring all your dead, make us all dread
we caused your country's' fate.
Show us life's blood, wounds mixed with mud,
show "Freedoms bloody mate."

Just a few poems of my thoughts
from times long in the past,
of Love and War and Little Children,
some stay and some don't last.

Poetic license was used at times
but the truth as I retain.
Tho emotions were tough to express in rhyme.
They became my healing pain
.

I know in certain poems I wrote
my pain flowed out as tears,
T'was quite unpleasant typing them,
my Shadow Ghosts from warring years.

Jimmie Joe
fishhook junction, Alaska

James Woods

"No Joy"

There is no joy in my writings,
in war there can not be.
The ones who suffer most from war
are the displaced refugees.

Some noncombatants sit back here,
so knowing all and smug,
they've never held a dying Child
who's hurt too bad to hug,

Nor held a dying Buddies hand
while terror thru him flowed.
They seem to think that war is grand.
Thank God I don't explode.

They've never had to kill a man
who's a "Boy" as young as you.
Our hopes and dreams are all the same.
His loved ones grieve him too.

There is no glory, only pain
in what we do and see.
You loudmouths on the barstools
all get contempt from me.

If you're the type who brags of war
or the people you have killed,
it's best you stop your reading now,
by my lines you won't be thrilled.

There are no glorious battle tales,
no courage like John Wayne.
Thru tortured writings by the Man,
Man exorcised the ghosts of war
and neutralized the "Boy's" stored pain.

A Healing

My two small Children play in peace
in Gods land beyond the sky.
Nurtured thru Love from Soldier "Boy".
The "Boy" who choose to die.

Jimmie Joe
fishhook junction, Alaska

Politicians in war devour their young
and quench their thirst with Mothers tears.
Only the vanquished foes are hung
but all sides fulfill a Mothers fears.

James Woods

"A Healing"

"I begin again"

"BOY'S" JOURNEY WAS LONG, HE WAS GIVEN NO MAP, NO COMPASS, NO directions and I had a great deal of trouble locating exactly where "Boy" was hiding. I searched behind the many walls "Boy" had built, the last wall was a son-of-a-bitch to break thru, I didn't want to enter, I was afraid to enter, but the courage came and thankfully I broke thru.

The following poem is dedicated to the combat Veteran, who in some shadowed area of his mind senses the loss of a small but vital part of himself, a part left on his distant battleground, a part that's his alone, a part unshared, a part protected.

Probably a result never anticipated is we, who faced our enemy in real battle, would be fighting him in our dreams at night for several years and facing "Boy's" flashing images in day most of our lives, images that keep us from a peace we don't quite find. We constantly push the images back; shun the "Boy" who left us in bloody battle yet subconsciously search for him, some for a lifetime. We need him home, to touch his pain, to let him know we're sorry and convince him, "it's okay Son, we're home", it's over, it's really over.

"I never knew him as a man"

I don't know where he went.
I knew him well tho as a "Boy"
and his dog we called "Old Gent".

This poem I wrote for a young man,
one I didn't get to know.
I knew him only as a "Boy"
from fifty years ago.

A Healing

I remember "Boy" from Childhood,
he was just a little Lad.
He kind of stuttered when he talked,
No, I'd say he stuttered bad.

When "Boy" was five a little puppy
came to be his pal for life.
When he was feeling sad or hurting
"Old Gent" smoothed away "Boy's" strife.

"Boy" and "Gent" seemed star crossed Buddies
and I alone would see,
with "Gent", "Boy's" stutter disappeared,
with "Gent", "Boy's" words flowed free.

That fine dog we called "Old Gent"
formed a sacred bond with "Boy".
They roamed the woods and fields together
and life became their special joy.

They would wrestle on the front lawn
and cut-up all about the farm,
spend summer days a fishing bluegill
in the lake beyond the barn.

"Boy's" stutter nearly ceased to be
along with shame from teasing days,
"Old Gent" stayed there beside the "Boy"
and helped "Boy" thru his stuttering ways.

"Old Gent" finally cured "Boy's" stutter,
then "Boy" talked like you or me.
That old Dog was really something,
how'd he set "Boy's" stutter free?

I'd like to think God sent "Old Gent"
to that childhood friend of mine,

James Woods

to love "Boy" down that stuttering road
and guide "Boy" thru that curious time.

"Boy" and "Gent" hunted the field mice
and rats and snakes were fun.
Later on was pats and rabbits
when he'd learned to use a gun.

"Boy" built huts around the woodland
made with spruce boughs and saplings bent.
They'd always share the game together,
"Boy" and his dog we called "Old Gent".

That "Old Gent" was something special,
I wish I had a dog like him.
I still can see them both together
but what will be is not what's been.

I remember "Boy" from high school,
he was kind of like a chum.
He was not inclined to studies.
I was quite sure he'd be a bum.

I was even surer "Boy" would be a bum when he quit school in
the tenth grade, not once but twice. The tenth grade was the last year of
high school "Boy" finished; he did get to play basketball those three
years. "Boy" was sort of dumb about some things but he caught up.

He was in on all the high school sports,
basketball was his favorite game.
His hands were quick, his feet were fast,
"Flash" became the "Boy's" nickname.

I think I sort of liked him,
he grew on you after while.
He had a laughing sparkle in his eye
and a slightly crooked smile.

A Healing

"Boy" skipped school to hunt the whitetail,
hunting deer to him was fine.
His biggest love was still the fishing
for fat bluegills on his line.

"Boy" skipped school a lot for fishing,
of course he took along "Old Gent".
Their life was peaceful carefree days,
much wasted time they spent

.

I shared in all his boyhood pranks
and there were quite a few.
I hung out with all his Buddies
and that fine dog named "Gent" too.

He poached the deer in numbers great,
he was devious as could be.
The game wardens couldn't catch him.
"Boy" was sneaky, "Boy" was free.

January 15, 1949

He joined the army at eighteen
I kind of tagged along.
We trained in mud and grime of Infantry
and life still sang "Boy's" youthful song.

""Boy's" orders for occupation duty with the 24th. Infantry Division in Japan was cut in May 1950. "Boy" began a 30-day home furlough the first of June where he met his lovely Helen whose essence still resides in "Boy's" heart.

When our eyes met we couldn't pry
our eyes apart, they're stuck!
We didn't even want to try;
Can Cupid run amok?

James Woods

"Boy" didn't know 'bout Cupids charms,
he was a bit naive.
Quite soon he'll hold her in his arms
and boy!! will "Boy" believe!

That furlough's where "Boy" fell in Love,
the first love of his time.
The Love would last throughout "Boy's" years,
unconsummated as rare wine.

Twenty-fifth of June 'twas on that day,
A day that changed "Boy's" life.
The North Koreans stopped "Boy's" play.
"Boy's" darling Helen will not be,
Will never be "Boy's" Wife.

"Boy" was a Lad of nineteen years
when we were sent to fight our war.
His mind of pain and death was clean,
it would change forevermore.

They shipped us out together
'cross that ocean wide and wild.
I was to become the fighting man
and "Boy" remained the Child.

(**bold** type denotes "Boy's" outfit)

The U.S. forces in the Far East at Mac Arthur's disposal included the four divisions in Japan: the 1st Cavalry Division, the 7th, **24th**, and 25th Infantry Divisions. Due to Congressional budget restraints the divisions were lacking over a third of their infantry, artillery units and most their armor units. Existing units were far under strength, weapons and equipment were war-worn relics of World War II and ammunition reserves amounted to about a month's supply.

None of the divisions had reached full combat efficiency nor were they building towards it, hell they weren't even close and to

67

A Healing

make matters worse their cohesive unit training had been scandalously neglected. The men had no idea of how deadly this lack of training would become. Occupation duties seemed to be all Congress, Mac Arthur and Divisional commanders was concerned with; to me this was dereliction of duty.

Pre-WWII in the Philippines and Hawaii also faced the real problem of being unprepared and many died needlessly, we court marshaled a few Admirals for Congress and Roosevelt's malfeasance of not funding the military for years. General Mac Arthur escaped without charges.

I write of wars small children dying
and the "Boy's" we left across the sea.
I write of an old man who's been trying,
to cleanse his war, his long past war
as he walks his mind where there's no peace,
thru times of inhumanity.

We headed north from Port of Pusan
on a bullet riddled train.
"Boy" and I crouched alone in a cattle car
as fear wafted across "Boy's" brain.

As "Boy" rode the train to our assignment
with the **24**[Th]. that day,
he thought of God and death and dying.
God don't let me be a coward,
please don't let me run away.

"Boy" answered now his country's battle call,
Politician's failures cause wars pains.
Boyhood fades in ancient mists of war,
soon I the Man must take the reigns.

We had intelligence data from several sources and should have prevented this war; at the very least we should have been much better prepared. Our Military at all times should be a well

James Woods

trained, well equipped, cohesive fighting force in top physical condition, anything less and we betray those we send to war, we cause some deaths as surely as if we lined those under-trained "Boy's" up before a firing squad.

The **34**[th] losses were more than 530 men out of its total strength of 1,549 present *at the city of Taejon alone*. The leadership losses were horrendous in the regiments they included four Regimental Commanders and two operations officers in just over two weeks. The 1st Battalion lost its executive officer and the **3/34**[th] lost two battalion commanders and its operations officer. The division commander, General Dean, was also missing in action. {He survived in the hills avoiding capture for about 45 days} General Dean was awarded the Congressional Medal of Honour for action at Taejon.

About the first of August, the **24**[th] Division deployed in positions behind the Naktong River on a 40-mile front, with the **34**[th], 21st and the Republic of South Korea's 17th Infantry regiments on line from south to north. The **34**[th]'s sector about 34,000 yards, along which were deployed the 493 remaining troops of the **3**[rd] Battalion, the average of one man every 300 feet can only be justified by the desperateness of our situation, we should have been wiped out. We were forced to learn by on the job training, I ask politicians to note the price we paid while learning.

We were not tin soldiers; we were flesh and blood and hope, we were and are the past and future dead of uncaring politicians, even tho we live, we've seen our dead who never knew of their betrayal. The POWs we left to their purgatory? They knew.

The regiment was critically short of vehicles, 4.2-inch mortars and, the mainstay of Korean War rifle squads, the Browning automatic rifle. Some 3.5 inch rocket launcher, a replacement for the wimpy 2.76 inch relic of WWII, arrived at Taejon but the effectiveness was miserably lessened due to the troops unfamiliarity with the weapon and the lack of any tactical training in its deployment against tanks in a city.

A Healing

Had the troops had this training they could have destroyed every Russian T-34 tank within Taejon as the tanks came in without infantry support. Several hundred lives would have been spared in this battle alone and possibly gained enough time for reinforcements to arrive.

On August 4, elements of the North Korean 16th Infantry Regiment staged an assault across the Naktong between Companies I and L, **3/34** Infantry, and overwhelmed most of their positions. Communist North Korean troops drove about five miles into the **24th** Division sector, bringing about the First Battle of the Naktong Bulge. This eventually involved the entire **24th** Division, the U.S. 1st Provisional Marine Brigade, the newly arrived 9th Infantry Regiment and 1/23rd Infantry (both from the 2nd Infantry Division) and the 2/27th Infantry. The struggle lasted until August 19.

The **34th** Infantry gave every thing it had, Company K stayed on its nearly 7,000-yard front along the Naktong alone until ordered out on about August 14. At the outset, the 1/34th launched a counterattack, but part of Company C was trapped in a gristmill, where the men valiantly held out until rescued. Captain Albert F. Alfonso, with remnants of Companies A, C and **L**, held a small perimeter at the nose of the bulge until ordered out on the night of August 8-9. Elements of the regiment took part in a number of counterattacks between August 6 and 18.

The **34th** made its last attack on the August 18th, during which Company C was reduced to 37 men and Company A to 61. Company **L** lost more than 20 men in a few minutes to a counterattack, when it was relieved by the U.S. 2nd Infantry Division on August 25, the **24th** Division numbered 10,600 men-- 8, 000 short of full strength.

On August 27, Lt. Gen. Walton Walker, U.S. Eighth Army commander in Korea dissolved the **34th. Regiment**, converting the 1/34th into the 3rd Battalion, 19th Infantry, and the **3/34th** into the **2nd Battalion**, 21st Infantry Regiment. Those who served and survived the first fifty-three days of the war should well remember our politician's years of drastically under-funding and the generals under training of our Infantry units.

The original "under-manned" regimental strength of the 34th Infantry Regiment when they embarked Japan was 1,898 men. After fifty-three days of battle 184 "Boy's" were left to carry on the fight.

The **34th**. Is not the norm, but it is one example out of many contributing to thousands of needless deaths in Korea. Deaths caused by politicians' distaste of spending money on research and development, new equipment and intensive unit training during our years of peacetime. *Making our military into cohesive fighting units is a leadership obligation of Generals and politicians, not the Grunts. We can be well-trained, well-conditioned, fight effectively and a few die. We can be poorly trained, fight ineffectively, panic, run and most die. We non-combatants have a sacred obligation to defend the need of training for the men who defend us.*

It's peacetime when Congress must stand behind our military, assure the budget is adequate and demand the units be trained as cohesive, effective fighting units. Again I stress anything less is a betrayal of the young "Boy's" we send to war, a needless death warrant for many. With well-trained Officers and Non-coms to enforce discipline the terror felt by some Troops would have been eliminated and nearly all panic prevented, the Troops would have known what to expect and how to execute the delaying actions when vastly outnumbered.

In a larger war young lives will still be lost in the slowing down of a foe while we draft and train civilians, but there will be thousands fewer of Americas young "Boy's" dying needlessly and coming home in body-bags as bits of Clay for their Moms.

From; I never knew him as a man.

> 'Twas along the bloody Naktong River
> that I noticed my Chum change.
> His eyes lost their laughing sparkle
> and his smile was not the same.

A Healing

"Boy's" conscious mind began to slow
from sights of man-kinds gore.
Subconscious mind recorded all,
enclosed in walls now being built
by the "Boy" they sent to war.

"Boy" thought much about his dog "Old Gent"
and the peaceful woods back home.
His dull eyes now hid the numbing sights
where future ghosts of war would roam.

His Granny wrote "Boy" a letter,
said his good "Old Gent" had died.
His dog. His Friend for all those years.
He just broke down ----- "Boy" cried.

It was about this time, August 1950, we had a vicious nighttime firefight the end result being three deuce and a half trucks with bodies thrown in filling them nearly to the top of the side racks. I walked on these dead young "Boy's" looking for my Buddies; I didn't find them, they must have been further down than I could uncover.

Walking on our dead did not bother me consciously at the time. I can, right now amazingly, see a few faces. They must have been seared far back in my memory cells, they were never part of my Ghosts, it's odd. I now feel sadness fifty years later. There must be a lot of survival pushed back beyond our brains and I just unwrapped a piece of time from mine. The sorrow is in the youngness, so very, very young; they really were little more than "Boy's" and so many in one night. *Lord I'm sorry.*

'Bout then in nighttime battle
or it could have been in day,
"Boy" just kind of up and disappeared.
He became a different kind of M.I.A.

James Woods

He would take no more mans warring hell,
that childhood friend to me so dear.
One minute fighting stoutly by my side,
then, thru cordites mists, "Boy" disappeared.

I think I tried to find him later on,
maybe for a year or two.
I don't know how or why he disappeared.
Guess "Boy" and I were thru.

He'd built his walls, he'd built them well,
enclosing Mans "demons" in the rooms.
While building walls and filling them
the "Boy" became entombed.

He could be somewhere I won't know
with his dog we called "Old Gent".
Roaming the woods and fields together
as in his peaceful youth he spent.

I still miss "Boy" just a bit.
Guess I miss his "Old Gent" too.
He bugged out on me in bloody battle,
the "Boy" I knew so very well
left with the man I never knew.

I'll not know what he might have been,
he would not be shaped by warring time.
His walls absorbed the shaping
and that boyhood friend of mine.

The "Boy" who left for war is gone.
He was never seen again.
Only I came home from battles.
Now a stranger 'amongst old friends.

A Healing

My ground battles all had ended
but for years they would remain,
enclosed in walls built by the "Boy",
Mans flashing, ghostly visions
from the "Boy" entombed with pain.

In sleep "Boy's" walls released the Ghosts,
Ghosts of long repeating dreams.
The first few years I would awake
as lips closed upon "Boy's" screams.

I'd push them back by light of day.
My nightly fight; God make them end.
I grew to dread my nighttime battles.
Always alone; No Comrade Friend.

No Comrade Friend to aid my fight.
No solace my soul could share.
Just I alone in twisted night
and death, not peace, awaits me there.

The "Boy" was trapped in self-made tomb
built to protect the Man.
The Man was trapped by social mores.
It took years to understand,
Manly men may cry.

One "Boy" died, one Man survived
those days so long ago.
One made it into Manhood.
Jim misses jimmie joe.

I kind of hope I get to meet them
in that land beyond the sky.
I'd like to see my dog "Old Gent"
and the "Boy" who choose to die.

Jimmie Joe, fishhook junction, Alaska

James Woods

My time of twisted nights

In the following dream artillery round kills me, the dream made no sense. On the nights I had this dream death not only awaited me in sleep, death took me in exactly the same way every time, as in all my repeating dreams, they seemed to be carbon copies.

Why repeating dreams that are not real?
Is there reality I won't recall?
Why could I cope in actual war
and in sleep not cope at all?

We are attacking a steep wooded hill in daylight; the trees are just beginning to turn so it must be fall. I sense my Buddies to my left but can't see them due to the thick brush. As we continue up the hill we begin taking machinegun fire from directly in front of me, I twist-pull the pin on a grenade, rear up and throw it.

I'll never know if I got the machinegun as an artillery round hit in the same place my body was dropping back down to and my whole world turned into a huge exploding flash of light, I was blown up and out from the hill and felt neither pain nor fear, I felt pure terror. I had no body, I was left with only a pair of misshapen lips emitting a muted primordial scream into a totally soundless black void; I would awake sitting bolt upright in bed shaking and sweating as if I had malaria with my lips closing on a fading scream I never heard. My wife would hear it and never quite understood, nor did I. This was the only dream causing me to scream. After nearly half a century I still vividly remember the hill, the leaves half yellow and half green, throwing the grenade, the explosion with its huge flash of light and being blown up and out. I have no desire to figure why; it's just the way times were.

In this repeating dream half the damn Chinese Army is chasing me along a ridge pockmarked and cratered from artillery. The trees are all snags and stobs from direct hits or airbursts. I am running without a weapon, the enemy is about two hundred yards

A Healing

behind me in a vee formation. In this dream I am feeling fear but I must try to stop them.

I come to a dead enemy soldier, pick up his bolt-action rifle, kneel, aim at the lead man and fire. The bullet goes about twenty feet out of the barrel and just falls to the ground. DAMN! I rack in another round, the point sticks in the chamber and the base jams in the magazine; I can't un-jam it so I'm off running again. I go thru the same thing over and over, they never gain on me and it's the same shredded trees, the same craters, I pick up the same rifle and the same formation keeps chasing me for what seems all night. I don't have this dream anymore but the years I did have it every detail seemed to stay exactly the same and as always I was alone.

The following repeating dream has to do with an attempt to rescue a fellow soldier in a bombed-out village; this is the only one I occasionally still have and it started years later then the others and it was not a disturbing dream.

This dream begins with me kneeling beside a section of wall left from a bombed out building, I am peering around the partial wall looking for the sniper who had just shot a fellow soldier. The soldier is laying face down and appears lifeless in the middle of what appears to be a town square. My eyes are searching the partially bombed out buildings across the square for the sniper when I appear standing beside my kneeling self.

My dumb standing self is in plain view of the sniper. The conversation is as follows:

Standing self: Go get him.
Kneeling self: I will.
Standing self: Go get him now!
Kneeling self: I will, give me a minute!
Standing self: You've got to do it and you know you're
going to do it. So do it now!
Kneeling self: I know I am, I will in a second.

We argue in this fashion for short while with dummy staying in full view of the sniper. In the next instant I am kneeling beside the soldier with my left hand on his left shoulder, my left knee on the ground and I hold the M-1 in my right hand with its butt on the ground. My head is turned toward the buildings across the square still searching for the sniper, I turn back to the soldier and start to turn him over --- the dream always ends there, I never get to see his face or see if he is alive and I remain asleep as this was not a bad dream.

After a period of time, two years or so, I don't recall now, as I merged into the distressing part of my dreams a voice would say, "wake up Jim it's just a dream" and I would awaken. The voice spoke earlier and earlier during the dreams, after while as soon as a dream began it would end. This basically ended my long battles while sleeping and my time of twisted nights. Only one dream had anything to do with my recollections of war, the three other repeating dreams, the ones recorded here, are a blank in my war remembrances.

Jimmie Joe
fishhook junction, Alaska

A Healing

"Why a bit of guilt?"

"Boy" could take no more mans warring Hell,
that Childhood Friend to me so dear.
One minute fighting stoutly by my side,
then, thru cordites mists, "Boy" disappeared.

With no conscious knowledge of "Boy's" leaving
I took his place in battles storm.
All the pain of killing, death and dying
I would accept as Warriors norm.

I would accept the death of fallen Comrades
with distant pain and zombie gaze.
This pain that always kept it's distance,
taps lightly in life's autumn days.

I've lived a life that's long and full.
I've had a Wife and held my Child.
Great-grandbabies walk thru my heartstrings.
I've caught those fish in places wild.

These wondrous gifts bestowed on me
were from a sky of mostly blue.
Wisps of guilt drift by when I ask the WHY,
why me my fallen Warrior Brothers,
why me instead of you?

Jimmie Joe
fishhook junction, Alaska

James Woods

"Boy's" foe

I would accept as sacred duty,
Honour-bound, to destroy our faceless enemy.
Their dead we'd strewn throughout that land,
if by chance we looked, with time we see,
most dead were young, ----- young "Boy's" like me.

THERE ARE NO WORDS TO EXPRESS MY THOUGHTS ON THIS; I GUESS I shouldn't have skipped so much school along with the fact of my not finishing high school. Words are so damn inadequate for conveying my feelings. I'm trying to say I'm sorry to the young North Korean and Chinese Soldiers who died or may have died by my hand. I do not apologize as the hands of politicians and fate put us together in combat, we did our duty. I had no remorse at the time, no joy, no hate, emotions were muted, a strange world combat. It's a stranger world in which I attempt to express my sorrow to the spirits of men who have been dead fifty years.

My reverent prayer is all young dead of war will be reincarnated, this may go against my Christian teachings but God could do it if he so desired and it is in my prayers God will. I pray they will know the joyous time of a full life with a true and loving Wife, little Children and Grandchildren to hold their finger as they walk together. May they catch those fish in places wild and live out their lives in peace.

So I say to the Spirits of those whose death I caused, my sorrow is I deprived you of all the joys in living I have known.

I care that you died.

Jimmie Joe
fishhook junction, Alaska

A Healing

"Boy's" deep sorrow"

I would accept the massacred civilians,
from Babies small thru tired old Men.
All across that "Land of Morning Calm"
lay tortured dead 'mongst slaughtered Kin

"CIVIL" WARS ARE NEARLY ALWAYS BRUTALLY VICIOUS, KOREA'S was exceptionally so. The North slaughtered whole villages rumored to be Christians or American sympathizers; Unknown to me at the time the South Koreans also slaughtered anyone even rumored to be Communist sympathizers. Our top brass, the State Department ECT, which must have included the top of the executive branch, knew of these massacres. It's a blow to realize ones cause was so corrupted by an ally.

Altogether the North and South Koreans massacred tens of thousands for no reason, Men, Women and Children were butchered. Our bombers killed tens of thousands in the north and altogether these added up to several million Humans dying in fear and pain. The heavy bombing of cities seem to have become a legitimately accepted type of massacre (collateral damage) starting with World War II.

Dumb, smart, incendiary, cluster or any other type of bomb we can think up and drop on population's centers is a coldly calculated massacre. No matter what nice "collateral damage" type name the spinners come up with the poor bastards are dead.

The surviving Children will develop pencil thin arms, legs, and distended stomachs; their hair may turn a bit reddish. "Their eyes", look in their eyes my friend, tell me what you see. I see a little Child whose eyes reflect no light, only the dullness of the dead, our little walking dead, little Zombies of politicians. Death will come slowly; at the end the Grim Reaper will become the caring parent. .... *Damn you bastards.*

Americans will continue getting the morning paper, having breakfast and "you know Ma" we blew the Hell out of 'em last night agin, this wars been going on a long time, by God you'd think we'd be runnin out'a bombs wouldn't yu? Oh well. Better get the Kids ready for Church, it's a nice sunny day lets have a picnic down by the lake this afternoon, I kinda feel like just relaxin, it's been a tough week.

October 1950,
From; "My Healing"

> Two small Children crumpled by a crossroads
> with no one else around.
> Two casualties of grown-ups war,
> soon little bodies in the ground.
>
> A little "Boy" of five or six
> with eyes dulled flat from pain,
> held littler Sister near the ditch.
> Her eyes held pain the same.
>
> Leaha's little head was on Kim's chest,
> Kim's arm round Leaha's shoulder fell.
> Four haunting eyes imploring us,
> this is getting tough to tell.

Americans, such as myself, have no real concept of the tragic misery of a war being fought where ones family and totally extended family reside. Some say " well hell ya that's bad but there ain't no rules, that's war ya know ". No I don't know! I do know Americans don't know shit about the suffering of wars real pain. That includes myself.

A few million more died from the constant friends and companions of war; starvation, disease and sadly, suicide. Somewhere between two and six million Korean civilians died, no one knows, they guess. Hell few cared and they still don't care. Damn the world's politicians; the safe, fat, contemptuous, flag waving bastards who consider a crime against Humanity as something only the loser can commit and be prosecuted for. The egotistical asses never contemplated the thought of even considering the initiation of a war itself is a crime against Humanity.

A Healing

I would accept the bombed-out northern cities
as justice for our enemy.
I would accept the maimed and starving Children
thru war dulled eyes that don't quite see.

To much death gave dead a neutral view
and thus they stayed as years rolled by.

Except two small Children clung to me,
inside my head they would not die
and I would feel the lost "Boy" cry.

In the nightmare mangles of mans warring
it seems there lurked a cowards spawn,
'cause in fact took nearly fifty years
'fore courage asked why "Boy" had gone.

I would accept without a spoken question
my country's apathy to "Boy's" war.
I would accept while never really knowing
the cause my Buddies had died for.

I would accept "Boy's" flashing, ghostly visions
and never ask or question WHY.
I would accept the damn repeating dreams
and unheard scream when I would die.

I would accept the dead and crippled Children
as "collateral damage" of mans wars.
With "Boy's" resurrection thru my writings
there's no acceptance anymore.

Politicians sent our "Boy's" to battle
in wars that held no victory goal.
Several million deaths they'll never question,
nor atonement for a Warriors soul.

James Woods

So for all my living wartime Buddies
and the ones fate chose to die,
forgive me Friends but I must ask,
asks our callous politicians—**WHY**?

In retrospect there was never acceptance of "collateral damage", as the word hadn't been spun yet. At the time my conscious mind was past being consciously traumatized by the sight of Children crippled and starving from our bombing North Korean cities. At this stage of the war we were quite well conditioned to Mans inhumanity to Man thru our earlier battles and the sight of many massacres of Men, Women and Children by the North Koreans.

Flat dull eyes (The thousand yard stare) and muted feelings are Mother Nature's way of letting us function without becoming a section eight (crazy), so I say there never was acceptance of the dead, the maimed or the starving. Our eyes saw the abject misery around us and stored all in our memory banks for future time when mankind's sanity returns and demands a necessary atonement. We're given only a temporary hiding, a semi-reprieve so to speak and a partial reprieve until WHY?

For some of us the time comes when we must ask WHY and than examine our war. Our very own war, *you know the one we keep inside, the one that so often appears unbidden, the one that hurts and you don't want to think about but the son-of-a-bitch is part of you and you weak kneed sniveling bastard. Yeh that's the one. Sorry Friend but that is the one.*

We won't know what to examine and we won't know the question but, ----- we must answer. My semi-reprieve lasted nearly forty years, when it ended in the fall of nineteen eighty-nine it was only by the grace of God that it didn't end with a very loud bang.

A Healing

My examination began aboard my boat in peaceful Halibut Cove, Alaska in mid-July 1997. I've found most of the questions and many answers thru the intervening years and the method that worked for me was writing and writing and writing, on paper white with pain in black. It was tough getting long repressed or suppressed emotions dug out and printed where I could see them in black and white, once written down I could no longer push them back behind my walls. The pain and tears flowed as words brought forth light to replace the darkness of the "Boy" imprisoned.

I would read the writings that were painful over and over 'til there were no tears. The worse by far was the poem about two small Korean Children who didn't make it. I one-finger typed forty to sixty thousand words before examining the house of dismay in my brain where those small Korean Children lived. Many times I had told my friends I was finished with my writings, I really thought I was but, "Boy" knew I wasn't, his tenacity took hold and it seems I was forced to write thru to "Boy's" completion. In truth I guess it was our completion together.

One morning I drove to Wasilla (Alaska), picked up typing paper, an extra ink cartridge and for some reason what turned out to be the most important item, a bottle of Jack Daniels, I drove home, set up the word processor, put on my glasses, opened the bottle and began my one fingered typing and one fisted drinking. Somehow I knew this was my time of courage, even tho it was derived, at the start, from a fifth of Jack Daniels whiskey.

I began the unwrapping of a piece of time about a small little "Boy" and a smaller little "Girl", It's been several years since I opened that bottle, now writing this part down for you my Friend I have wet eyes, not of guilt or unresolved conflict, the writing has triggered a deep sadness for Kim and Leaha who have somehow, in my heart, became my Children.

James Woods

I must have been quite a sight after a few hours, silent tears streaming down my cheeks, my shirt astonishingly wet, fumbling for the letters on the keyboard, wiping my glasses, wiping my eyes, trying to see the keys, and about killing that bottle.

I didn't accomplish much in the writing but I did break thru a wall, it was painful thru its later writing and stayed painful thru the many readings after completion, but it was the key to nearly all. With time it gave me the peace I had cried out to God for in nineteen eighty-nine and some part of my brain may have been praying for much longer.

I retain a sorrow with love when I think of my Kim and my Leaha, I quite believe the sorrow will stay 'til I pass thru this veil of life and enter the land beyond the sky. In a burst of Love the sorrow will be gone and those I've loved, those who have loved me, will greet me. And *two small Korean Children will rush me with arms outstretched for their hug.*

I'm not interested in wars glory,
the recounts I quite despise.
Try telling your war stories
thru my Kim and Leaha's eyes.

Jimmie Joe
fishhook junction, Alaska

A Healing

"Remembered"

M-1 rifle upside down,
Korea, 1950 late September.
Fixed bayonet stabbed deep in ground,
I'm one that does remember.

Helmet placed atop the thing
to mark his lonely grave.
One dog-tag on chain does swing,
The name on it reads "Dave".

Between his teeth the other tag
As rain washed blood away,
back then we had no body bag,
no more will Dave and Jenny play.

The rain, this death of late September,
will Jenny understand?
I won't forget, I will remember
when Jenny lost her Davie man.

His Jenny also will also remember
the sadness of this day.
One rainy day in late September
God took her Dave away.

With entrenching tool we dug his grave,
our emotions hidden and suppressed.
Interned in it one Warrior brave,
dying in rain I just detest.

On his back the lad was placed,
his eyelids we did close.
Rain poncho protects his face
and covers bloody clothes.

James Woods

This Buddy that died in the rain,
in the rain of late September.
Jenny your name was last word said,
he loves you Jenny, I remember.

Graves registration I hope will show
and exhume this lonely grave
and take him home --- I just don't know.
A White Cross for Warrior brave?

Throwing earth in seemed obscene,
rain made the earth quite muddy.
Six days from now he'll be nineteen,
Happy birthday Warrior Buddy.

All his hopes and dreams or strife,
in the sixty years he should have lived,
ended here with one short life.
He has no more; No more to give.

Mom and Dad will shed some tears
as with sad times they must cope.
For losing him in his young years
their tears fall down --- So does their hope.

Grandkids for them not a one,
'tis sad but it is true.
An only child, an only son.
Their line of life thru time is thru.

True love Jenny he'll not wed,
their plans are now awry.
They'll not share a nuptial bed,
alone at night Jenny will cry.

His Jenny's pain is part of war,
For a while she'll question why,

A Healing

> her country sent her Dave to war
> and God let her Davie die.
>
> He sailed here from 'cross the sea
> this country to defend.
> Now Mom, Dad and Jenny's memory.
> So few do care, so few remember,
> one rainy day in late September.
>
> I dedicate these rhymes to Dave,
> buried I don't know where
> and all our Combat Vets in graves.
> Not to this land that didn't care.

The loneliest sight I've seen so far in life was that grave on the treeless barren farmland and us leaving it. I suppose any grave under those conditions would appear as lonely but this one sure has been burned into my brain.

Jimmie Joe
fishhook junction, Alaska

James Woods

Small White Crosses:
Our MIAs

There are no Crosses row on row
for many Warriors brave.
No Flanders fields, no poppies grow
on unknown far off graves.

The internment of our Warriors
near the death camps of our foe,
will interest very few of us.
Most just don't care to know.

POWs and MIAs,
buried where none can say,
in most cases they won't be found.
A price their loved ones pay.

The loved ones have no place to kneel
beside a small white Cross.
No special ground for solitude
in weeping for their loss.

There is no special place for flowers,
no stone to bear a name.
We have the tomb of unknown soldier
but somehow it's not the same.

These Warriors names are not unknown,
we know their names quite well.
Why are there no white Crosses
for these men who went thru hell?

No name inscribed in Cross of stone
to show their sacrifice thru time?
Erase them from their homelands view.
Erase them from our mind.

A Healing

Our national cemeteries 'cross this land
have their rows of Crosses white.
Our Warriors who just disappear?
We leave in darkness of our night.

I've not had a son missing in War,
if so I'd want his Small white Cross.
I'd want my place to kneel and pray.
Alone to weep my loss.

I now speak of our brothers Wall,
with names inscribed in marble black,
with names inscribed of Warrior dead.
All who didn't make it back.

As I observe this wall of honour
and the caring with their pain,
I seem to feel the Warriors spirits
as they drift across my very soul,
pang my heart, mist thru my brain.

This black marble wall gives off a power,
I choke back tears, why do I cry?
Those names inscribed in marble black
are much too young in their short years,
and much to young to die.

What spirits do and where they roam
this old Vet cannot say.
'Near sixty thousand names on marble wall?
Somehow I feel an urgent need,
an urgent need to weep and
an urge to kneel and pray.

The tears along the wall infect me,
puts painful turmoil in my head.

James Woods

It was not my war ----- Was not my fight.
Still I feel these comrades dead.

I feel the time they didn't have,
like my dead comrades of old.
Why do I feel those Warriors spirits
who make old memories unfold?

Why do I feel this sense of comradeship
with Warriors not known by me?
It's all the names, dead young "Boy's" names.
They lived a while --------- and then they died.
Tell them our "Freedom's free."

A formation of standing Warriors statues
will never be the same,
they are not true, they cannot be.
What's true is a Warriors name.

A name tells us the Warrior lived,
tells of time that wouldn't be.
Tells of rights we must protect,
proves our "Freedoms are Not Free."

Our dead were not tin soldiers,
our dreams were all the same.
Do not give us statues.
Damn it give us our Buddies names.

Jimmie Joe
fishhook junction, Alaska

A Healing

No Small White Cross
8,177 Missing In Action
Korea 1950 - 1953

On the Island of Oahu
where eternal summer dwells.
Is a place we call the "Punchbowl"
for our "Boy's" who went thru hell.

Our missing from the Korean War
who's remains could not be found,
have their names inscribed on tablets
in this warm and peaceful ground.

The ground is never frozen
and the grass is always green.
We honour missing Buddies there
in that Hawaiian bowl serene.

There is no stench of summers death,
no grotesque shapes of frozen dead.
But a sad something will remind us,
deep back inside, hid from all view,
old Visions in our heads.

I honour you my Warrior Brothers,
I'll join you in a while.
Will you welcome me as Comrade brave
or will there be no smile?

Have I upheld your sacrifice and death
as I lived time you never had?
Is our Homeland as Free as when you left?
By "Gods own truth" your answer is -----------?
Your answer friend ---------- is mine.

Jimmie Joe

James Woods

"Those left behind"

Those left behind whose tears will fall
on new formed mounds of clay.
They accept the carefully folded flags
on their loved ones funeral day.

They'll accept the flag with tear stained hands
and it never will be said,
the coming weeks or months or years,
the pain, the loss won't leave their head.

The degree of pain will vary
and get less with passing years.
The pain will always be there,
"inside those hidden tears."

Those left behind now pay the price
of the freedoms we retain.
Those left behind are the only ones,
for us a lifetime carry pain.

An exception is the combat Warrior
who survived the bloody land.
I've covered that in other lines
and the caring understand.

Jimmie Joe
fishhook junction, Alaska

A Healing

"Forgotten Mothers of our fallen Brothers"

"A Small White Cross"

Gods gift to me that morning,
was a fine strong baby "Boy".
I held little fella to my bosom
and my heart near burst with joy.

As I breast fed my little fella
our eyes locked tight with love.
He'd always clasp my finger,
my Gods blessing from above.

I helped him with his first steps
and I'd catch him when he'd fall.
Dear God I loved my little fella,
so full of love I 'most could bawl.

I'd walk him to the school bus.
I'd hold his little hand.
Dear God I loved my little fella,
he was his Ma'ma's little man.

He grew up strong and healthy,
six foot two or a bit more.
Dear God I loved my little fella.
Then they sent him off to war.

I prayed for him, oh how I prayed,
I prayed both night and day.
Dear God protect my little fella,
please don't take my "Boy" away.

M-1 rifle upside down
fixed bayonet stabbed deep in ground.

James Woods

Helmet placed atop the thing,
one dog-tag on chain does swing.

My body's here sweet Mother dear
but my spirit's soared away.
I've left wars hell and I will dwell
with you when we would play.

I'm here with you and Jenny too,
I'm still your little man.
I love you Mom and I'm not gone,
I just came home --- left warring land.

God took my little fella
and I'll always question why.
My country sent my joy to war.
My God let my "Boy" die.

Now I kneel beside Little Fellas Cross,
a Cross so powdery white,
I pray to God, hold my "Boy's" hand
and hug him extra tight.

Hug him the way I hugged him
in those days not long ago.
Hug him God, really hug him
and my "Boy's" heart will glow.

Now I see the other Crosses,
a million, maybe more
and a million grieving Mothers.
I had not seen before.

I see the Crosses now so clear,
I can't comprehend just why.
How did I miss those crosses,
'til while kneeling here I cry?

A Healing

The cross I kneel by's not alone,
there's crosses all around.
All those Little Fellas crosses.
Sons who died on warring ground.

Does my homeland see these Mothers
kneeling by their crosses white?
That mound of earth now's all their worth?
You can't see crosses in the night.

Beneath those mounds rests freedoms clay.

Jimmie Joe
fishhook junction, Alaska

James Woods

Moms' "bit of clay"

About a million weeping Mothers
since our nations birthing day.
About a million tear stained Crosses
placed above Moms bit of Clay.

How quickly we forget our wars
and the white crossed mounds of earth.
How quickly we forget the Moms,
forget their Gold Stars filled with pain.
What can a mound of earth be worth?

Moms loss will lessen thru the years,
it will never go away.
The love they shared throughout His rearing,
a telegram --- a bit of Clay.

What thoughts these Mothers do not speak
as we let Freedoms drift away?
Honour?
Honour is now a strangers word,
Honour rests enclosed beneath the mound
enclosed within Moms bit of Clay.

This bit of Clay the final product,
this price of Freedoms holding sway,
from flesh and blood and loving Son, to this,
this I hold in Warriors sacred Honour,
Moms precious bit of Clay.

Jimmie Joe
fishhook junction, Alaska

A Healing

"Daughters of our fallen Brothers"

"Little Daughter, Daddies Daughter"

Little daughter, Daddies daughter
back when arms held Daddy tight,
Little Daughter, Daddies Daughter
Daddy was her wondrous Knight.

Her wondrous Knight in shining armor,
she was Daddies special joy.
Daddies glad that she's his Daughter,
she's sure glad she's not a "Boy"!

Little Daughter held Dads finger
after walking time began,
Little Daughter hugged her Daddy,
hugged him tight, hugged him again.

Little Daughter caught the rainbows
fishing from her Daddies lap
and she almost seems an Angel
as she slips into her nap.

Little Daughter missed her Daddy,
after Daddy left for war,
Daughter hears her Mother crying,
what is Mommy crying for?

The word death to her means nothing,
not when she is only three.
At night she hears her Mother crying
and she misses her Daddy.

The missing sadly stays a while
'cause Daddies not around

James Woods

as she plays beside his white cross
why is Daddy in the ground?

Her loss will lessen thru the years
and child that is only right.
Time will hide the hurt of Daddy
not being there for hugs at night.

As Daughter grows into her teen years
Dad's a faded memory,
I am sorry Daddies Daughter
but that's the way a life may be.

Now she's a woman fully grown
and tomorrow she'll be wed,
Today she's drawn to Dads white cross,
drawn to Daddy so long dead.

By Dads Cross this Daughter's kneeling
as she talks to Dad that day,
Her mind opens repressed memories
of when together they would play.

Once again she is a small girl, bouncing,
laughing with her Dad,
Bouncing, laughing, now she's missing
all those years they never had.

For nineteen years the tears don't flow,
now tears flow like a stream.
Tears of healing comprehension,
Daddies real not just my dream!

As the memories flood thru her
a great change will soon come on,
What was lacking, what was missing, soon,
quite soon will most be gone.

A Healing

Daddy tomorrow is my wedding day,
now I know that you'll be there.
Up in front real close beside me
there will be one vacant chair.

I now feel my God's in heaven,
I know Daddy with me abides,
I know the chair will not be empty,
Daddy will see me as a Bride.

I seem to have a special sadness for little Daughters who have lost their Daddies in war. The bonds a Daddy and his Daughter may accomplish in her first few years of life are sacred to the core of both lives.

I survived the battles and raised Daughters and as the Daughters approached their teen years, I as a Daddy, missed the little Daughters I remembered so fondly. My grown Daughters remember nothing of those long ago times, those memories are still precious to me. There were no questions of "Who am I?", "Why am I here?", "What is the meaning of Life?" On many occasions and times that were all to short, I knew exactly the answer to those profound questions.

I miss those Little Daughters, my heart and my head miss those hugs at night. I miss the walks with a little hand holding my finger. It has been a lonely missing but the memories still cause my heart to glow a bit, so I am, in certainty, blessed.

Love, Dad

Jimmie Joe
fishhook junction, Alaska

James Woods

In memory of 1st. Lt. Bert W. Justus Jr.
From his daughter,

"Mary's Poem"

World War II called out to him
And that was all it took
But he was there when I was born
I saw my baby book.

When I was six he left again
He looked into my eyes
"I'll be back with hula skirts"
And then he said good-bye.

His uniform was crisp and green
He held me in his arms
I knew he wasn't coming back
No Dad, no skirts, no charms.

And though I was a little girl
I cried upon his shoulder
I knew deep down this was good bye
He wasn't getting older.

I felt so old, so wise that day
I still can feel the shame.
The family gathered round and played
I thought they were insane.

Twas Christmas day and he was gone
Korea was the name
Two months later MIA
No words can share the pain.

A Healing

Fifty years have come and gone
Since we received the letter
He never came back home to us
It never does get better.

I need to tell the story
Because old men forget.
It's not just soldiers that we lose
their families are bereft

They hold a family update
To pacify our hurt
And then they send more babies
Out to die on foreign dirt.

It's not that I'm a pacifist
I'm not against all war
But I'm for talk and talk and talk
And then you talk some more.

The wars may be inevitable
And we will be prepared
But war should be the last resort
So little girls are spared.

I could not locate "Mary" to obtain her permission to include this only poem not mine. I had to include it here after my Poem "Little Daughter, Daddies Daughter" dedicated to the Daughters who lost their Daddies in War.

----- James Woods

James Woods

"To Mary"

Mary's Poem is the answer
to what my poem's about.
My heart now falls in sadness,
seems I have to let pain out.

I'm sorry Daughters have to write
such a sad and poignant poem.
Could I be God I'd wave my hand
and send all the Daddies home,

Daddies would stay at home with you
And give hugs to show they cared
Daddies would never be allowed in war
And "little Girls" would all be Spared.

Bless you Mary
James Woods
i.e. jimmie joe

A Healing

"For the forgotten Fathers of our fallen Brothers"

"A Small White Cross"

In Flanders field the poppies grow
beside the Crosses, row on row.

Those rhymes I learned in grade school
in year nineteen twenty-three.
White Crosses then meant nothing
to a small young lad like me.

They drafted me in world war two,
even tho I had a son.
I was stationed on the home front,
I was a lucky one.

Those Crosses placed around the world
meant nothing to me still.
I'd never been in combat.
Never seen the young "Boy's" killed.

We were hero's back on V- J day.
The Country partied 'bout a year.
White Crosses still meant nothing.
I saw no death and felt no fear.

Now I kneel here beside a Cross,
so white in light of day.
Now I kneel here beside a Cross,
'neath it my son does lay.

'Twas along the Naktong River
in far off Korea land.
God took my son at just nineteen.
White Crosses now I understand.

104

James Woods

I understand the pain they hold,
each and every one.
Forgive me God, I didn't know.
Until you took my Son.

I slowly raise my eyes to heaven,
the White Crosses catch my eye.
Rows on rows of Crosses
and my heart, my Soul does cry.

They stretch beyond this graveyard,
beyond the county, cross this land.
A million small White Crosses.
I beg you God please stop them.
Please God, I understand.

Jimmie Joe
fishhook junction, Alaska

A Healing

"The Veil"

Mom tell my Dad please don't be sad,
I really am all right.
I still reside there by Dad's side,
bass fishing in the night.

I 'm still holding Daddies finger
back when I was two or three.
I'm still riding on Dads shoulders.
I am Love; My spirit's free.

God's gift of life dwells near *"the veil"*,
I'm now beyond life's tears,
in a place of peace, of joy, of love.
A wondrous place my after years.

I've passed thru the veil that binds us there,
no more war nor hell from man.
My passage thru our veil was quite okay,
a burst of love was there to greet me
and at last I understand.

This time after my life on earth,
I travel now on rays of time.
I gather joyful stardust from my past,
from those I've loved so very much,
from those I left behind.

My dog "Old Gent'" plays by my side
in this tranquil land beyond your sky.
He radiates our love from Childhood years;
For me, our country's Soldier "Boy".
For I've a Soul that did not die.

Jimmie Joe
fishhook junction, Alaska

James Woods

"A Healing"

"Little Children" --- "Grown-ups War"

I HAD NO CONSCIOUS PERCEPTION OF THE EMOTIONAL STRUGGLE I would endure as I forced myself to initiate, and then complete this poem. My mind was protective and possessive of certain contents within its hidden walls full of flashing thoughts suppressed for nearly fifty years, memories full of long stored pain. It covers this concealed pain, repressed guilt and pieces of uncharted time, the suppression of which was a burden I could no longer carry, I'm going to weep while I type long stored tears.

At some point I felt a demand in my heart to adopt and name two small Korean Children who died from their wounds in the fall of 1950. I gave the little boy the name "Kim", the little girl I named "Leaha", as my lines freed them from my guilt and pain, somehow with God's mercy I've come to love them; the years of distress were too long, to hidden and much to painful.

This was the last poem written while my soul still held the unforgiving torments of war, after forty to sixty thousand words my subconscious allowed the walls to break, the tears of a nineteen-year old Soldier "Boy" to flow. Unlike the tears of Nineteen eighty-nine these were healing tears, tears stored in the silent loneliness' of time, tears from a "Boy" held in banishment for nearly fifty years by my ignorance and fear. (The fear was groundless; I didn't have the courage to endure emotional pain.)

I'd received no map to find my way to "the healing time", there were no directions to fall back on and, regretfully, there was no one to ask. A real "man" would never admit to this non-adjustment or the desperate need of healing. It took nearly fifty years for my stiff upper lip to break down and the "flash" images of my Korean Children's haunting eyes to close. I can no longer consciously recall those eyes, I try and I visualize happy Children holding my hands as we walk in a peaceful land, the fields are

107

A Healing

green and there is no longer pain, there is sadness, a sadness now surrounded by a feeling of love.

The two Korean Children left my conscious mind soon after we'd departed the crossroads in 1950 and didn't appear for over three years. They first appeared in dreams after the Korean War ended in Nineteen-fifty-three. The dreams went away but the visions of the children, exactly as they huddled by the ditch in nineteen fifty, stayed clearly in my mind for many years. The vision of their broken bodies slowly faded away leaving only their pain filled haunting "eyes", those eyes, accusing, silently pleading for help I could not give were what I battled, a battle I could not win.

I don't understand why this one piece of time should stand out so vividly thru the years. There were probable a few hundred incidents of civilian, enemy and comrade dead. For some reason my Kim and my Leaha would not leave, they would spontaneously appear inside my head with neither rhyme nor reason. My mind would run from and try to shun them but never had complete relief until I had written the following poem. There were more silent tears shed in this one poem than I had cried in my entire life, they were tears from my very soul. This human's mind seems to be a bit complicated.

I never talked about them; I couldn't talk about them. Putting them on paper was probably the most painful experience of my life. It took all the courage I could muster to finally start and complete these writings about two small Korean Children, my Kim and my Leaha.

They trained us how to fight in war,
to kill and perchance we die.
They didn't train us for aftereffects.
What about our time to cry?

James Woods

I know little ones, as I wrote this poem I knew it was finally my time to cry, to grieve for you, to grieve for "Boy". I cried the tears you didn't cry. I cried tears on your little hands so small and trembling. I cried tears for my inability to do anything to save you. I cried tears for leaving your little sleeping forms to die alone and I cry inside for the years I fought to ignore and hide your existence. I was wrong. I didn't have the courage to face you any sooner, the path thru the labyrinth was much too difficult. I couldn't find my way. I ask your forgiveness little ones.

I read the poem below many, many times before the tears completely ceased to wet my shirt; the odd thing is I never made any sound, only tears streaming onto my shirt. I now read it with wetness only in my eyes. I feel love for and from my Kim and Leaha, this I did not expect, if it's all in my head I accept that, it's still a healing ----- my healing. This I will be grateful for unto the grave and as I seek our Lord, I thank our Lord.

Jimmie Joe
fishhook junction, Alaska

A Healing

"My Healing"

"Little Children" ---"Grown-ups War"

I'm not interested in War glory,
the recounts I quite despise.
Try telling your War stories
thru our little Children's eyes.

Have you seen the little Children
in our man-made warring lands?
Have you seen their fear strained faces?
Held their trembling little hands?

These rhymes are mostly of my Children,
"Leaha" and "Kim" long in the ground.
Will you adopt some Wars' dead Children?
Mans' made enough to go around.

Will you hold Wars' bleeding children?
Will you help them as they die?
Will you grieve for Wars' dead Children?
In your sorrow even cry?

Tell me it isn't fair to ask you this,
these dumb questions you abhor?
Ask all your favorite politicians
just before we go to War.

Ask about the little Children,
the ones you will never see.
The unnumbered maimed and dying Children,
the ones so far from you or me.

Some of them are Chinks you know,
or Japs, Ragheads or Gooks.

110

James Woods

There's Ni**ers there in Africa
and Spearchuckers and Spooks.

There's Infidels and Sloops and Kikes
and names not known by me.
Worlds' drums of War will always claim
they're subhuman enemies.

So we'll ignore these little Children,
not quite human, not like us.
We have a name; "collateral damage",
a small mistake, no need to fuss.

Well, I've held collateral damage,
My little Leaha and my Kim.
Multiply these deaths by millions.
Politicians' genocidal Sin.

Have you seen the haunting eyes of Children?
Won't reflect as does a mirror.
Only Warriors there to comfort them
and ease their pain and fear.

Have you seen the Children bleeding
and you couldn't help at all?
Have you held the dying Children?
Damn it! I've begun to bawl.

It's really weird how tears can flow,
near fifty years have passed.
I shed no tears on warring ground,
why now at this long last?

No sound I make but a small lake
forms from these eyes of mine.
I didn't know I would hurt so
typing little Children rhymes.

A Healing

This is going to cause myself some pain,
a bit more than I thought.
But I must write of little Children
in that land where War I fought.

Those refugees in miles long lines
trudged thru our lines each day,
there's certain sights so clear to me
like they happened yesterday.

Old men and women in those lines,
little Children by the scores.
Some with Grandfathers and Grandmas,
some left orphaned by mans Wars.

Some Mothers trudged along with them,
little Babies they did hold.
Not one young Dad was sighted,
all conscripted we were told.

This was along the Naktong River
where we made a desperate stand.
Once the refugees got thru our lines
they would be safe again.

These sights were sad, but not as bad
as they'd be when we broke out.
As we sallied forth and headed north
mans' atrocities all about.

Dead Babies in dead Mothers arms
by the hundreds maybe more,
Dead Grandmothers and Grandpas.
Grim reaper smiles at mankind's War.

These sights were bad for Warriors young,
in our war numbed minds they'd hold.

James Woods

They might take years to reappear,
with a vengeance when we're old.

The worse by far were living Children
and their deadened haunting eyes,
The hopeless eyes of little Children
that stay with us 'til we die.

Have you seen the frantic Mothers
as their Babies death draws near?
We may not speak their language
but we cry the same sad tears.

Their anguished tears of pain and sorrow,
all emotions are the same.
Their little Children are our Children,
this slammed home in rhyming game.

I've learned the most from Children's eyes,
the living not the dead.
The painful, awfulness of War
in eyes of Children I have read.

Those haunting eyes I won't explain,
thru life those eyes I see,
I won't discuss those haunting eyes
except thru rhymes by me.

North of Hague, 'mongst farming lands,
along a forlorn and dusty road,
we were moving fast in a deuce and a half
with a heavy ammo load.

Two small Children crumpled by a crossroads
with no one else around.
Two casualties of grown-ups War,
soon little bodies in the ground.

A Healing

Stragglers from the North Korean army, separated from the retreating Red Army or guerrillas, would zero their mortars in on crossroads to harass and/or destroy our troops as we pushed their army northward. This harassing fire was probably the cause of these Children's fatal wounds. Why they were all alone I have no idea, it could be their Mother was killed somewhere else and they were left by the crossroads hoping someone would rescue them.

War is very much more than our young "Boy's" bodies coming home, Americans have never understood war from the perspective of "their entire family" facing death from bombs, starvation and disease.

All the pains of War are failures by our world's politicians, those nice, safe, fat, and self-righteous flag waving Bastards.

They didn't scream or cry or such,
they never made a sound,
just locked with us their dying eyes
as grim reaper hovered 'round.

Gave them morphine, could not do more,
I held their little hands.
Gave them morphine 'til they slept,
We played their God in warring land.

I do know they slept, if we hastened their death with too much morphine I just don't know. I had no idea back then I would carry those four pained and haunting eyes mirrored in my head for most of my life, my secret pain and hidden sorrow. I pray they didn't awaken except to Gods caring arms in heaven.

We had to leave them to die alone,
they died alone in sleep.
I knew no way could I atone
for years my soul would weep.

In this War they were a small sad part
of innocents who died.

James Woods

Out of several million, just these two
within my soul abide.

These were the toughest rhymes I wrote,
for years I'd fought the visions,
Took many years to set them free,
'twas a needed, painful decision.

I had a little Son who died
in nineteen fifty-four.
My pain was great, but I now state
my Korean Kids hurt me more.

Little Jimmy died a natural death
not from mans inflicted pain.
The mangled dying of those two Children
welded ghosts within my brain.

The only flashback War gave me
and it took 'bout Forty years,
were two Small Children I won't free
'Till I have shed their Tears.

In Nineteen Eighty-seven, my mind seemed to produce what
appeared to be a physical restoration of Kim and Leaha as they
appeared that day in October of Nineteen-fifty. I dropped to my
knees to enfold them before my brain caught up with my arms.

While the vision only lasted long enough for my arms to
encircle empty air I was completely caught off guard and my
reaction after was one of mild confusion mixed with sadness and
a little anger, I have no idea why the anger nor why this should
happen thirty-seven years after the event.

My writings somehow have helped me,
after I'd reread them many times.
The guilty pain has left my head,
My therapy thru rhymes.

A Healing

There is still a sense of sadness
that dwells within my heart,
but we've erased the guilty pain
and Loves' had room to start.

Their eyes no longer dulled by pain,
a sparkle's what now shows.
They walk while holding hands with me,
we walk in summers sunshine
and we play in winter's snows.

They are now my little Children
and I'm not a Warrior man.
We walk thru peaceful fields of green,
laughing Children hold my hands.

Of course it's all within my mind,
to my soul it is quite real.
My lines absolved near fifty years
we shared that dying field.

I've welcomed these two Children
to live their lives thru me.
I truly welcome them with Love,
for this Love has set us free.

If you really want to stay,
honest Children it's okay.
I've had you here a lot of years,
in many dreams, thru many tears.

When I find sleep in resting ground
and my soul soars I know not where,
I kind of hope you're still around.
I pray you'll meet me there.

Love, Daddy

James Woods

I'm not interested in war's glory,
the recounts I quite despise.
Try telling your war stories
thru my Kim and Leaha's eyes.

Jimmie Joe
fishhook junction, Alaska

I wish to publicly thank our Lord for letting me live long enough and giving me the courage to cope with the emotional turmoil of completing these painful but healing writings. A nineteen-year-old Soldier "Boy" has been released from a very long battle against a foe no one had trained him to recognize.

I don't believe most will understand how events that far in the past can be hidden from the world's eyes so many years then hurt with such intensity when exorcised in print. It doesn't seem quite normal.

The relief I have been given is something I've wanted very much before I died, I am no longer alone with the part of me that never left the battleground. This one poem about my Little Children, my Kim and my Leaha has led to Peace. Now perhaps I can find that which I seek but for some reason have eluded thru life, ***my God.***

A Healing

"We Still Fought On"

I looked for God on battleground.
I could not find God my friend.
I prayed there with a Chaplain.
No message would God send?

The Chaplain said I must believe.
He could not tell me how.
Picked up my rifle took my leave.
Grannies Hell awaits me now?

There are no atheists in foxholes,
I've heard that since World War Two.
What of us who try but lack belief,
what is our Soul to do?

We seek the calm of sureness,
a knowing of our Lord.
Is it our fault we do not find Him
fore we die by bloody sword?

Does a Warrior have his lords compassion
if he tries to believe in God?
If a Warrior dies in bloody battle
will Heavens peaceful streets he trod?

Does it take more than love and Honour
to walk thru Heavens Gate?
If we feel we've never found our God
will hell be a Warriors tortured fate?

Are we too lacking to be worthy?
Why don't we feel God in our heart?
I asked for Him but couldn't find.
I could not find the start.

James Woods

Chaplains didn't have my answer,
I must put finding God on hold.
A young Warrior in Gods wilderness,
fights on thru stench of summers death
and frozen dead in winters cold.

Fights on with death around him.
No thoughts of Heaven nor of hell.
Fights on with mind in limbo.
Where will my soul now dwell?

Will my "Just cause" give Redemption?
How speaks God of my foe?
It's to damn complicated
for this old Vet to know!

I could see Gods stars above me,
they stood out like precious jewels.
My mind was blank 'bout God in Heaven,
could be the blankness of a fool.

What fate awaits me should I die?
Where is the place I'll go?
Will devils laugh? Will Angels cry?
This young Warrior did not know.

If life blood ran out on warring ground
and soaked into stinking sand,
would this fearsome God I hadn't found
take jimmie by the hand?
Say "It's all right Son" I understand?

Jimmie Joe
fishhook junction, Alaska

A Healing

"Ticking Clocks"

"TICKING CLOCKS" IS NOT PLEASANT NOR IS IT INTENDED TO BE. IT is quite candid about the years after ground battles ended and mind battles began. The mind battles caused by the ground battles were the more difficult of the two as they lasted nearly a lifetime.

I thought only I had visions in my head and thoughts flashing in and out thru the years, thoughts hidden from the world until now. I would be constantly pushing them back and arranging them inside walls, building, patching and rebuilding. I felt a bit of shame with my perceived weakness and a bit of fear of ending up in a VA mental ward. In those times, for a military man or Veteran, a section eight was equated with the same fear we had for death or cowardice on the battlegrounds.

I never thought to examine the period of time which forced me to build walls, to try and consciously recall certain memories from my days of combat was a constant struggle to avoid. I was ignorant of therapy, any need of therapy or even if therapy existed. I was alone with this aspect of my life and quite unaware that in truth I was lost, some years later when I would occasionally admit to myself my "demons", I seemed to lack the "courage" to confront them. I left "Boy" with his pain in a separate compartment in a darkened corner of my mind, manly 'Men" still didn't cry or at the very least they cried alone, out of sight of prying eyes.

With use of the Internet in 1998, I found many Combat Brothers still carried pain. I wasn't alone. I thank those who responded to my poems. Except via the Internet I never knowingly met a combat Infantryman from the Korean War, the forgotten war really was or tried to be. Men who fought in Korea didn't talk about their war; it took the fiftieth anniversary for our country to recognize our vicious Korean War and the deaths of over fifty-four thousand American "Boy's".

James Woods

A few hundred thousand South Korean troops, over a million Chinese and North Korean's soldiers and several million Korean civilians died.

"Ticking Clocks" is for all Veterans of combat; others who read the words may yawn and set it aside. Some, who have been there, will read it, understand and put it on their bookshelf. A few may cry and not put it down until they have absorbed it. I will not be the cause of their tears, like mine, their tears will be from a young "Boy" who disappeared on some distant battleground, the "Boy" who would not accept the unacceptable reality of war, the innocent "Boy" of our youth who bugged out on us in bloody battle. We miss him. We search for him. We need him home.

I never knew him as a Man

'Bout then in nighttime battle
or it could have been in day,
"Boy" just kind of up and disappeared.
He became a different kind of M.I.A.

I think I tried to find him later on,
maybe for a year or two.
I don't know how or why he disappeared.
Guess "Boy" and I were thru.

When the last of my Children left home the house became an empty lonely place, when I retired from my working years the house was doubly lonely. I could cope with my Ghosts while raising Children; I could cope with my Ghosts while working. I could not ignore or cope with my Ghosts in being alone. In my ignorance there was much I didn't know about the phase of my life that would be played out in the next few years.

1989

My formerly peaceful cabin on the banks of the Little Susitna River became a place I dreaded coming home to each night after the Fishhook Bar closed. I bumbled along for about four years in a steadily more confusing state of limbo, never

A Healing

realizing the deadly course the fates had chosen. I didn't know there was a nineteen-year old Soldier "Boy" hurting and cringing in a darkened corner of my brain. A "Boy" who never left the dying field of a distant battleground, nor that one autumn night in nineteen eighty-nine I would come within a whisker of being a casualty, by my own hand, of a war nearly forty-year-old.

I still don't know why my ability to cope left my control; I can't even pin down quite when. I'm probably a classic case of something but damn if I know what. The important point is I made it thru this distressing and dangerous period of my life. Below is my version of this battle, my buildup to the final facing of the fates.

"Ticking Clocks"

I rhymed in Reality and Wanderings
my release of anger and pains of war.
I can not express my reasons
for suppressing warring season.

My memories are not repressed
'cept a few times I can't recall.
It's emotions I would not express,
from Childhood little "Boy's" were told;
Real Men do not bawl.

I don't know if those who read them
will care or understand.
I know I must write all this down,
the years after my killing land.

If I don't express my thoughts to well
as you peruse my rhymes,

James Woods

please believe I tried like hell.
Can you read between the lines?

In Wandering adjusting of Combat Vets
is mentioned frequently.
These odes cover suppressed ghostly flits
my mind refused to free.

As emotions flowed out from my mind
on paper white with pain in black,
my strong built walls back there in hiding,
my walls of war began to crack.

My walls took over forty years in building,
the patchwork was like stone.
It took several years of painful typing
'fore part of me from war came home.

It took 'til old age, all those years,
for me to get things right.
Now old Man cries a young "Boy's" tears.
He'll cry alone, adjust, atone
as he frees subconscious from its night.

Back during times of warring days
conscious mind takes a sabbatical.
Death almost becomes a normal way,
'til our ticking clock we battle.

The battle went on within my mind
after the warring land.
The ground battles end, no peace I find.
I couldn't try to understand.

They take a lad of just nineteen
and send him off to war.

A Healing

His mind of pain and death is clean,
it will change forevermore.

Dead buddies locked inside his head,
dead and crippled children too.
Massacred civilians all long dead
but the visions stay quite new.

Throughout time flitting ghosts will roam,
it's tough to keep them in.
Clean nineteen when he left home
to join our fighting men.

Clean nineteen no more is he
but few will understand.
They'll say he went away a "Boy",
look now and see our Warrior man.

They're so proud to see him standing there,
gosh Dad, he looks so brave and strong.
They can't see inside his crew cut head,
just ticking clock knows something's wrong.

He'll probably live his life all right,
with visions stored in back of mind.
There will be war dreams in the night,
they'll end given some time.

His dreams began in fifty-four,
ghostly death stalked him in sleep.
For several years he'll dream of war.
Societies code inscribed in stone.
Manly men don't weep.

He'll awake sitting bolt upright
as lips close on fading a scream.

James Woods

He ends another nighttime battle.
It's nothing Hon, it's just a dream.

His little Child sleeps in his arms
and causes his heart to glow.
His ticking clock ticks out the harm
and sights of Children long ago.

The long dead Buddies who gave their life,
even the young enemies that died,
they'll not hold a Wife, nor have a Child,
nor catch those Fish in places wild.

I mention this a lot in rhymes,
his visions from long ago.
Unforgiving Ghosts from warring times
drift out from cracks in walls you know.

He'll get real good at hiding pain
but the years after his kids are grown,
fates clock keeps ticking in his brain.
Ticks faster when he's all-alone.

He retired from his working years
and his Children left his house.
His time drew near to fight his Ghosts.
Twill be an unknown mental joust.

He knew nothing of this at the time,
did not know what lay ahead.
It will take a few confusing years
to face his predatory dead.

He may not have been a drinking man
with his Children in his care,
now Ghosts bounce off echoing walls
as clock ticks down to face them square.

A Healing

It'll take about four years or so,
clock ticks slowly at the first.
He'll begin frequenting the Fishhook Bar
and the cause will not be thirst.

This friendly bar where Ghosts won't roam
kind of soothed his besieged life.
This friendly bar became his home
and somehow smoothed his strife.

He'll learn to play pool games quite well,
as slowly he drinks more.
While wannabe's brag of their hell
he keeps his own in store.

He didn't tell his war stories,
no heroic deeds he'd done.
He'll play pool, drink and listen to
other mothers drunken sons.

Twelve hours a day in bar he'll drink,
He doesn't think about the why.
As clock ticks down toward fates brink
some part inside him grieves to die.
He not yet knows it's time to cry.

He'll head home at closing time
to walls that echo grief.
It'll take a few years more before he knows
ticking clock in bar won't bring relief.

Sleeping will become a real tough chore
as protecting walls begin to crack.
He's filled with hopelessness and more,
forty years his ticking clock turned back.

James Woods

No Children's laughter, no joy rings out,
no loving mate to hold,
he's sort of lost what life's about,
the Pipers pain will now unfold.

He'd tried the booze it didn't work,
I think he knew it from the first.
His ticking clock caught up one night
as his confused mind caved in.
Ticked time had come to end his fight.
Is old warriors suicide a sin?

His forty-one mag he took to bed,
silently told his friends good-bye.
Cocked it and pressed it to his head
about an inch behind right eye.

His ticking clock was speeding now,
time was nearly at an end.
A bit more pressure on the trigger
and I will lose my lifelong friend.

His Children appeared inside his head
back when they were young.
What are you doing part of brain said,
put down your killing gun.

Pressure on trigger slowly increased,
no thoughts of Heaven nor of Hell.
His ticking clock wants deaths release
for reasons only God can tell.

Your Children and your friends will hurt
if you do this deed,
You've never picked the cowards way,
please Dad your love we need.

A Healing

He didn't know how long it took,
this argument for escaping or for livin.
For livin trigger pressure relaxed,
for escaping pressure was givin.

His clock would pause then pick up speed
and the sear was he knew not where.
To cry or die? His unknown need,
the sear didn't really care.

Visions burst from the old Warriors head
that he'd fought to hide thru time.
Those Furies nearly made him dead,
now ticking clock caught warring slime.

He sees despair in men's eyes there,
just before they cloud.
Deaths wounds exposed he sees deaths throes
as men take on deaths shroud.

Children with missing arms or legs
caused by death bombs from the sky.
Orphaned Children with no Mommies.
Starving Children;.......... Children die.

He feels the fear of yesteryear
as men charged 'cross no-mans land.
Sees blood that pumps from legless stumps
as life's force spurts out in sand.

Four haunting eyes locked and staring,
now accusing with their pain.
Will he still feel their accusation
after death relieves his brain?

Will they still appear when he is dead?
Those eyes from long ago.

James Woods

Eternally harbored in his head?
God, please God don't let it be.
Please don't let that be so.

He sees eyes burned out, hears screaming shouts
as white phosphorus burns men blind.
He feels the pain, sees the insane
as brave men escape their minds.

He sees his Children home at play,
hears their laughter, feels their joy.
Now he's holding little bloodied hands.
Holds mangled Dying Children
locked in time with soldier boy.

Now visions raced and visions stopped,
Blurred visions raced once more.
Reality fought time and space.
Pushed back the tearless visions.
Stored his tearless Ghosts of war.

He thought of who would find him dead,
his Daughters or a friend.
Pressure on trigger he slacked off,
can't let them see this kind of end.

Then slowly pistol left his head,
the living won despite his grief.
Those he loves beat warring dead
as his soul cried out for some relief.

Damn it God won't you help me,
I don't want to die alone.
I am lost in pains direction.
The road is long, please God, please help.

A Healing

The demon fates had nearly taken him
to that land beyond the sky.
His Angel touched him just in time:

jimmie Joe, **Hey!** *jimmie Joe.*
Come on "Boy" it's time to cry.

For forty years he'd hid deaths tears
from kin and all he knew.
For forty years he'd hid deaths tears
and from himself he hid them too.

He didn't know the why of tears.
Confusion reigned supreme.
Now he felt "Boy's" long hidden pain.
Mans flitting visions; warring dreams.

Tears gushed from the old Warriors eyes
but they were not old Warriors tears.
The tears were from a soldier boy
who's age was nineteen years.

Tears from that far and distant past.
Young tears from eyes of old.
The Pipers being pain at last.
Thru soundless tears past times unfold.

Tears flowed for little Children
with their eyes clouded from pain.
Tears flowed for their senseless dying.
Tears stored back beyond his brain.

Tears flowed for little children's hands
which he'd held so long ago.
Tears flowed out his mournful sorrow
mixed with tears he didn't know.

James Woods

Tears of guilt flowed for the leaving.
Dying Children tears did mourn.
Questioned, never understanding.
Questioned God, why were they born?

Question why the dying Buddies
in that Land of Morning Calm.
Question reasons for their dying.
Only tears, no soothing balm.

His Daughter found him the next day
huddled and sobbing in his chair.
Ask no questions, just held her dad,
she helped a lot, his times were bad.

I recall only one of my thoughts that night, the rest were too scrambled. The one thought I would not forget as I squeezed the trigger were the words I kept saying over and over as I applied pressure; A little more won't hurt ……. A little more won't hurt……… A little more won't hurt. ……………won't hurt. ……………… hurt…I figured it out years later, I'm a little slow sometimes.

I know my thoughts were bits and pieces of my later rhymes, involved with, a time of conscious need without subconscious release. A time to bring back the "Boy".

*Twas along the bloody Naktong River
that I noticed my Chum change.
His eyes lost their laughing sparkle
and his smile was not the same.*

*I'll not know what he might have been,
he would not be shaped by warring time.
His walls absorbed the shaping,
and that Boyhood friend of mine.*

A Healing

The "Boy" who left for war is gone.
He was never seen again.
Only I came home from battles.
Now a stranger 'mongst old friends.

One "Boy" died and one survived
in those days so long ago.
Jim made it into Manhood.
Jim misses jimmy joe.

I hope I get to meet them
in that land beyond the sky.
I'd like to see my Dog "Old Gent"
and that "Boy" who choose to die.

Jimmie Joe
fishhook junction, Alaska

I gained very little therapeutic help from that distraught night; I did gain enough to save me. I unknowingly gained the knowledge of there being a way out, of some nearly fatal flaw with which I must come to terms.

My Angel had given me a reprieve and the time I would need to find my way, it would be nine years before I found the route leading home, my thoughts continued hiding from family and friends. They are now recorded for all to see. Putting pain on paper forced me to examine and squarely face my "demons" as I read and reread my printed words until no tears were left.

Eisenhower's Papers which I read in Nineteen ninety-seven demanded a response. With sadness, disappointment and anger it's spread throughout my poems. History is so different when viewed with knowledge gained with time.

Adjusting began as I attempted my response to the treasonous acts of our leaders. The abandonment of our POWs, became America's sacrificial victims of political expediency in a War which, after November 1950, we had neither a plan nor any intention of winning.

James Woods

A forgotten War? It was. by most that weren't involved in it, or lose a Son, or having been there as one of the Korean peoples.

The final poem " Little Children—Grown-ups War" was my road leading home, a forty-seven year saga along a twisting, sometimes straight, smooth, sometimes-bumpy road. I'd have found my way sooner but I was never given a road map and the journey was thru lands I had never traversed. My vision sometimes became quite blurred, all making the journey more difficult and time consuming. The first few years were mostly dead ends; my road was a rat's maze. As I bounced off many roadblocks I slowly learned to put up walls of directions and distress so I would not take those turns again.

When I had built enough walls I was able to feel my way along and my road smoothed out for many years with only unexpected potholes. I would work around them and continue on, remembering their locations and ministering the blisters of my soul.

Near roads end all the potholes from my journey combined to form one huge hole with no way around, I was forced to fill it in with "Boy's" precious protective walls. As I tore the walls down Kim and Leaha's tears began to flow from my eyes, four little helping hands appeared to assist me in the filling, two small Korean Children paved it with Forgiveness, understanding and yes, I felt and still feel their Love. My imagination? My heart says no. My saga has ended and I shall not pass that way again.

> Took a few years but worked out fine.
> He can see it as he reads my rhymes.

I am very thankful my friend didn't end his life in Nineteen eighty-nine and I thank the Lord for what ever saved him. A lot of Vets don't make it past their crisis point. —Sadly, their life ends in despair. I am quite ashamed I never considered or thought about the series of events, that in an instant of time with no one interceding would cause a Brother to end his life.

A Healing

I now realize "demons" can lurk for years, keeping the "Boy" away and patiently waiting, waiting for that one instant, his time of despondency and confusion, to kill him in a war that is thirty, forty or fifty years old. ---- I know it happens. —I do not know why.

The way out can not be that instant in time, only an Angel, luck or whatever you care to call it will save you then. The way out is to realize that instant in time will, does or can exist, believe me it can. Get help long before you reach this stage, otherwise you may cause family and friends pain you have no right to put them thru.

Again I say putting my pain on paper, where I was forced to face it, was for me very healing. I pray "Ticking Clocks" will help some Brothers before they face their instant in time. Please know you are not alone. I'm not a shrink; my story is the best I can do. May God bless and guide you.

A lot of Vets have died by their own hand,
none really know the reason why.
Damn clocks ticked down from killing land.
We just tell our friend good-bye.
We're sorry Buddy

Jimmie Joe
fishhook junction, Alaska

James Woods

My journey to a view of responsible citizenship

I TOOK SIXTY-TWO YEARS TO LEARN THE CORRECT SPELLING OF Republican; I needed to go from being raised a Democrat (forty years), thru "the hell with it" stage (ten years), and thru the independent stage (twelve years).

I finally learned damnrepublican was not one word and Republicans are not all rich, some are almost like you and I except of course they are quite a bit uglier.

There will be those who will take umbrage with some of my writings, ultra-conservatives or ultra-liberals may agree or disagree, they can write me off as a whiner or a warmonger I could care less, nearly anything with ultra preceding it I don't seem to care for.

The liberals' agenda is that which I fear most, thru their policies my Children, Grandchildren and Great Grand-children, each generation has known less and less freedom. To each generation their moment in time is the status quo; they'll never know that which has been taken from them. What I see as intrusion on Freedoms they will see and accept as normal.

The Liberals have been the ones in power, in both houses of Congress and the Executive Branch, each time we went to war in the twentieth century, minus of course Desert Storm.

I was born a democrat, my parents, grandparents and every relative I've known has been a democrat. I actively campaigned in Alaska for President Johnson against Barry Goldwater in 1964 and was proud when Johnson won the election. I was afraid Goldwater would get us into a war. I never dreamed what Johnson would turn Vietnam into with his Gulf of Tonkin lie.

I also never dreamed the Johnson administration would set the wheels in motion for the subjugation of my Alaska. The appointment of Stewart Udall in the mid-sixties as secretary of the Interior would begin the environmental and liberal lobby which would eventually run the war to shape my Alaska into an

A Healing

image projected by themselves, an image of their concept of the *"Last Frontier"* totally disregarding the desires of ninety percent of the population living in the Great Land. The promises in our statehood compact of nineteen fifty-nine have been rendered null and void over the last four decades; the equal treatment clause of our constitution has not been met as it applies to Alaska. Liberals have made my Alaska much less free and caused great mental anguish among us, Alaska's Children.

Because of the huge build up of ground troops and the general vast escalation of the war in Vietnam I joined the Alaska Army National Guards "38th Special Forces" in March of Nineteen-sixty-six. With my Country at war I felt an obligation to at least be ready to do my part even tho I had seven children.

With LT. Calleys massacre at "My Lai" along with the cover-up of "My Lai" by Captain Medinas, I finally had to much of liberalism and its' lies. The massacre at "My Lai" caused great turmoil in my soul, it cast a pall on the honour I personally felt about our government. I live by my code of Honour and I expected my government's code to be no less. MyLai was the last straw for me. With knowledge from time and history I have been forced to conclude our governments code of conduct is quite flawed at times and the Democrats had run government most of my life.

Prior to the year 2000 AD my expectations of our *politicians honour* was not met in Korea, Vietnam, Panama, Afghanistan, Sudan, Serbia and Kosovo. Honour has left us thru the death of innocents who had nothing to do with what the executive branch and congress perceives as its God given right. The right to use our armaments; bombs, rockets and cruise missiles on innocent peoples in the wars we were actively engaged in or later as a lesson to terrorists, abducting a leader of a sovereign nation for his part in the drug trade. We kill innocents in all cases, it is sad, for a while I lost the belief in America I once carried so proudly.

James Woods

I am totally appalled by the lack of honour on our domestic front in the years 1993 thru 2000, all the liberal excuses and lies to justify Clintons very existence as the perjuring head of liberal liars.

All I had seen as an adult in the running of our country by the liberals were questionable wars in which several million civilians were killed and over one-hundred thousand of Americas young became a bit of clay in flag draped coffins.

Johnson's war on poverty's a joke, a damn expensive joke I might add, we've trapped past generations into dependence on and total need of taxpayer largesse, Liberals have kept them as children. Liberals have kept them as voters. I was worried about Goldwater being president? We were unprepared for World War II even tho it was well known we would be at war with Japan and Germany, well known by Roosevelt and the higher echelons of government whose only plan of preparation was hiding the American public's head in the sand so as not to get them upset prematurely. The military basically remained under-funded, under-trained, under-prepared and the top peoples, especially Roosevelt knew war was coming. We were set up.

They knew that by being so unprepared some of our young "Boy's" in the military would be sacrificed and they knew it would take that sacrifice to bring America fighting mad into World WAR II. *They were correct*. Enlistment offices were mobbed on Dec. 8, 1941.

Our young "Boy's" paid the price at Pearl Harbor and worse yet in the Philippines, those "Boy's" died defending the Philippines without adequate armament, ordnance, training or a chance in hell of winning. A little over half survived the Bataan Death March, the ship transports and the Prisoner of War camps to return home nearly four years later.

The Bataan Death March, was a forced march of 70,000 (About 12,000 were American) and Filipino prisoners of war captured by the Japanese in the Philippines.

A Healing

On Dec. 7, 1941, Japan attacked Pearl Harbor. The American Pacific Naval Fleet suffered heavy losses in lives and ships. The Fleet was incapacitated and could not, in that state, defend American interest in the Pacific Rim and in Asia. Only eight hours later on Dec. 8, 1941 Japan launched an aerial attack on Philippines.

Most of the American Air Force in the Philippines was destroyed while the planes were on the ground. Eight hours after Pearl Harbor our planes were caught on the ground? A few days' later, Japanese forces landed on the Philippines. The Japanese landings were in Northern Luzon and in the Southern Mindanao Islands. Inexperienced troops failed to stop the Japanese at the landing. Mac Arthur had to revert back to the original plan, withdrawing the Filipino-American forces into the Bataan Peninsula. By the January 2, 1942, the Northern Luzon forces were in-place for the defense of Bataan.

The Filipino-American Defense of Bataan was hampered by many factors: A shortage of food, ammunition, medicine, and attendant materials. Most of the ammunition was old and corroded. The AA shells lacked proper fuses, as did many of the 155mm artillery shells. Tanks, Trucks, and other vehicles were in short supply, as was the gasoline needed to power these items of warfare.

Poorly trained Filipino troops, most of who never fired a weapon, were thrown into frontline combat against highly trained Japanese veterans. Americans from non-combatant outfits: such as air corpsmen and, in some instances, even civilians, were formed into provisional infantry units.

The Defenders of Bataan continued to hold their ground, without reinforcements and without being re-supplied. Disease, malnutrition, fatigue, and a lack of basic supplies took their toll. On March 11, 1942, Gen. Mac Arthur was ordered to Australia, Gen. Wainwright took his place in Corregidor, as Commander of the Philippine forces and Gen. King took Wainwright's place, as Commander of the Fil-American forces in Bataan.

Around the latter part of March, Gen. King and his staff assessed the fighting capabilities of his forces, in view of an impending major assault planned by Gen. Homma. Gen. King and his staff determined the Fil-American forces, in Bataan, could only fight at 30% of their efficiency, due to malnutrition, disease, a lack of ammunition and basic supplies, and fatigue. On April 3, 1942, the Japanese launched their all out final offensive to take Bataan. On 9 April 1942, Gen. King surrendered his forces on Bataan, after the Japanese had broken through the Fil-American last main line of resistance.

More on Bataan see URLs below.

"http://home.pacbell.net/fbaldie/Outline.html"

"http://home.pacbell.net/fbaldie/In_Retrospect.html"

We had the lead-time, damn it we had over two years to be well prepared, there was no excuse for the Generals and politician's complacency, and many thousands of deaths should not have been. These deaths rest on the backs of politicians and show the disdain liberal politicians hold for our "Little Tin Soldiers" when we are in a small war or at peace.

Less than five years after the end of World War II we were again at war, this time in Korea, a poor, rural, impoverished country about the size of Minnesota, a Civil War so to speak. The Democrats controlled the House, the Senate and the Executive branch, as you might have guessed we were again unprepared, possibly more so than at the onset of WWII.

Young "Boy's" again died needlessly, we didn't learn. Politicians of mostly Liberal bent had been willing to trade lives of young "Boy's" for smaller defense budgets in peacetime. They still believe a well trained, well-equipped Military is not needed in peacetime. *They will not/do not learn. Liberals still say today; " we aren't at war, we don't need so much for defense; "Hell no one is a threat to us now, or lets use the Military to stop drugs*

139

A Healing

along our border with Mexico." The most important aspect of an individual Warriors survival will be lost: [Constant disciplined Cohesive Unit Training]

I ask in all sincerity;

" Have you seen "Boy's" panic, run, and die due to the lack of cohesive unit training?"

"Have you seen "Boy's" die due to outdated armament or being untrained to improvise/repair in the field?"

"Have you seen "Boy's" die due to the lack of supplies, or ordnance that would not do the job?"

"Have you seen "Boy's" die due to the lack of well trained, well disciplined Officers and Noncoms?"

"Have you seen "Boy's" die?"

I ask those questions and most Liberals will not connect their answer to my questions they do not equate: The reality of death on a battleground to the lack of constant cohesive unit training, or The Honour of a Rangers Black Beret' to a whole damn army of black berets'.

The liberals have lowered standards in basic Infantry training so females could compete in a ground combat role. "Hell we can do less training, give 'em all a black beret' and we'll have some fine looking fighting men", oops I mean persons. Social engineering should not be attempted where the results on a battleground will be unknown, if females desire to become "Amazon Warriors" let it be in an all female battalion or division. The lowering of intensity and difficulty of training will only increase the number of needless deaths when Troops enter combat.

Liberals see our Warriors as charging up a hill with bayonets fixed, they know we aren't quite real people; real people wouldn't do such a damn thing! Thousands died needlessly due to liberals being in power and shortchanging the military thru the past sixty years and if Americans are aware of this they don't give a damn.

Gulf of Tonkin? Politicians even lie to each other to get us killed. Johnson's LIE, this lie would live thru the last ten years of the Vietnam War. A Democratic Congress every year would fund the lie and a Democratic Congress every year would fund the killing. Flower children would be spitting on our returning Warriors; A Democratic Congress would be funding basic training for their newest crop of young American males.

Johnson was totally responsibly for the huge build-up of ground forces and for the criminal tactic of "free fire zones" with a predictable result of a "My Lai". In a war where the enemy wore "black Pajamas" and you never knew who was the enemy it is a tribute to our Troops that there weren't more "My Lai's".

Nixon becoming President in early Nine-sixty-nine and the expanding of the war into Laos, Cambodia and bombing the hell out of North Vietnam does not say much about the Republicans attempt at a peaceful resolution, again winning, right or wrong, was the unquenchable demand of their egos. Losses of life become quite secondary when politician's egos are involved. The same type of damn egos were involved in the last two years of the "Korean Police Action", again we had a Democratic House, a Democratic Senate and Old Harry. In the North we bombed the hell out of the cities for twenty-six additional months. Near the Thirty-Eighth Parallel we would take the same hills and ridges, lose the same hills and ridges, over and over again for twenty-six months as the death toll mounted, a million? Two million added deaths? No one knows. None really cared then or question it now. We only know for sure more Warriors died, many more innocent Civilians died as their are more of them when the bombs fall on cities, their are more of them to die from disease, from suicide and from starvation. I sincerely doubt if you will find many Soldiers who died of starvation. Soldiers have the guns, they eat first.

Vietnam, 1962 - 1975, a Democratic Congress would not stop the war nor demand the winning of it, just authorize it's continuation, year after year after year after year. Can you get it thru your heads flower children? It was Congress not the Grunts, the Grunts Died. Politicians devoured them and sent the Bones home in Flag draped Coffins to become a mound of earth,

A Healing

honoured by our government in Death, disdained by flower children in life.

Flower children burned, pissed on and stomped our flag and by proxy those mounds of earth. Gold Star Mothers knelt and prayed beside those mounds, a bit of wet clay for Mom as a gift from the caring altruistic flower children.

See page 12

As of 1998 over 200,000 Vietnam Vets had committed suicide and joined their Buddies in those mounds of earth, in part put there by you flower children, your actions of over thirty years ago keeps killing them. We did not have this high rate of suicide following either the Korean War or World War II.

It was Congress damn you Congress, not the Grunts. I believe you knew. I think it was the in thing and you were in. No danger of jail for harassing the Grunts and no guts to truly take on our politicians.

While you did have a large part in the stopping of the war in Vietnam your methods had a larger part in the death thru suicide of Warriors who fought in the Vietnam War. As Warriors must cope with the memories of war itself, they must also cope with the treatment their country gives them when they arrive back in the States. Their country and their peers for many years betrayed them.

We fought and died for you America
and your Warriors you will curse?
Our Buddies dying hurt quite deep
but your attitude hurts worse.

Our adjusting we had to face alone,
there was no counseling long ago.
A few inside their minds did not come home,
their minds still hold what you won't know.

James Woods

For the two hundred thousand plus Vietnam Veterans who have committed suicide (as of the year 2001) the Wall of Honour either came too late or their Ghosts were to demanding. Sadly their names will not appear as "killed in action" even tho in reality many of them were.

Jimmie Joe
fishhook junction, Alaska

A Healing

The Wall

THE VIETNAM MEMORIAL IS NEARLY SACRED IN MY MIND; IT causes sorrow to well up in my heart that is far and above any other memorial, book, movie or any thing I can name in this world. The Vietnam Black Wall of Honour seems to hold an aurora of Spirits that are to me tangible. Those Spirits are there for us, they heal us, be we Vietnam Vets, Korean Vets or any combat Vets. It is a Wondrously unique and therapeutic oasis for the hidden recesses of a pained soul, a soul who has lived the reality of a war zone and survived, survived to discover his war didn't end with his return from battle. We all need an oasis such as the; "Black Marble Wall.

My shoes will fit most Grunts, some will pinch and some will walk right out of them. Some will have Ghosts and no shoes, I'll try to lend them mine for a short while, and mine are broken in and without the blisters of nearly fifty years.

Jimmie Joe
fishhook junction, Alaska

James Woods

Young Warrior ---- Old Veteran

I can't remember my rotation
from that bloody killing land.
Can't remember leaving Buddies
and I don't understand.

Subconscious mind will not release
in leaving should I atone?
The living friends I left to fight,
to fight and die alone.

I was not aware these thoughts were there,
must have been repressed back thru time.
While typing thoughts, my soul to bare,
my guilt flowed out in rhyme.

I remember being on a ship
While crossing the wide Pacific.
Euphoria filled my mind with peace,
I felt really terrific.

Safe and going home was I,
I'd survived that killing ground.
I'm going to live, not going to die,
mixed emotions did abound.

That might seem kind of nuts to you
but to me was a revelation.
I now was thru with death and war,
I'd survived that bloody warring nation.

I knew I might now have a wife,
could have and hold a child.
Again I'd see my Mom and Dad
and catch those Fish in places wild.

Jimmie Joe, fishhook junction, Alaska

A Healing

"Arriving "Home"

I've made it home the battle's over,
I can't believe it's true.
The stench of death and rice paddies
and dying friends are thru.

As I ride home on plane or train
or on a greyhound bus.
I look around and life is normal,
my war has caused no fuss.

I noticed as I travel
thru this homeland of the free,
there's none that care, they all ignore,
"Boy's" dying 'cross the sea.

.

Back then the thought was not disturbing,
at least not in a conscious way.
I now was thru with mankind's war
and my life in peace would be okay.

Friends and family were 'near like strangers,
something was not as it should be.
Home was the same as when I left.
The stranger friend was me.

My world was somehow different
but it wouldn't register for years.
My war I'd force way back in hiding.
Till I released the long stored tears.

I know how odd to some this seems,
my subconscious was locked tight.
Took two more years to start war dreams
and fight alone in dark of night.

146

James Woods

In the daytime I'd seem normal,
folks wouldn't see that all's not well.
Later on in sleep, I'll scream, I'll weep.
My war's now fought in nighttime's hell.

I began to hate the sleep time,
with the same dreams without an end.
Always alone with nighttime battle,
always alone, no Comrade Friend.

They train us "Boy's" to fight in war,
train us to kill and maybe die.
They don't train us for aftereffects.
What about our time to cry?

So we go for years always on guard,
that wall must be strong we know.
Caught by surprise with chance remark
and tears nearly begin to flow.

We patch the breach quite quickly
and feel embarrassed for our friend.
We scribe a note inside our heads,
this subject won't come up again.

I thought something was wrong with me,
a weakness I must hide.
The hurting, flitting ghosts I'd see,
I must push back deep inside.

Other combat Vets don't feel this way,
with these damn Ghosts in their head.
The other combat Vets all seem okay,
we never know 'cause nothing's said.

Nothing's said 'cause no one knows,
alone we drift thru years.

A Healing

'Round and 'round the clocks hand goes,
alone we suppress tears.

For many years the ghosts hide deep
and flit out now and then,
should not take forty years to weep,
even for Warrior men.

Now that I have let them out
thru sometimes painful, tearful rhymes,
Vets who've read my poems know it's about
they're not alone with hurting times.

The guilt and pain is standard fare
to some Warriors from their war.
The sharing when our souls we bare
might help someone's hidden inner core.

The Shadow Ghosts began to roam
and flit out now and then,
there was no peace in coming home,
my warring dreams began.

You've read about the two small kids
back there in Shadow Ghosts,
Of three or four repeating dreams
by far those hurt the most.

I'd wake from dreams a crying,
at times in them I'd scream.
I'd dream of Buddies dying
or little Children and morphine.

Subconscious mind slipped out at night,
of that I'd no control.
I'm tired of this, this endless fight,
I don't want dreams; please not tonight.

148

James Woods

This time of life it held no joy,
for me, his country's soldier boy.
Outside my head I seemed all right,
some inside part held dark of night.

I'd dream of things that were not real?
At least I can't recall.
Why could I cope in actual war
and in dreams not cope at all?

The dreams went on, I can't remember,
a couple years I guess.
It was a quite confusing time,
my mind in sleep won't rest.

Those dreams all really scared me,
they scared me thru and thru.
Dear God don't take away my mind,
I don't know what to do.

Please God it's up to you.
Later God might have helped me,
a voice in my dreams would say,
"wake up jim, it's just a dream."
I'd awake and be okay.

Dreams came less and less and less,
less tears, less fears; no screams.
After while I was back to
my flying jumping dreams.

The visions here within my head,
I know that they will stay.
Was better then to cope with them,
When dreams finally went away.

A Healing

You're not alone in how you feel
with Ghosts of War that roam.
My prayers for you my Friend are real.
At long last I say, Son Welcome Home".

War is a deadly serious undertaking, our young Warriors will not realize this in the beginning, they will learn quite suddenly as they see their Buddies fall. The young "Boy's" will have an excuse, all thru our history, the fact defending ones country, the awarding decorations and medals has been seen as an initiation into manhood. Valid or not this is what may very well subconsciously tempt many young men to expose themselves to the dangers associated with harms arena, we as men are expected to be defenders as were our forefathers and their fathers.

The draft fulfills a demanded patriotism and I doubt if the above applies, but to the draftees that are sent into harms way and survive the result will be the same. The rites of manhood will have been met, it's a fallacy of course but a fallacy accepted in general by all societies.

Far back in time men were by necessity the protectors of the family group, later they became the protectors of their Clan, their Tribe and later still their Country. I believe, out of necessity, thru the ages we've built upon this "ritual of manhood". When countries came into being politicians had a ready made, deeply rooted cause for gathering the men they would need for armies, need for power, and need for war.

In all our wars since the end of World War II we have been a little unclear about the real threat our enemy actually carried. We were unclear about any danger to our Family, our Clan, our tribe or our Country, we neither observed nor felt danger, yet it was demanded we join in battle with an enemy half way around the world. We battled an enemy contrived by politicians (ours or theirs), a war against an enemy who was no threat to us except in the ideologically paranoiac minds of *some politicians*. cold war anxiety attack? Maybe, but our wars have caused the death of millions of innocent Humans, and sadly it was an official game of

150

James Woods

domino effect. A game played by politicians for nearly half a century, a game where all concerned found playing necessary to "their" political survivable.

We still carry our primordial "tribal distrust" of other tribes into modern day warfare involving hundreds of million to a tribe (country). Today we kill them every bit as viciously, even more efficiently and in numbers known only to God, our tribal ancestors would have been quite proud of our accomplishments in warfare. ...... Politicians take another bow!

Jimmie Joe
fishhook junction, Alaska

A Healing

"Tears of Rain"

"A MOUND OF EARTH IS ALL THEY'RE WORTH?"

1776 -------------- THRU TIME

OVER ONE MILLION YOUNG MEN HAVE GIVEN THEIR OATH AND their lives to defend the constitution of these United States of America; They gave their lives upholding this sacred oath, for our country, all who have lived in our history, all who now live, for our freedom and their honour. Their honour is eternal, ours is being tested and the test will continue as long as we remain a free Country, as long as we have "Boy's" such as these who will die to keep us free. We should be extremely humble, exceedingly thankful our land produces Men such as these "Boy's".

Although our Warriors were young men, in my olden mind we were "Boy's", with much honour and respect I will refer to them as such. I honour these young "Boy's" who gave their lives for this country, this long line of young "Boy's" from the revolution to now, one million strong. Most of them never knew our joys, the joy of a loving Wife, the joy of having their little Child hold their finger as they walked together, never knew the joy of being Grandparent, the simple joy of a full adult life.

They knew only death while preserving our freedoms thru time, our freedoms right down to each individual, to you now alive in America. Each of us, every one, has a million dead young "Boy's" who gave their lives for the freedoms we still enjoy. We have a sacred obligation to not let these freedoms slip away, an obligation to inform the next generation thru our home and schools of these sacred sacrifices made for us.

My Children have no idea how little intrusion there was by government in my younger days, the present status quo is their reality and accepted as the norm. This slow eroding of freedoms caused by creeping intrusion of our government into many aspects of our lives will slowly evolve to freedoms demise as

James Woods

each generation passes. Once lost these freedoms will not be given back or regained by politicians. Politicians are at their best when people threaten them the least, are not answerable to the people, and have nearly total control of the people.

Only politicians can remove our freedoms, only the American people can prevent it from becoming reality. At the very least we should teach "Our Constitution and Bill of Rights" in grades four thru twelve. Has anyone ever questioned why educators ignore this document, this blueprint of our freedoms?

Neither our politicians nor the American peoples are above exchanging our freedoms for the perceived safety of our persons. The mess created by Johnson's Great Society has been coming home to roost for over thirty years. We are obligated to the infirm and truly disabled, those who would be adults have a severe and sacred duty to their own maintenance, the care of their families and the care of the infirm, No more and no less. Taxation higher then needed is partial slavery as we are forced to work part of the time for free.

"Our Bill of Rights Amendment number ten" has been the one most corrupted by politicians, they are aware it is the one that gives States the Right to, nay demands, holding the power of the federal government in check. All other "Rights" become progressively more vulnerable as the "Tenth Amendment" becomes more degraded. Power over the States (people) is the agenda federal politicians have been slowly building for one hundred and forty years.

States now are basically powerless; their Constitutions, which were accepted by the Feds at statehood, now mean nothing in the halls of Congress or the U.S. Supreme Court. Statehood compacts have become one-way streets leading to a way of life where one shoe fits all. We have a D.C. dictatorship, an elected dictatorship whose yoke is a heavy burden placed on amendments one, two and ten.

You will notice I use the plural of freedom in my poems, freedom is not a singular right. We will continue to lose freedoms one by one 'til singular could be all we have left.

A Healing

For our million "Men of Honour" the ultimate sacrifice was required. They were true to their oath.

Mr. President and Congress! Honour our Constitution and Bill of Rights.

Article X.; The powers not delegated to the United States by the Constitution, nor prohibited by it to the States, are reserved to the States respectively, or to the people.

The ones in power slowly devour
the freedoms for which men died.
The enemy's not 'cross the seas,
inside the beltway they abide.

James Woods

"Tears of Rain"

There's a price we pay for freedoms
and for some the price was high.
Our long dead Warriors paid this price,
for our freedoms they did die.

Most do not care 'bout their death there,
a half a world away.
Most give no thought to price that bought
the rights we have today.

Some should take heed and do not read
these rhymes in "Tears of Rain."
The graphic speech is meant to teach
freedoms cost in death and pain.

It's rhymed to show the debt we owe
our long dead Warrior men.
Deaths debt unpaid, payments not made,
thru time debt will not end.

We're guardians now, I fear somehow
for our constitutions decree,
as time travels on I feel we're pawns
of feds back in DC.

In congress halls freedoms do pause
their oath of office they have spurned.
An oath's that's made is a debt unpaid,
it's time the bastards learned.

It's up to us, deaths debt of trust,
our constitution to defend.
Freedoms loss is slow and some politicians know
it just takes time my friend.

A Healing

Each freedom lost dishonour costs
the ones who make the rules.
Honour will drain from despots brains
as we remain their childish fools?

When people choose freedoms to lose
for their own uncaring gain
and freedoms call has left us all,
our Warriors deaths will be in vain.

For my country dear I hold great fear
as federal intrusion grows.
Infringement on life is cause for strife,
still we go with status quo.

The ones in power slowly devour
the freedoms for which men died.
The enemy's not 'cross the seas,
inside the beltway they abide.

I am well aware that damn few care
'bout Warriors death in bloody pain.
Memorial Day's a day for play
not for Warriors who were slain.

Dead Warriors cause should make us pause
and question why they gave their life.
Question why men die as loved ones cry,
question why men faced such strife.

Throughout the years with pain and fears,
young men have gone to die.
Freedom meant more than death in war
and freedoms did survive.

Our freedoms now near lost somehow,
slowly they slipped away.

James Woods

Like melting snow in spring they go.
Charge us a Judgment Day.

Rise up, rise up our Warriors dead,
your resting days are thru.
Your country needs you once again,
lost honour calls for you.

Thru history our enemy
you defeated back thru time,
You faced wars strife and gave your life
for your loved ones and mine.

In honour you died, to death you tried
and did your job damn well.
But now my friends, my long dead friends
our honour slips toward hell.

Most only know the status quo
of government today.
Of freedoms lost, the ones we've tossed
they comprehend no way.

There are no fights for lost states rights,
the opposite is a fact.
Our men who fought 'twill be for naught
'til freedoms we earn back.

Did you die in vain? It's with great pain
I call you from your sleep.
Rise up from graves our Warriors brave,
the ones who care now weep.

Your song of life ended in strife
and your spirits drift in sky,
joining those before who died in war,
forming clouds as freedoms die.

A Healing

As dark clouds form spirits will mourn
freedoms loss and feel more pain,
They'll face once more their death in war
and tears will fall, their "Tears of Rain".

Us who now live please do forgive,
we've let freedoms slip asunder.
We need you friends, dead Warrior friends,
unleash your cannons' thunder.

Bring all your dead, make us all dread
we caused your country's' fate.
Show us life's blood, wounds mixed with mud,
show "Freedoms bloody mate."

For freedoms cause you didn't pause,
show the price that kept us free.
Show buddies dead, ripped wounds that bled,
show legs blown off at knees.

Show us the fear of yesteryear
as you charged 'cross no mans land.
Show blood that pumps from legless stumps
as life's' blood spurts out in sand.

Show eyes burned out and screaming shouts
as white phosphorus burns you blind.
Show us the pain, show the insane
as brave men escape their minds.

Show Warriors brave in lonely graves
ten thousand miles from home.
"That mound of earth now's all their worth?"
Preserving freedoms will atone.

None lay a wreath, none cry their grief,
none tend the mournful graves.

James Woods

Few truly care 'bout their death there.
Forgotten Warriors brave.

Show machine-gun rip from neck to hip
as slugs rake a buddies life.
Above his hair in helmet there,
photo of one to be his wife.

His last act will be to try and see
this picture of his love.
Last words we hear are Jenny dear,
spirit leaves for sky above.

M-1 rifle upside down
fixed bayonet stabbed deep in ground,
helmet placed atop the thing,
one dog tag on chain does swing.

My body's here sweet Mother dear
but my spirit's soared away.
I've left war's hell and I will dwell
with you when we would play.

I'm here with you and Jenny too,
I'm still your little man.
I love you Mom and I'm not gone.
I just come home ---- Left warring land.

Mom tell my Dad please don't be sad,
I really am alright.
I still reside there by Dad's side,
bass fishing in the night.

I 'm still holding Daddies finger
back when I was two or three.
I'm still riding on Dads shoulders.
I am Love; My spirit's free.

A Healing

God's gift of life dwells near the veil,
I'm now beyond life's tears,
in a place of peace, of joy, of love.
A wondrous place my after years.

I've passed thru the veil that binds us there,
no more war nor hell from man.
My passage thru our veil was quite okay,
a burst of love was there to greet me
and at last I understand.

This time after my life on earth,
I travel now on rays of time.
I gather joyful stardust from my past,
from those I've loved so very much,
from those I left behind.

My dog "Old Gent'" plays by my side
in this tranquil land beyond your sky.
He radiates our love from Childhood years;
For me, our country's Soldier "Boy".
For I've a Soul that did not die.

Show moms torments when word is sent
her little "Boy" has died.
Show sad tears flow and pain won't go,
show hurt there deep inside.

I implore again dead Warrior friends,
show freedoms are not free.
Show the dark side and do not hide
painful death and misery.

Show artillery pound as you hugged the ground,
show Warriors torn asunder.
Show spirits fly for peace in sky,
leaving shrapnel, hell and thunder.

James Woods

Show us despair in men's eyes there,
just before they cloud.
Deaths wounds expose and show deaths throes
as men take on deaths shroud.

Show sweet sickening smell of death from hell
as shrapnel slices Buddies down.
Show dripping parts and blown out hearts
and blood sucked up by ground.

Show death march north of Twenty-fourth
after the divisions ripped to shreds.
Show those of God who couldn't trod,
old Nuns and Priests all dead.

Show death camps there under "tigers" care
where starvation did abound.
Show "Johnson's List" the ones death kissed
and graves that won't be found.

Let us know of death in snow,
show grotesque shapes of frozen men.
Show frozen feet and then repeat
dead grotesque shapes again.

Young bodies froze in life's last throes,
camera clicks eternity.
For us that live please don't forgive
if we think freedoms free.

Show intestines ripped and hands that grip,
bloody fingers force them in.
He went thru this all for freedoms cause,
primordial scream ----- amen.

Show wounds suck air from lung shot there,
show choking on life's blood.

161

A Healing

His voice not found, just gurgle sounds,
show deaths from warring crud.

Show men that run from death by gun,
show stark terror in their face.
Those not too daft will dodge the draft,
someone else must take their place.

In summers rain show torturous pain
where reeking bodies swell.
In summers heat show rotting meat
of Buddies blown to hell.

Show the damn flies we all despise,
show the maggots as they crawl.
Show all these things, make ignorant cringe
at the price of freedoms cause.

Show bayonets flash as the blades clash
in combat hand to hand.
Show life just wilt as to the hilt
blades stuck in gut of Warrior man.

Show blood run cold in your foxhole
as artillery slams you 'round.
Show damn air burst that was the worse,
mixed your blood and flesh with ground.

Show mustard gas as you breathed your last
in France in world war one.
Show lungs on fire, when one desire is air;
but life is done.

Show how you hold Buddies near cold
as eternity draws near.
Show this my friend, how at the end
Some cry out for, Ma-Ma Dear.

James Woods

Line up your dead, show wounds blood red
since days of nations birth.
Dead shuffle along, one million strong,
show price of freedoms worth.

March down our streets, slow funeral beats,
your tortured dead from war.
Some aren't aware, most just don't care
'bout freedoms you died for.

Let out your groan, in deaths pain moan
as you limp by us the living.
Make uncaring see what's kept us free
deaths' debts of freedoms giving.

Surround those there who do not care,
make them view your pain dulled eyes.
Make them touch blood,
wounds caked with mud,
demand they apologize.

I'll ask all why freedoms slide by
that I died for long ago.
Does no one care 'bout my death there?
No, long dead son; just let it go.

They won't understand, they love this land,
we are now our country's' bane.
They'll take deaths shroud and form those clouds,
those clouds, dark "tears of rain."

Show our constitution and bill of rights
for which you died so long ago,
place them in the pool of blood
of your million dead or so.

A Healing

Dark clouds despair, show all deaths there,
place above that pool of pain,
Force us to see what's kept us free,
your deaths, so freedoms would remain.

The sun shone thru after world war two
on the pool and constitution where
the golden light made glow what's right
and we in our land showed care.

Dark clouds close in and it's a sin,
our constitution fades toward gray.
In this land of mine it's tough to find
in this pool of blood a ray.

The ray is there, if enough care
our constitution will shine once more.
Protect it we must, fulfill our trust,
to those who died, our debts of war.

Open our eyes, our children's eyes
to your deaths long time in past.
You left in "trust" freedoms for us,
with uncaring it won't last.

The dead my friend won't rise again,
there can't be such a thing.
If they could I know they would
cry out; demand that freedoms ring.

I end this part with tired heart,
with sorrow and deep pain.
Good-bye my friends, dead Warrior friends
and welcome now dark "tears of rain."

James Woods

This long line of our dead young Warriors, over one million strong, stretches back from time, to not just you and me, but most directly to those who represent us thru our free elections. Elected officials, local, state and especially the federal are the only ones who have the power to assure that dark clouds don't form,
Tears of Rain won't fall.

Jimmie Joe
fishhook junction, Alaska

A Healing

Preamble to our Constitution

We the People of the United States, in Order to form a more perfect Union, establish Justice, insure domestic Tranquility, provide for the common defense, promote the general Welfare, and secure the Blessings of Liberty to ourselves and our Posterity, do ordain and establish this Constitution for the United States of America.

The (Our) Bill of Rights

Article I: Freedom of speech, religion, press, petition and assembly.
Article II: Right to bear arms and militia.
Article III: Quartering of soldiers.
Article IV: Warrants and searches.
Article V: Individual debt and double jeopardy.
Article VI: Speedy trial, witnesses and accusations.
Article VII: Right for a jury trial.
Article VIII: Bail and fines.
Article IX: Existence of other rights for the people.
Article X: Power reserved to the states and people.

Article I.
Congress shall make no law respecting an establishment of religion, or prohibiting the free exercise thereof; or abridging the freedom of speech, or of the press; or the right of the people peaceably to assemble, and to petition the Government for a redress of grievances.

Article II.
A well-regulated Militia, being necessary to the security of a free State, the right of the people to keep and bear Arms, shall not be infringed.

Article III.

No Soldier shall, in time of peace be quartered in any house, without the consent of the Owner, nor in time of war, but in a manner to be prescribed by law.

Article IV.

The right of the people to be secure in their persons, houses, papers, and effects, against unreasonable searches and seizures, shall not be violated, and no Warrants shall issue, but upon probable cause, supported by Oath or affirmation, and particularly describing the place to be searched, and the persons or things to be seized.

Article V

No person shall be held to answer for a capital, or otherwise infamous crime, unless on a presentment or indictment of a Grand Jury, except in cases arising in the land or naval forces, or in the Militia, when in actual service in time of War or public danger; nor shall any person be subject for the same offence to be twice put in jeopardy of life or limb; nor shall be compelled in any criminal case to be a witness against himself, nor be deprived of life, liberty, or property, without due process of law; nor shall private property be taken for public use, without just compensation.

Article VI.

In all criminal prosecutions, the accused shall enjoy the right to a speedy and public trial, by an impartial jury of the State and district wherein the crime shall have been committed, which district shall have been previously ascertained by law, and to be informed of the nature and cause of the accusation; to be confronted with the witnesses against him; to have compulsory process for obtaining witnesses in his favor, and to have the Assistance of Counsel for his defense.

A Healing

Article VII.

In Suits at common law, where the value in controversy shall exceed twenty dollars, the right of trial by jury shall be preserved, and no fact tried by a jury, shall be otherwise re-examined in any Court of the United States, than according to the rules of the common law.

Article VIII.

Excessive bail shall not be required, nor excessive fines imposed, nor cruel and unusual punishments inflicted.

Article IX.

The enumeration in the Constitution, of certain rights, shall not be construed to deny or disparage others retained by the people.

Article X.

The powers not delegated to the United States by the Constitution, nor prohibited by it to the States, are reserved to the States respectively, or to the people.

James Woods

"A Cause that's Just"

A Cause that's "Just" in my mind is a cause where we are defending our homeland from a foreign power with which America's very survival is at risk.

When a government is committing **Genocide** against its' neighbors or its' own citizens we definitely have a "Cause that is Just" with our intervention to stop it and restore a "Just" government to the people. To ignore such a situation would make us an enabler to such crimes and share, to some degree, in the guilt of said genocide.

Another cause that's "Just" may have been our defense of South Korea after the North Koreans invaded on the Twenty-fifth of June, Nineteen-fifty even tho in effect this was a "civil" war.

With our defeat of the North Korean Army by November Nineteen-fifty and China committing her army on the North's behalf the picture changed drastically. China warned our State Department she would not stand for a super power's army on her border. There were skirmishes between our army and the Red Chinese army in Northeast Korea about the last of October 1950. China withdrew, *at this time diplomacy should have taken over*. Mac Arthur refused to heed this warning and ordered the push on to the Yalu River, at this point wisdom became lost and the war became "unjust" in my mind.

The war could very well have become "unjust" when our army pushed across the Thirty-Eighth Parallel and carried the battle into North Korean territory, altho I question this as The North had been the brutal aggressor. I believe we were obligated to change a regime that committed genocide and other war crimes on such a large scale.

We had intelligence on the ground about the buildup of Red Chinese forces. We had air superiority and we should have observed quite well the buildup of Chinese troops across the Yale River. Our troops on the ground may have been surprised by the Chinese hoards that smashed across the Yale River, Mac Arthur and certain others most assuredly should not have been.

A Healing

The Politicians and State Department could have ended the war in October or November, they didn't. Whether from their own malfeasance or the total belief in Mac Arthur I don't know. I do know at this point our politicians failed in their sacred duty, we were no longer fighting for "A Cause that's Just". An *extra two to three million Civilians died*, about one million more warriors, all because of one general with an ego like a God and politicians with no courage except one, "Old Harry" and his showed up to late by five or six months.

The proof of an unjust war is when a vast majority of the homelands population no longer has a caring about the men involved in said war. An uncaring homeland that doesn't have the intelligence to comprehend it's not the warriors but the politicians, thru their failings, cause the wars and then draft the most recent crop of young "Boy's" to die in their "Just Cause". Young sacrifices are politician's renewable resources, about every twenty years the crop is again ready to be harvested. It's man-kinds insanity! You get Johnson's "Vietnam" and his damn "Gulf of Tonkin lie" believed and approved by Congress with only Greuning from Alaska and Morris from Oregon voting no! Bush had his Panama and Clinton threw missiles at four different countries, all acts of war without congressional approval. An incalculable number of humans have died in wars that should not have taken place and that accounts for nearly all wars.

View the film of some World War Two combat men who never recovered from "shell shock", "battle fatigue", "post traumatic stress" or whatever you care to call it, who died in institutions as near zombies They fought a "Just Cause" and still could not cope. This film was deemed to disturbing to be viewed by the general public was never released. (It caused deep sadness in my heart) How can we expect young "Boy's" to cope in a war where a large percentage of our peoples protest against it? How about the near totally unjust causes where you have mass protests? Some ware we should possibly not have engaged in fighting but don't take your bullshit out on the Warriors we send in harms war to do said fighting.

Jimmie Joe

James Woods

August 2004

"They" are killing us again;

Politicians such as Senators, John Kerry, Ted Kennedy and all the ultra liberals who publicly show the enemy the split of vicious dissension that exists in our country are without any question in my mind giving aid and comfort to our enemies. As in Vietnam this dissent leads to the enemy being convinced of a victory if they can keep killing more Americans and more innocents. They were correct in Nam as the American public bought the false and self-serving stories of men like John Kerry. His sworn statements before a Senate Committee could have caused the deaths of a few thousand more "grunts". During the first few years after our withdrawal a several million innocents died in Vietnam and Cambodia.

The honeymoon ended for President Bush a short time after 911, dissension was creeping in even as our dead were being searched for in the bowels of the world trade center. Iraq was the trigger for those wishing to make political hay from a course of action in which they had all voted with the administration. More young Americans are again dying, more outlandish public outcry by our political leaders is again taking place, and more innocents are again being killed and maimed by our foe. I hate to even have the thought that not only are our politicians aiding our foe, perhaps our foe is aiding our politicians as happened in Vietnam. We have the same generation in power now as the liberals who gave up Vietnam and Cambodia to the killing fields and in following years caused the death by suicide of thousands upon thousands of young Veterans by their own hand. The young liberals from the Vietnam era are now those in power and their words are again killing our young Warriors and of course the innocent civilians.

There is a very important difference in how Warriors will adjust thru the years after the battles have ended; a "Just Cause" and a "caring population at home is that difference. Compare the number of suicides of World War Two, Korea and Vietnam combat Vets, the less America supported a war the greater the

A Healing

percentage of suicides thu the adjustment years. It is a terrible sin to send our "Boy's"" to a war and abandon them during battle, it is a every bit as bad to abandon their emotional healing after their return from battle. It is imperative Warriors have a "Just Cause" to justify and cope with the carnage and death we witness, otherwise a lot of men's minds will not be able to accept or adjust. I speak of Warriors who were in actual combat for prolonged periods. -- ----The Grunts, may our Father Bless and Heal them all.

Jimmie Joe
fishhook junction, Alaska

James Woods

A Cause that's Just

I am convinced all our wars in the twentieth Century started out justified and with honour. While some may not have ended that way, we who battled the enemy, were not allowed by America to feel Honoured for having served in those causes. Wars began by politicians ten thousand miles away in Washington D.C., Messed up by politicians ten thousand miles away in Washington D.C. and we were not allowed to win because of politicians ten thousand miles away in Washington D.C. who had no problem abandoning the millions of innocent civilians we went to war to rescue from the tyranny of our foe.

There are many in this America I Honour greatly, reverently even and it's that mud covered hurting son-of-a-bitch whose home is a fox-hole, whose tools of trade are his rifle, a few frag grenades an entrenching tool and he lived in the steaming jungle of Vietnam or the Frozen hills of North Korea.

A Cause that's Just

Our last "true Just Cause" was World War Two
'near sixty years back in time.
To save this world most Warriors
knew it was worth their warring slime.

These men came home to cheering throngs,
the tired Warriors earned the cheers.
The next two wars when men returned
by their countrymen were spurned.

I'm not qualified to write of Vietnam,
about their war I will not tell.
Still I'm trying to tie together,
times of "all" our non-adjusting;
Of why our non-adjusting hell?

A Healing

Our country didn't care about Korea,
about Vietnam they cared much less.
Their contempt and their uncaring,
left our "Just Cause" quite a mess.

A "Just Cause" is really needed
for the Warriors who survive.
In our heads we need a reason,
to free our ghosts of warring season.

A reason for foxhole Buddies
who didn't make it home.
A reason for dying Children
who as "Shadow Ghosts" still roam.

.A reason for a Congress
who said "stepped War's a go".
An extra fifty thousand dead in Vietnam
'cause Congress can't say no.

You looked on our wars as all quite small,
not real like World War Two.
As grim reaper struck our buddies down
there was no support from you.

America didn't seem to give a damn
about her fighting men.
They had their fill in World War two,
to this I say "Amen".

A bullet killed us just as dead,
hot jagged flying shrapnel too.
We still held dying Buddies
as you did in World War Two.

The only difference was a "Just Cause,
that was on your side.

174

James Woods

You saved our Freedoms for us all
and you came home with pride.

You came home to millions of
cheering parties all across this land.
We came home to silence.
No, "thank you "Boy"; No band.

We didn't win in Korea
and your Warriors you would blame.
There was no all out war 'gainst China,
"Politicians take your shame."

Vietnam Vets came home to bastards
who spit on some Warrior men.
They came home to worse than silence.
Some spewed hate ---Damn it! Amen.

We pushed North Korea to the Yale River
Nineteen fifty in November.
We won the war in just five months,
then China hit and none remember.

We fought and died in numbers great,
South Korea we had freed.
We would have been home by Christmas.
Politicians let China intercede.

Mac Arthur wanted one last laurel
to be pinned upon his chest.
Free China from the commies
and he tried his level best.

All of China was Mac Arthur's goal,
too late Truman set him right.
We were already engaging China
in a bloody winter fight.

A Healing

That's the trouble with Infantry
when politicians do not try,
we're the ones who have to cope.
We're the ones who die.

Naive were we and Warriors young,
who thought our country always right.
At first we thought our Cause was just,
took years to see the light.

We fought them to a stand off,
the War ended in a tie.
For one damn General's ego
a few million more would die.

After November of Nineteen-fifty
all of the Korean wars long dead,
by a count of several million
rest on politicians heads.

We believed in God and country.
We believed in Mom and apple pie.
We believed in Causes that were Just.
We believed the bastards lies.

Pride for many years evaded us,
none was shown us here at home.
No gratitude to fill our minds
to displace the "Ghosts" who roam.

The Korean Warriors said nothing,
our battles we would store.
Deep back inside a pain filled wall
We hid with our Forgotten War.

It was forgotten by our countrymen,
forgotten by our Kin.

James Woods

It hid deep inside our Warriors heads.
No Just Cause; Our hidden sin?

The Korean War stayed hidden rather well,
'til we had Internet in our homes.
Then we found we weren't the only ones
where "Ghosts of War" at demand roam.

Because of Vietnam's Gulf of Tonkin lie
under Johnson's tender care.
Many thousands of our Warriors died,
many Vets have vacant stare.

A lot of Vets adjust just fine
but the homeless I can't name,
the ones who wander thru this land
are proof of this country's shame.

The "Just cause" the warriors needed
was nowhere to be found.
How can we justify the pain and dying
of all our Comrades in the ground?

Again we believed in God and country.
We believed in Mom and apple pie.
We believed in "Causes that were Just".
Why did we believe their lies?

Congress has the power to make the rules
about "A Cause that's Just".
Since World War Two they've not done well,
in malfeasance they do trust.

Adjusting to carnage and death
is tough enough to do,
it's only hopelessness that's left
when homeland spits on you.

A Healing

We're done, we'll leave, we're out of here.
We'll go we don't know where.
The hell with you, we'll disappear,
you sent us over there.

There are a lot of homeless veterans
who wander thru this land.
Looking for an answer,
to help them understand.

A Cause that's Just they were denied
by our politicians here.
Our reasons for Comrades who died?
Our reasons disappeared.

Adjusting isn't easy
when men first come home from war.
Adjusting isn't easy
when these young men you ignore.

When you spit on us and hate us,
this hurt we're forced to hide.
In back of mind with other hurts,
those War hurts deep inside.

Please don't do it,
our minds already sore.
You sent us off to War.

To a War without "A Cause that's Just"?
a War built on politicians lies.
That little "Gulf of Tonkin" fuss
caused millions more to die.

Politicians should carry all the blame
for pain and guilt from "Unjust Wars".

James Woods

Instead they have no answer.
We're not needed any more.

America will back "A Cause that's Just"
and politicians please take note,
we deplore you for our unjust Wars.
We deplore you with no vote.

We deplore you for our Buddies
and all the innocent who've died.
We deplore you for not caring
about our lives, our pain, our pride.

We deplore not stopping Mac Arthur
'till he had drawn the Chinese in.
We deplore you for "Gulf of Tonkin" lie,
We Damn you for those sins.

Because of you we have our homeless.
For thirty years our streets they roam.
It's too late now to help them.
Too late you said "Son Welcome Home".

The p.t.s.d. type of our homeless
are difficult to verify.
So many wannabe's on our streets
who never saw their Comrades die.

I only rhyme about our combat vets,
the phonies I disdain.
I only care about the Vets
who faced wars death and pain.

Adjusting some just cannot do
they never stood a prayer.
On the streets they'll live and die alone
because their country didn't care.

A Healing

I don't blame them, I'm blaming you,
the VA, congress and me too.
Had we given them A Cause that's Just,
their numbers would be few.

Counselors today are everywhere,
They converge on every tragic scene.
For each traumatic exposure
near civilians they are seen.

I think this is needed and fine
but this caring is quite new.
They went thru trauma just one time
not for a year or two.

Our adjusting we had to face alone,
there was no counseling long ago.
A few inside their minds did not come home,
their minds still hold what you don't know.

Alone we drift to VA counseling
and we drift back out again.
For our "unjust cause" we get no answer,
No answer? our subconscious sin?.

Next we visit the VA hospital
for help to ease the pain.
To the physic ward we stop a while
and the Bastards fry our brain.

We give up!, there is no help,
our answer can't be found.
We go back to the street and cardboard boxes,
not quite ready for the ground.

Now drugs and alcohol fry our brain
and numb the Ghosts we hide.

James Woods

They take away the nagging pain,
give back some phony pride.

Kinda makes us feel okay
with a full bottle in our shed.
Hides those Ghosts, those God Damn Ghosts,
that sneak out from our head.

I'll make it thru the day,
just a little drink or two.
Maybe heroin in the vein
or coke or crack will do.

It kind of takes away my pain.
It makes me feel all right.
See those dark clouds?
Those Tears of Rain.
Hope it doesn't rain tonight.

We fought and died for you America
and your Warriors you will curse?
Our buddies dying hurt quite deep
but your attitude hurts worse.

That's the life we gave to Vets
The "Unjust War" syndrome.
Not all, but some truly needed;
"Good to see you Welcome Home".

Your "Cause was Just" my Warrior friend,
the damn politicians lied.
If you fought their war with Honour,
than hold up your head with pride.

If you helped the little Children
in that far off warring land.

A Healing

Hold up your head with Honour,
us Grunts all understand.

If you held a dying Buddy
as he took on deaths shroud.
Hold up your head with Honour
of you us Grunts are proud.

If you despise carnage and death,
be it friend or be it foe,
Hold up your head with Honour,
you're a Just man us Grunts know.

To hell with politicians lies;
to hell with Unjust wars.
If you fought their lying war with Honour.
God will not ask for more.

Jimmie Joe
fishhook junction, Alaska

James Woods

"A Cause that's Just"?

SOUTH KOREAN SOLDIERS AND POLICE EXECUTED MORE THAN 2,000 political prisoners without trial in the early weeks of the Korean War. It causes outrage to me as some executions were observed by American Army officers who didn't have the honour to stop it, or possibly they did try and couldn't. Mac Arthur could have, the State Department could have and Truman sure as hell could have.

Four different times the battles raged thru the central section of Korea, four times Civilians were caught up in the waves of massacres. I'll grant the North Koreans committed most atrocities but the South Korean army and police apparently committed some unknown number. We will never know the true numbers, I find in what I can dig up estimates ranging from two to six million Civilians died in the war, either number is an abomination on all who participated in the intentional murdering of innocent Humans. There is not a need nor any excuse those kinds of bastards can give, it is genocide and a crime against Humanity. Hell all wars are politician's failures, all are crimes against Humanity. The soldiers committing atrocities are no more despicable than the politicians who stage the war.

Gen. Douglas Mac Arthur was aware of some of the mass shootings, according to documents classified "top secret" and released thru our freedom of information act. Hundreds of civilians were put aboard ships, taken out to sea, shot and their bodies dumped overboard. Mac Arthur commanded the South Korean military at the time; he referred this report on its actions to American diplomats "for consideration" and "such action as you consider appropriate."

American witnesses reported that 200 to 300 prisoners, including women and a girl 12 or 13 years old, were killed by South Korean military police on Aug. 10, 1950. Korean soldiers placed 20 prisoners at a time on the edge of a cliff and shot them in the back of the head, some did not die immediately, three hours after the executions were completed, some of the condemned Humans were still alive and moaning.

A Healing

U.S. Army attaché Lt. Col. Bob E. Edwards reported that 1,800 political prisoners were executed over three days at Taejon. It pained my soul to learn my war was so corrupted by the actions of the South. I had much soul searching and many questions about the civilian casualties resulting from our bombing of the North Korean cities. I now must add South Koreas criminal conduct, with our knowledge, and ask WHY did we allow it to happen, a question that will remain unanswered.

Damn the world's politicians, those safe, fat, contemptuous, flag waving bastards who consider war a crime against Humanity as something only the loser can commit. The egotistical asses never even consider that war itself is a crime against Humanity.

God alone knows the number murdered by the North Korean Reds or the South Korean dictatorships military and police. After we entered North Korea near Hague a prison was torched by the retreating Red army, burning alive the hundreds of prisoners inside. The murdering bastards executed several hundred old Men, Women and Children in a ditch near the town.

Outside town at the base of a cliff was a pile of Human remains fifty or so feet high, the bones near the bottom were quite old, near the top quite new. All this in one small area of Korea, God alone knows the total for the entire country. I remember a group of townsmen armed with axes, hoes and clubs marching a large group of their oppressors out of town to what I presumed to be their execution. When we were beaten back by the Chinese a few months later I would guess the avengers met the same fate. Our three-years of bombing North Korea also contributed greatly to the terrible carnage of innocent deaths.

War equals bombs, then comes the starvation and disease. Thru it from the start come the massacres, the rapes, the suicides and all manners of carnage against the innocent. I pray the bastards and the humane will be well sorted on judgment day with justice for all.

Jimmie Joe,
fishhook junction, Alaska

James Woods

Atonement?

ATONEMENT IS A QUITE COMPLICATED STATE OF MIND TO ACHIEVE. If I have been able to atone thru my writings it has to have been with help from God, a God I have never been able to grasp and believe in the way I feel I should.

I never killed the wounded, the undefended enemy or civilians. I have seen literally hundreds of old men, women and Children who had been massacred by the North Korean, and possibly (the South Korean army as I learned fifty years later). As we headed north I viewed the maimed survivors from our bombing of the North Korean cities.

Somehow I have felt a degree of guilt about these deaths, deaths I had nothing to do with. How does one atone for the enemies or his own country's' methods of warfare? The burden is great and complicated for one Grunt.

Throughout our wars there have been an abhorrent number of dead innocents. Between two and six million civilians died in Korea and roughly one and a half to two million soldiers. Fifty years later the number of civilian deaths is still growing due to the North Korean unbending regime. Starvation and disease, which are a large cause of death in any war, is still occurring in North Korea, all from a war of fifty years ago. There are so many countries on this earth where, the fact of just being born there Humans seem predestined to a life of suffering and early miserable death.

Atonement? I try, but don't know. I've done the best I can.

Jimmie Joe
fishhook junction, Alaska

A Healing

"Atonement"

I end these lines of warring times
'cause Ghosts I have set free.
I've ended pain locked in my brain
from my days across the sea.

My mind had control 'til I grew old
and retired all alone.
With just me home the Ghosts would roam.
The booze did not atone.

Near fifty years I'd suppressed tears,
manly men don't cry.
I'm here to tell I cried like hell.
My choices? --- Cry or die.

The Shadow Ghosts who'd been my host
since times long in the past,
thru lines by me are now set free.
Shadows no more they cast.

Children's haunting eyes for years despised
have softened now to Love.
They hold my hand in a peaceful land,
I thank our Lord above.

Buddies long dead have left my head
and rest where they belong.
Where pain did swell just sadness dwells
'bout ending young life's song.

No more do rhymes cause tearful times,
my soul's typed out it's grief.
I'm glad I'm thru; Bet you are too,
old Warrior's had his Ghost relief.

James Woods

I hope readers see what's kept us free,
tho rhymes may not be first rate.
Men died for you and the next line's true.
Our Freedoms had a Bloody Mate.

Jimmie Joe
fishhook junction, Alaska

Our treatment of Vietnam Vets.
"America's Shame"

They sleep and die in door ways,
it bothers us as we walk by.
We wish that they'd just go away,
their disgraceful to our eyes.

We don't care for decrepit warriors
or their non-adjusting fears.
What kind of fighting men were you?
Hell, it's been 'most thirty years!

So we'll leave them to die alone
with their hepatitis "C"
or maybe aids from needles shared
or maybe they'll just freeze.

It doesn't matter how they die,
they'll be away from you and me.
When their spirits soar for peace in sky,
then all their Ghosts will flee.

A forlorn spot in paupers field,
no tombstone marks his grave.
"A mound of earth NOW's all he's worth."
His country's warrior brave.

A Healing

It's hard to believe that derelict
fought a war to keep us free.
It's hard to give that man respect,
hell, he's not like you or me.

He was once, about thirty years ago,
he came back from war, did his bloody tour.
Good bye young man; Get out, go home,
it's warm above the sewer.

A cardboard box is good enough,
You're now a "Vet" === Hell man you're tough.

James Woods

THOSE YOUNG "BOY'S" FROM VIETNAM, FRESH OUT OF HORRORS most people will never see, were treated as no other servicemen in America's history. The pains many of them still carry are a direct result of their treatment by America's young. Mobs would harass them on their return from combat, calling them baby killers and spitting their spittle and shouting their hate.

Riots against the war took place at the democratic convention in Chicago in 1968; this action was well justified for those convinced the war was unjust. It should have been carried to the halls of congress and into the oval office, not against our Warriors.

Our homeless Vietnam Vets are the direct result of their treatment upon their return from war and for years after. Politicians gave us what some considered an "unjust war" and the troops were blamed by ignorant asses, most have no concept of the lives they are responsible for destroying, the number of suicides they have caused, suicides which continue with over 200,000 and counting as of 1998.

Jimmie Joe
fishhook junction, Alaska

James Woods

Jimmie Joe's thoughts on Bastards

NEWLY DISCLOSED DOCUMENTS SUGGEST THAT AS MANY AS 900 U.S. servicemen were left behind in North Korea after the United States and North Korea exchanged prisoners following the Korean War. The Dwight D. Eisenhower Presidential Library released the declassified papers. There were a total of eight thousand two hundred missing in action in Korea.

The public didn't know about those left behind, but it is clear that Eisenhower did. Five months after the war, in a document dated December 22, 1953, Army Secretary Robert Stevens met with President Eisenhower and told him the Defense Department had the names of 610 Army people and over 300 Air Force prisoners still held by the North Koreans.

A number of people confirmed the reports, citing their own experiences. Retired Colonel Phillip Corso, a former intelligence aide to Eisenhower, watched the exchange of prisoners at Panmunjon, and talked with some of those who came back. "Our own "Boy's" told me there were sick and wounded American "Boy's" not 10 miles from the camp, and they were not exchanged," he said.

A former Czechoslovakian general and Soviet intelligence agent, Jan Sejna, defected to the United States before the end of the Cold War. He told Congress that he saw some of the prisoners being used in gruesome medical experiments. "The top-secret purpose of the hospital was medical experimentation on Americans and South Koreans. The POWs were used to test the effects of chemical and biological weapons, and test the effects of atomic radiation," Sejna said. "The Soviets also used the American prisoners to test the psychological endurance of American soldiers. They were also used to test various mind controls.

The Eisenhower documents suggest that although the administration was concerned about the possibility it had abandoned POWs, it did not make the issue public for fear of a nuclear confrontation with Russia or China.

A Healing

None of the preceding is of any import to the vast majority of Americans nor should it be, it is some degree of import to us who fought and remember our missing comrades and these events that should not have been part of our history, become in our mind a distant but deep betrayal by those who were our leaders.

"Our betrayed"

Nine hundred ten who fought for us
in Korea and were captured long ago,
were abandoned to a dreadful fate
this traitorous act at last we know.

Those men we left, we left to death
and tortures we can't comprehend.
My country in my mind won't find
atonement for those warriors end.

For us they fought and 'twas for naught,
in untold pain they all have died.
Politicians back then betrayed our men,
where is their honor? where is pride?

We were well aware that they were there,
politicians and some generals too.
I can't believe how they deceive,
for politicians that's not new.

My heart does weep, fury runs deep,
the bastards left our combat men.
None seem to care and I'm aware
given time it will be done again.

Politicians lies I just despise,
their deception isn't rare.
To date it's such a common trait
and so few in this land care.

James Woods

Our founding fathers would rebel
against our government today.
They'd wish the bastards into hell
and help them on their way.

Jimmie Joe
fishhook junction, Alaska

*O*ur Korean war POWs

THE AVERAGE SURVIVAL RATE OF OUR POWS UNDER JAPANESE control was 74%, under German control 96%, and POWs of the Korean War, who after up to three years in captivity only 49% survived to make it home. Somewhere in there were over eight thousand of our MIAs that if counted would make the survival rate a deplorable 20%, yet we hear absolutely nothing of this. The difference seems to be Americas attitude about anything connected with the war in Korea, as if the war never took place!

As far back as 1953, retired Lieutenant General James A. Van Fleet, who had commanded the U.S. 8th Army in Korea (and whose son was among the POW/MIAs), was quoted in the New York Times as saying that "a large percentage of the over 8,000 American soldiers listed as missing in action are still alive."

Van Fleet was not alone in this assessment. General Mark Clark, former U.S. commander in Korea, upon his sudden resignation from Army in 1953, accused the communists of holding several thousand American servicemen after the prisoner switches supposedly had been completed. But even such blunt comments from well-respected leaders evoked no results; indeed, the remarks were soon forgotten and America went on feeling quite good about herself.

A Healing

A few POWs "turned" thru brainwashing by the Reds, a methodology unknown in our militaries prior history. None were prepared or trained to cope with this unknown. America and the military did a great and uncalled for injustice to the survivors of the communist death camps.

Because of the few who succumbed a pall was cast over all, few Americans responded to the unjust critics. This must have been a time of great distress to those brave Warriors. After going thru years of hellish inhumane treatment where over half their Buddies died America put them thru polluted bullshit and treated them all like the few that turned.

Near fifty years have passed and many of these survivors are still receiving counseling. In part some this is due to their treatment by America thru the months and years after their return. It took years before the degree treatment was recognized as needed, by the Veteran himself or by the VA. I cannot apologize for America. I will apologize for myself. When I came home from the ongoing war in Korea I tried to shut the war out, it would flit in and out but I kept it hidden as best I could, until nineteen ninety-seven when I read the Eisenhower Papers. I couldn't believe what I read; I had to believe what was to me unbelievable. The documentation is there in those damn "Secret files", released 28 years after Eisenhower's death in 1969.

Cold rage slowly built up with the realization that my country could/would do this to her Warriors, rage at the news media that gave it very little coverage, rage at America then and those who don't care now, disappointment in myself for not facing the reality of the Korean War. I should have been more involved with my comrades in arms. I am ashamed for all the years I spent in the limbo of self-imposed ignorance of forgetting and offered no helping hand to my Brothers who faced so much more than I, so much more than I can even imagine.

James Woods

All POWs who survived the death camps of North Korea are very exceptional people. The will and courage to keep putting one foot ahead of the other day after day for up to three years while coping with cold, malnutrition, dysentery, mental and physical torture and watching over half their Buddies die, have been and are to this day truly Heroic survivors. I Honour you my friends, I pray God will grant you the Peace of mind we denied you. Forgive me.

I despise the politicians without honour who abandoned our Warriors. Eisenhower was not the only one, our other political leaders, our State Department and some of our own military must have known. In reality we were and always have been their expendable "tin soldiers" whose courage on the battleground was always demanded in the name of Liberty, Loyalty, God and Country. Loyalty: A one-way street to torture, death and abandonment via the route of political expediency while the traitorous bastards wave Our Flag for votes. The very Flag they have desecrated thru abandonment of those who took the risks for our freedoms. Wave it at political rallies and tell us how we have the greatest country in the world. Ask the men we knowingly left to a fate known only to God and our enemies, tell me again about our country and it's greatness. Our Constitution is where the greatness has, does and will live. What politicians do with it is???

> The ones in power slowly devour
> the freedoms for which men died,
> The enemy's not 'cross the seas,
> inside the beltway they abide.

Jimmie Joe
fishhook junction, Alaska

A Healing

"A Bit of Wandering"

THE FOLLOWING POEM WAS MY FIRST, THE TITLE TELLS YOU I HAD no idea where I was going or why. I could go thru and make the flow better and make some thoughts more clear but I won't, when you read this poem I would like you to observe I stayed away from or went around subjects/emotions lurking behind the shadows. Anything written in prose was added later.

January 15, 1949 enlisted in the Army.

RA 16 307 188 mos 1745
Basic in 2nd. Infantry Division., Ft. Lewis, Washington
Desert training 2nd. Infantry Division.
Amphibious training 2nd. Infantry Division, Hawaii
Air transportability training 2nd. infantry Division.

Orders cut in May, 1950 for assignment to occupation duty in Japan with the 34th. Infantry regiment of the 24th. Infantry Division.

"A Bit of Wandering"

Back in May of Nineteen-Fifty
the Army made a decision,
Lets transfer Corporal Jimmie Joe
to the "Twenty-Fourth Division."

That idea was fine with me,
I couldn't wait to go.
I'd never crossed the great wide sea,
but first a home furlough.

For thirty days I'll have some fun
and all that sort of thing,

James Woods

by chasing Girls in summers sun
to make this lads heart ring.

I met one thru my cousin Jack,
her face all could adore.
She made my heart flip off it's track,
had not been done before.

When our eyes met we couldn't pry
our eyes apart, they're stuck.
We didn't even want to try;
Can Cupid run amok?

I reached and took her hands in mine,
them softly I did hold.
Our probing eyes sought out divine
as we viewed each others soul.

Both of us just standing there,
eyes would not break away.
Just holding hands, just holding stare,
I miss it still today.

Almost our eyes seemed to reveal,
a knowing back thru time.
Almost a love, was almost real,
Soul Mate with hands in mine?

Some past life, could it be
in a place I know not where,
Helen was holding hands with me
in a lifetime we did share?

Didn't know then 'bout Cupids charms,
I was a bit naive.
Quite soon I'll hold her in my arms
and "Boy" will I believe!

A Healing

While holding Helen close to me,
on my chest her head does rest.
My heart does sing but it's not free,
Those feelings were the best!

It's tied and bound by Helen's charms,
the Charms are ropes of Love.
Entwined with Helen in my arms
I felt peace as Noah's dove.

For two more weeks, both day and night,
a time our hearts did glow.
We walked and talked, held hands, held tight.
My heart just seemed to grow.

I couldn't know in one more week
as love flowed thru my heart,
a war would end what my soul does seek
and forever we would part.

We talked about our future life
and babies, four or five.
How someday we'd be man and wife,
'twas great to be alive.

Twenty-fifth of June 'twas on that day,
A day that changed my life.
The North Koreans stopped our play.
My darling Helen will not be,
will never be my Wife.

That night as we strolled around
in sorrow we did walk.
In sadness Helen's tears flowed down,
to miserable to talk.

James Woods

This was a sadly painful night
and for life our hearts did yearn.
Let me survive this warring fight.
Please God let me return.

We held each other much, much more,
our hearts mixed love with woe.
It's very sad to leave for war,
ten thousand miles away I'll go.

Just one more night of her warm arms,
we held each other tight.
Just one more night of Helen's' charms,
we held and held all night.

Today I have to catch a bus,
a sad time this has been.
No family there just two of us,
don't let this be the end.

I sailed to Sasebo and then
on to Pusan, my war began.
34th. Inf. Regt./21st Inf. Regt.
24th.Inf.Div. late July, 1950.

A far off land long, long ago,
thru summers heat and winters snow.
The North Koreans fit and trim,
sponsored by Russian Commies,
with commie cadre' discipline
modern equipped by Russian army.

Blitzkrieged south June, twenty-five,
South Korea won't survive.

So good "ol Harry" used his pen,
which he was nippy to do.

A Healing

The "Twenty-Fourth" it must go in.
Cannon fodder's nothing new.

You must go old Harry said,
or perhaps some other guy.
"tis better to be dead than red",
dear God don't let me die.

Men in Japan for occupation,
living the easy soldier's life.
Not well trained to fight a nation,
soon must deal with soldier's strife.

So they packed up you understand,
kissed their Geisha girls good-bye.
Guess it's time to be a man,
there, there Geisha girl don't cry.

The "Twenty-First" will join the fight,
have no idea what's ahead.
Left for combat the next night,
two days later near half were dead.

Task force Smith's four hundred men,
out numbered over thirty to one.
Only one way the fight could end,
less than one day the fight was done.

Delaying action near Suwan,
Infantry 'gainst commie tanks.
"Bout half the men won't see the dawn.
South Korean monument gives thanks.

What's that the politician said?
Safe at home in USA
These "Mothers children they're not red."
Too young to be a bit of clay.

James Woods

Dying there in fear and pain,
they'll never see their Moms again.
Nor hold a Wife, nor have a Child,
nor catch those fish in places wild.

They fought thru "Taejon," it was mean,
those ill trained and bloodied men.
In the mountains lost our "General Dean,"
barely slowed the commie war machine.

Just after that out gunned retreat
the Naktong River seemed real neat.
We'll hold them here the generals said,
"'tis better to be dead than red."

That sayings cute in congress halls,
those brave men way back there.
So far from war, so far from death,
bright eyed no vacant stare.

It's hardly cute as it can be
when so many "Boy's" are dying.
Ill equipped men of Infantry
'cause politicians were not trying.

My Helen wrote me every day,
love thru her pen would flow.
Her longing, loving hopes she'd say.
Dear God I missed her so.

War was a very lonely place
in that far off killing land.
Her letters let me see her face,
in my mind I'd hold her hand.

None knew when mail call would be,
the front kept shifting 'round.

A Healing

But always letters there for me,
from this Soul mate I'd found.

Mail call's really quite a treat,
letters from home are super neat,
waiting there with bated breath
until there are no letters left.

The ones whose names they didn't sound
would walk away with eyes cast down,.
they'd set alone and kind of stare
and wonder 'bout their loves back there.

I'd be busy reading mine.
My first love Helen, damn she's fine,
in ten more months if I'm not dead,
when I get home that girl I'll wed.

My heart's so full of lonesome love,
I thank the Lord whose up above.
for my sweet Helen way back there
who keeps me from that lonely stare.

May I explain what letters mean
to lonesome soldiers I have seen?
The letters take us far away
to places where we use to play.

To girlfriends who we tried to fool
around with out behind the school.
To night time bass fishing with Dad.
Want it again, want it real bad.

The only pleasure we receive,
the only thing that will relieve,
the loneliness we feel clear thru,
are letters from back home—from you.

James Woods

The "Thirty-Fourth" that one was mine,
I joined them in late July.
As battles raged outside Pusan,
I was exposed to men who die

Twenty miles? and that's not much
Mac Arthur's edict, hold your ground.
The ocean will be the end of us,
we hold or die or drown.

There will be no Dunkirk here
General Mac Arthur said.
Our ships will never rescue you,
hold fast or you're all dead.

That order we could quite despise,
things are not as they should be.
Damn it! real bad we need supplies
if we are to stop our enemy.

Red Army front, Guerrillas rear,
water, ammo and food are low.
Sure wish we were out of here,
we have no place to go.

Slowing commies down was tough,
untrained "Boy's" died while trying.
There's not too many left of us,
a lot of Warriors Mothers crying.

My biggest fear, my greatest dread
and I've just turned nineteen.
Is where I'll go if I get dead,
'cause preachers hell I've seen.

Back at home when people pray
God seems to help them on their way.

A Healing

>Me, God seems to quite ignore,
>perhaps it's just this awful war.

>Maybe dying? I can't tell.
>There's no way I could know.
>Spend eternity in Hell?
>I'm afraid that might be so.

>I know one thing I'd like to feel,
>that God and heaven both are real.
>Saying I believe won't do,
>Why did your God answer you?

>Oh! God! I'm scared the young "Boy" cried,
>Sarge I'm scared of Grannies hell!
>"I want my Mama" --- then he died.

>There is much more I need to say,
>there is no way to tell.

A repeat;

I now to speak to our Christian Brothers, since our revolution we have sent young "Boy's" into battle, first to earn and than retain our Freedoms. If our Lord had not yet sought them out, or they had not heard, or did not answer, is their fate eternal Hell as they die in battle? There have been over one million who have died in our wars, we demanded the lives of these young men in the name of Freedoms we retain. Was the price many paid their lives plus eternity in Hell? Their sacrifice is not of great significance to most of us, it was vital to those who died.

The chance of our hearing "Gods Call" exponentially raises as we age, our young Warrior dead do not age. You who send our young to war before the Holy Ghost has touched their Hearts and Soul, You who's words would condemn to Hell those Warriors not "Saved" or "Born Again", yet you accept their deaths as your right. Nay, You have and will demand the sacrifice of their

James Woods

lives/souls as protectors of Your Freedoms. You who are so sure of your place in Gods Love leave some seekers adrift in fear. I believe the bridge you lay out between man and God is exceedingly narrow. God would not build a path so few could find or trod. God's path will hold all seekers of His light. Your narrow path is a torture of Man and a disservice to our Gods Love, Understanding and Compassion. I, as a seeker believe you wrong us.

I hope God took him by the hand
and eased his soul from bloody sand,
held it tight and took him home.
So many deeds I must atone.

Guerrillas round Pusan would roam,
well trained for killing in the night.
Sent a lot of Warriors spirits home
in confusing mixed up fire fights.

The day after the killing stopped,
for some reason I felt no pain.
Trucks filled with bodies to the top,
thrown in back like sacks of grain.

Protecting walls in brain were new,
the reasons why I'll never know.
All those dead were neutral view,
as conscious mind let feelings slow.

Sometime before, not after that,
it took years to understand,

my eyes turned dull or dead or flat.
Conscious mind fogged up the killing land.

There is no way I can explain
what takes away the conscious pain.

A Healing

and stores it way in back of head,
for future times or 'til we're dead.

Subconscious mind can hide away
the sights and pain thru warring days.
As the months or years slide past,
the piper will be pain at last.

Another scene flits thru my mind
winding down those dusty roads,
refugees in miles long lines,
with those loads, back breaking loads.

All they'll own upon their backs,
eyes reflect despair and fear.
Fleeing from the Reds' attacks
only safety's south of here.

Those who think communism is fine,
view those peoples fleeing home.
Why heading south those tragic lines?
With many children all alone.

Two thousand men in "Thirty-Fourth,"
quite happy in Japan.
'Bout nine July they ventured forth
into that killing land.

Those under-trained troops quite soon would see
as they watched their Buddies die,
the training they all didn't have
made the price in lives quite high.

All of us, we will remember
of the original two thousand men,
one-eighty left by mid-September.
A lot of Mothers cried back then.

James Woods

Some might break down when Buddies die,
most will just have dull stare.
To much death will make the eyes
unseeing, flat, dull, no glare.

Mother nature seems to know
when we have seen to much.
Conscious mind will kind of slow
and "hold our mind in trust."

We lost our colours fighting there,
'cause to many men were dying.
Not many know, not many care,
but damn it we were trying.

The "Thirty-Fourth" ceased to exist,
our numbers were to few.
The "Twenty-First" next on my list,
their numbers were down too.

Bed Check Charley in BI-wing plane,
sounded like a wash machine.
Caused a small amount of pain,
Bed Check was brave and mean.

Some nights at sundown from the West,
he'd drop his bombs on what seemed best.
One night at sundown he glided in,
I guess we seemed what's best to him.

Bombs from plane came swishing down,
wounded all my squad but me.
Caught us out on open ground,
million dollar wounds, whoopee!!.

They're going home and they're okay,
a long life should be theirs.

A Healing

> Won't have to fight, not one more day,
> they're thru with warring cares.
>
> Crossed the Thirty-eighth parallel
> in this land of war torn strife.
> Near a small town viewed Warriors hell,
> commies had no regard for human life.
>
> POWs with wired hands
> behind their backs were tied.
> Face down in bloody stinking sand,
> murdered is why they died.

A saying at this period in our history was " Better to be dead than red" orated mostly by flag waving politicians who never had to face the truth of their garbage. They never adequately funded the Armed Forces at Infantry Division level (who must fight on the ground) 'til after we were at war, our tactics and training were as lacking as our worn out World War II armaments.

The lines "these Mothers Children, they're not red" express my total disdain for politicians who send young "Boy's" to a war for which they have not been prepared in tactics or arms. The apathetic bastards in the early stages did not even supply us with enough ammunition for our rifles and machine guns. There were no replacement barrels for the machine guns, we wore the rifling out and were left with smooth bores that sent the tracers ripping thru the air like a wounded duck, causing inaccuracy in direct and overhead fire as the result.

It was many years before I realized monetary support for peacetime military was a non-priority item for our liberal Congress. A great deal of funding went to the Air Force in research and development, the Grunts on the ground? Just enough for occupation duties, this was a deep betrayal to all Grunts who were/are the most expendable. Not one politician has or ever will answer for these betrayals nor even recognize death can be

James Woods

caused by lack of funding for adequate continuous training and armaments.

Again I declare we have executed some percentage of our own under-trained "Boy's" as surely as if we lined them up before a firing squad and Congress gave the order to "FIRE". Some will disagree. One good aspect is our dead will never know of their betrayal nor that the system of government they fought to defend was in fact their nemesis, a motherland that, at times such as these, devoured its young.

Bullet holes in back of heads,
We'd seen this crap before.
these mothers children, they're not red.
God I hate this stinking war.

But on we went to whip a nation,
could do nothing for these men.
Left them for graves registration,
a quick prayer then --- amen.

Civilian dead seem every where,
killed by retreating Commies.
Two or three hundred in one ditch,
Grand-parents, Kids and Mommies.

In dead Mothers arms Babies held close,
killed by the Commie slime.
These visions plagued my mind the most
after I'd left my warring time.

Even after all these years
of pushing back the "Ghosts."
Most times are fine and not yet tears,
visions of Children hurt the most.

A Healing

Many "Ghosts" flit thru my head,
can't hide them all the time.
'Cause I'm not dead, nor am I red,
they flit out from warring slime.

I do feel sad 'bout those in ground,
who were little more than "Boy's".
I do thank God I'm still around
and tasting all life's joys.

The flitting "Ghosts" within my head,
kinda sneak out when guard is down.
I force them back, beats being dead,
it's the only way I've found.

We headed north still going fast
our war was nearly won.
Had the commies whipped at last,
previous months have not been fun.

Should be soon I'll cross the sea
and hold this love who stole my heart.
My first love Helen waits for me
and our life together we will start.

Arms, warm arms and much, much more,
I have missed my Helen so.
Generals said we're home by Christmas.
A happy Soldier jimmie joe.

Some thanked God upon their knees,
in fairness that seemed just.
God answered with the Red Chinese,
who is this God we trust?

Thus began the longest retreat in American military history.
Please note this retreat did not take place under the Grunts orders, the

James Woods

Generals and I assume very high politicians were the ones responsible for the ordering a "tactical withdrawal".

Our supply lines were far to long to take on the Chinese Army, we in many cases had to fight our way thru encirclement to even make a retreat. Supplies become critical quite quickly under those circumstances.

Without a withdrawal we would have been wiped out with losses in the tens, possibly hundreds of thousands. There wasn't a chance of ammo and all the supplies needed would reach us in time or in continued abundance we would need against such numbers.

Some Divisions held as ordered while other divisions moved thru to the south as ordered, some suffered heavy casualties in this holding so others could escape. The Second Infantry Division was one of the holding divisions and took heavy casualties.

Half a million more or less,
of Chinese "volunteers"?
Again we're in an awful mess,
more Mothers shed more tears.

Bugles, whistles in the night,
this is not a pleasant place.
Guess we'll have a fire fight,
there's egg on Mac Arthur's' face.

Artillery pounding, light by flares,
cordite fumes abound.
Sure is an eerie night out there,
hot shrapnel slices 'round.

Tracers streaking 'cross the sky,
machine-gun barrel glows near red.
wave on wave they come; they die.
Can't believe unnumbered dead.

A Healing

Our ammunition's getting low,
can't hold out too long.
Soon, real soon we'll have to go
or death will end life's song.

Chinese withdraw, regroup a bit,
gave us respite from this fight.
"Politicians full of shit"!
I'm sure I said that right.

They kissed their god (Mac Arthur's ass),
your "Hero" from the "Big" war.
Politicians caused what's come to pass,
what are we dying for?

Politicians could have ceased
the war by mid-November.
Instead the damn thing just increased,
in sad anger I'll remember.

While politicians pissed themselves
Mac Arthur had his way.
A half a million Red Chinese?
We'll just scare them all away.

We must have scared them to distraction,
perhaps we were a fool.
We scared them in the wrong direction,
south to south of Seoul.

That's the trouble with Infantry
when politicians do not try.
We're the ones who have to cope,
we're the ones who die.

They cut us off last of November,
do not know the date.

James Woods

Kind of hazy, can't remember
don't like these hands of fate.

I know we had a huge air drop,
the planes in waves flew three abreast.
Cargo drop on old rice crop,
Those Pilots were the best.

Wave on wave as they flew past,
c-119s tipped up their nose.
They dropped us what we need at last,
There were no winter clothes.

Ammo, hand grenades and food,
our outlook was improving.
Sure put us in a hopeful mood,
once more we'll get a moving.

Gasoline for trucks and tanks,
mortar rounds and we gave thanks
for cargo drops from overhead.
Now most of us won't end up dead.

Turkeys here for us the living,
most were not quite done.
They dropped us some for our thanksgiving,
we ate them every one.

Ice-cream (melted), can't believe
we would get this now.
Surely eyes of mine deceive,
a last meal? Holy cow!

We made it out to safer ground,
there's not much more to tell.
Chinese no more us do surround
but it's getting cold as hell.

A Healing

Christmas Eve, cold full moon night,
Artillery lobbed no harassing rounds.
Twenty-four hour truce from fight,
we had peace but cold abounds.

Christmas Eve, Nineteen-Fifty, was the most beautiful I have in my memory, the full moon reflected light off the cold white snow so bright the sky seemed to have a dark blue hue. Small, white puff clouds drifted lazily past the moon and across the dark blue sky. It was deadly cold, deathly silent and absolutely beautiful when combined with the twenty-four hour truce from battle. The guns all along the front were silent, without even the distant sound of harassing artillery fire.

It would be nearly fifty years before a full moon and Christmas Eve would next be wedded in the heavens. I would be an old man remembering the peace a "Boy" felt when the sounds of battle ceased and the moon shone full and bright on this night of peace. It was a grand Christmas Eve, carried in my head for some reason as a special beauty thru time.

Carols streamed 'cross no mans land,
'twas beautiful to hear.
Ladies voices, big brass bands,
hadn't heard them in a year.

Tonight my Helen I really miss,
how I long for her embrace.
To hold her close, to share a kiss.
To touch my Helen's face.

Chinese speakers to make us sad,
guess they were not too bright.
They screwed up, it made us glad,
took us home for just one night.

We crossed the Han in dead of night,
the bridge was later blown.

James Woods

Formed our lines dug in to fight,
I'm cold wish I was home.

We heard the blowing of the bridge across the Han River from a distance. While researching the Korean War I learned nineteen ninety-eight the bridge had been filled with refugees and stragglers from South Korean military when the charges were touched off. If this was done accidentally or intentionally I don't know. They would have blown it intentionally while loaded with innocent Humans had they thought the Chinese might save the bridge. I would not have believed this at the time, there is no question in my mind now.

It seems we could have defended the approaches to the bridge until all the refugees had crossed then blow it when the Chinese were on it. At this late date I find there was, in far too many cases, too much disregard for the helpless confused refugees caught and killed in the turmoil of a war not of their making. Where is the glory?

There is much an Infantryman does see in war, there is much more garbage taking we never know about, a place far beyond the foxholes, its only years later we may discover the true extent of horrors in "our just cause", plus the extent of some politicians involved in the politics of war.

We held our lines against our foe,
can't remember firefights?
How we did it I don't know
but we must have done it right.

Damn it was cold, In can't believe,
twenty some below I'm told.
The clothes we had could not relieve
that penetrating cold.

213

A Healing

Fingers and feet were always numb
and frostbite did abound.
It was a bit unpleasant place,
that cold Korean ground.

A fox hole in the winter time
can freeze one's hands or feet.
It's not a place I'd call sublime.
Why do I think Alaska's neat?

Spring offensive time to go,
frozen foxholes are behind.
Still two feet of melting snow,
it's warm now so that's fine.

On we went again toward north
fighting the Chinese Reds.
The whole UN all blasted forth
this time we have less dead.

The first time in almost a year
we left the forward lines.
Division went division rear,
that peace was really fine.

Our Flag flew there beside a tent,
it stood out in the breeze.
I finally felt what My Flag meant,
My heart My Flag did please.

Forget what politicians say,
for re-election it's a spin.
Our homeland it is far away,
far from us fighting men.

Our Buddies dug in left and right,
those who danger with us share.

James Woods

Are reasons why we stay and fight,
are reasons why we care.

I don't know why my Flag did cause
My throat to lump, my heart to pause.
I really do not care a wit
for politicians full of shit.

My first loves letters they were fine
they helped me thru the warring time.
They came for seven months or so,
thru summers heat and winters snow.

The last one came in early spring,
the sky was clear and blue that day.
Black was edged around the thing,
My heart, my soul, my world turned gray.

It was the worse time of my life
and not at all the way We'd planned.
My soul torn out by pen's dull knife,
Will my soul survive this warring land.

My darling Jim's how it began,
I left it; Went to no mans land.
Sat out there 'twixt foe and friend,
Just wanting hurt, the hurt to end.

Hand on gun and head on knee,
war and killing so long around,
My Buddies came and rescued me
as I thought peace is in the ground.

I thank them now, I didn't then,
deep despair within me swelled.
Just wanted hurt, the hurt to end.

Jimmie Joe fishhook junction, Alaska

A Healing

The pain of that "Dear Jim" letter was quite deep; under combat conditions there was neither room nor time for the grieving. My writings of "my Helen" triggered the release of grief forty-six years later. I also grieved my Helens death twelve years after the fact. I carried my love for Helen mixed in with my memories of war for far too many years, I didn't get rid of the longing for her and hurt of the "Dear Jim" letter until a year or so after my second book, I suddenly realized one day I hadn't thought of her in a very long time. It is a bit weird; I guess she was entangled with "Boy" so deeply I couldn't separate them until I retrieved "Boy" from his long-term exile.

We didn't whip the Red Chinese
did push them back to north.
We didn't do it all alone,
the whole UN sallied forth.

Politicians say we can't wage war
north of the Yalu River.
As China's population soars
this war could go on forever.

To those who say we didn't win,
every Harry, Dick or Tom,
did you suggest invade China?
Maybe use the "Atom Bomb"?

You dishonor us who fight for you
when total victory's all you crave.
You dishonor us the living.
You dishonor us in graves.

It's a bit troubling to me the way most of the American public considers we didn't win in Korea. We did win in the sense of freeing South Korea from the North Korean invaders, which in the beginning was the goal. We had them pushed back across the

James Woods

thirty-eighth Parallel in October, Nineteen-fifty, we had fulfilled the United Nations mandate in a little over three months.

The decision, by Truman, Mac Arthur and God knows who else to reunite the entire Korean Peninsula by force of arms was the triggering mechanism that caused China's becoming engaged. China was paranoid about a world power charging toward her border long before we reached the Yalu River. Flush with her victory over the Chiang Kai-Sheck army only a year earlier she may have also felt the need to puff up the dragon to a size the world would notice. She did exactly that.

The cost in American lives in winning an all out war with China could have been a few hundred thousand. The costs in innocent lives of Chinese Civilians could have been in the millions, possibly tens of millions as we incinerated their cities with thermonuclear bombs. *Quite disturbing is, there were at the time and still are, a number of Americans, from Mac Arthur down to some average Joe's, who believe total victory is/would be worth the costs in other peoples lives.* In my mind only people in the last stages of a degenerative brain disease would trade the "standoff" we accepted with China for a total victory at such a price in Human suffering. Victory is and should remain the objective of armies; total victory at any costs is and should remain in the arena of despots of Hitler's' ilk. There should always be room for a diplomatic end to a war.

"Old Harry" and others were wrong in supporting the push to the Chinese border to achieve the re-unification of the two Koreas. "Old Harry" was correct in striving for and Eisenhower was correct in accepting the much-delayed process of peace via a stalemate and because of this the Korean War Warriors historically have been seen by many of America's World War II Veterans (especially the non-combatants) as not quite up to snuff, just didn't meet the Warrior status of their World War II brothers.

A Healing

A bullet killed us just as dead,
hot jagged flying shrapnel too.
We still held dying Buddies
as you did in World War Two.

I would ask you to keep in mind the Grunts didn't have anything to say about the political policies of international problems or anything to say about their solutions. The conduct of wars is political processes of both parties and will remain such. The solutions are political processes by both parties and will also remain such. In a war where one party demands unconditional surrender, such as World War II, the solution is still a political process, albeit a bit one-sided. I ask all politicians to take your bow; you've accomplished much thru my lifetime with the tens upon tens of millions of innocents you've killed in the name of God and Country.

The Grunts returned home some with broken bodies, some with broken minds and some with both. Win, lose or draw our country should have cheered their homecoming, acknowledge their sacrifice.

We were heroes back on V- J day.
The Country partied 'bout a year
White Crosses still meant nothing.
I saw no death and felt no fear.

The Grunts from the Korean War returned to a silence we 'most could hear and we kept hearing it for decades. The Grunts from Vietnam returned to a vicious, thankless Goddamn nation, they weren't ignored in silence, as were the Korean Grunts, they will remember being cursed and treated with disdain. Even tho not all treated them such, their remembrances of events surrounding their return are seared in their memory banks. Many could not cope with the war they carried in their heads plus the war we gave them here in the States.

218

James Woods

So far well over two hundred thousand Vietnam Vets have died by their own hand, but we, their Country's peoples, were the ones who squeezed the trigger. Over five times as many Vietnam Vets have committed suicide as died in the actual war. There is a reason America.

We fought and died for you America
and your Warriors you will curse?
Our Buddies dying hurt quite deep
but your attitude hurts worse.

Until recently the Department of Veterans Affairs, i.e. the V. A. hospitals have had no real agenda for analyzing and treating of wounds other than physical. The root causes of wounded minds were not treated; the Veterans were guinea pigs for the new experimental drugs. Drugs that managed to mask the problem not cure it, and in the process they managed to fry the brain, not heal it. The wisdom in the treatment of our Vets lacked caring. The caring in the treatment of our Vets lacked wisdom.

Next we visit the VA hospital
for help to ease the pain.
To the physic ward we stay a while
and the Bastards fry our brain.

The many wounded nurses serve
in any warring land,
takes courage and a special nerve,
I salute them they are grand.

Day after day I could not do
or face their awful chore,
what Mercy Angels must go thru
to heal "Boy's" wounds of war.

219

A Healing

They comfort all us Warriors there,
to us they are divine.
I thank them for the way they care
for us at dying time.

I know that some will later dream
of certain young "Boy's" dying.
I pray someone will hold them close,
give them comfort from their crying.

Ship takes me home across the sea,
I hope my Buddies follow me.
Some will die but most should live,
for leaving them please God forgive.

I had a Wife and that was fine,
my Children numbered right at nine.
Most my Grandkids make me smile,
I've caught those fish in places wild.

I've had a real good life you see
Since I sailed home from 'cross the sea.
But thru that life 'most every day
the "Shadow Ghosts" come out to play.

They flit around. They hurt a bit,
and "politicians full of shit."

Jimmie Joe
fishhook junction, Alaska

James Woods

In sad reflection --- We did not know

TO ALL "PRISONERS OF WAR" WE MAY NEVER HEAR ABOUT WHOM have been "abandoned by our politicians" in our wars, this includes our "cold war" with the Soviet Union and World War II (left in the Soviet Union at the end of the war, we knew damn it, we knew they were left and did nothing.). **Korea** (Known POWs left nine hundred and ten; two to four train loads of POWs sighted heading north out of Korea by several sources), POWs were used for experimental purposes as far away as Czechoslovakia and as near as the Yalu river; sworn statements by a former Czechoslovakian general before a Senate sub-committee, some of his sworn statements are bloodcurdling. God alone knows the fate of the 8,200 MIAs from the Korean War.

Vietnam claims there are no POWs retained in their country, there are about 2,500 MIAs unaccounted for from their war.

I doubt if any POWs have survived all these years, we must still strive for an accounting and we must never again allow our country to abandon our Warriors we send into harms way.

Credit;
James—Brooke
July 19, 1996, The New York Times

> *Numbering in the thousands, the list of Americans sent to Soviet labor camps is long and varied. They include left-wing Americans who emigrated to the Soviet Union in the 1930s only to be arrested as spies during Stalin's xenophobic sweeps; hundreds of dual nationals sent to Siberian labor camps after Stalin annexed Latvia, Lithuania, and Estonia in 1940; about 500 American military prisoners kept after World War II by Stalin as bargaining chips; about 30 F-86 pilots and crewmen captured during the Korean War and transferred to the Soviet Union in a secret aircraft industry intelligence operation; and as many as 100 American airmen who*

A Healing

survived downing of spy planes over Soviet territory during the Cold War. Continued on URL

"http://www.kimsoft.com/korea/mia-russ.htm"

Credit:
1996Nando.net
1996 TheAssociatedPress

Less than two years after the Korean War, a high-level Soviet defector told White House officials that American prisoners of war in North Korea had been taken secretly to Siberia to be exploited for Soviet intelligence purposes, according to a newly declassified U.S. government document

Entire article: *"http://www.kimsoft.com/korea/mia-us1.htm"*

Below is the possible fate of some who defended America.
[I don't know if the General Sejna's sworn statement is trustworthy.]

Statement of Jan Sejna

Before the Subcommittee on Military Personnel
Of the House National Security Committee

September 17, 1996

At the end of the Korean War, there were about 100 POWs who were still considered useful for further experiments. I believe all others had been killed in the

James Woods

process of the experiments because I do not recall ever reading any report that indicated that any of the POW patients at the hospital left the hospital alive—except the 100 that were still alive at the end of the war. These 100 were flown in four groups first to Czechoslovakia, where they were given physical exams, and then onto the Soviet Union. I learned about all this from the Czech doctors who ran the hospital, from the Czech military intelligence officer in charge of the Czech operations in Korea, from Soviet advisors, and from official documentation that I reviewed in the process of responding to a Soviet request for Czechoslovakia to send medical doctors to the Soviet Union to participate in various experiments being run on the POWs who had been transferred to the Soviet Union. I also reviewed reports on the results of autopsies of the POWs, and received briefings on various aspects of the experiments

During both the Korean and Vietnam Wars, the Soviet Union, assisted by Czechoslovakia, used over a thousand American POWs as guinea pigs in military medical intelligence experiments. Experiments were run to determine the limits of physiological and psychological stress the captive GIs could endure. The Soviets justified these tests, Sejna explained, on the need to determine how well the Americans could stand up to the rigors of all-out war.

American and South Korean and South Vietnamese POWs were exposed to chemical warfare agents and biological warfare organisms to test their susceptibility to the different agents and organisms. The Soviets wanted to learn if the American GIs were any more, or less, vulnerable than the Soviet soldiers to the experimental agents they were developing. The Soviets also wanted to know if there were any differences between the races—black, white, Hispanic and Asian— in their biochemical vulnerability to the agents.

A Healing

The captive GIs were also used as subjects in testing the effectiveness of military intelligence drugs, including a wide variety of mind-control and behavior-modification drugs, which, incidentally, were used during the Korean War to cause American servicemen to speak out on the evils of capitalism and on the benefits of communism.

The Soviets exposed GIs to atomic radiation to determine how much radiation was needed to kill or incapacitate a man. Tests to determine the long-term consequences of sub-lethal dose levels also were run. Lethal doses were administered and then the GIs were watched to determine how long soldiers could function and to learn if there were any drugs that could be used to prolong their ability to perform military tasks before permanently succumbing to the radiation.

Finally, autopsies were performed on the servicemen who did not survive the experiments to determine ethnic differences in biochemical makeup and to verify the effects of different drugs and biological organisms on the body, the heart and brain in particular.

Czechoslovakia's participation began early in the Korean War. The Soviets directed the Czechs to build an experimental hospital in North Korea. Ostensibly, the hospital was built to test new medical procedures for treating military casualties and for training young military doctors. This was its overt mission.

Covertly, the hospital served as a test bed in which captive American and South Korean servicemen were used as guinea pigs in the types of medical experiments described above. The Czechs also built a crematorium in North Korea to dispose of the remains.

Sejna discussed the operation with the deputy director of military intelligence for strategic intelligence who was in charge of intelligence operations in North Korea at the time and with the doctor who actually ran

James Woods

the experimental hospital in North Korea. The hospital was designed to handle two hundred "patients." In operation, the hospital was often overcrowded. One year six hundred patients were treated. The hospital was so crowded that two patients were often required to share one bed. Sejna never encountered any indication in any report or discussion that suggested that any of these hundreds of POW "patients" were ever returned back to the North Koreans.

In 1954, after the armistice was in effect, the Soviets decided to terminate operations in North Korea and turn the hospital over to the North Koreans. The roughly one hundred remaining American POWs were shipped back to the Soviet Union for long-term and more sophisticated experiments. For example, one of the experiments was to determine the long-term effects of sub-lethal doses of atomic radiation. To the Soviets, "long-term" usually meant several decades; fifty years was typical. In the case of the sub-lethal radiation effects, the Soviet interest included effects of radiation on the soldiers' reproductive organs and on their subsequent children and grandchildren.

The POWs were shipped by air, with a stop over in Prague, where the GIs were first examined for fitness before being sent on to various experimental medical test facilities in the Soviet Union. The stop over lasted typically about a week. The purpose of the stop over was for security to "break the trail" so that the Soviets could subsequently deny any claims that POWs were shipped to the U.S.S.R. from North Korea. This is also why the experimental hospital was a "Czech" hospital. These deceptions were all part of a carefully designed plan to mask the movement of GIs to the Soviet Union and mislead people about what was really happening and who was responsible.

(For complete report on Senate Select Committee see URL)
"http://www.aiipowmia.com/reports/dglssmalfe.html"

A Healing

The Americans are particularly interested in the Korean War when Moscow and North Korea had close ties. 8,177 Americans remain missing in action from that conflict.

The U.S. delegation has also sought information on American pilots who disappeared, nearly two hundred, while on spying mission over the Soviet Union. *Ten spy planes were shot down between 1950 and 1965 and about 90 crewmen from the spy planes alone have not been accounted for. We denied the flights and we denied their existence.*

The families of some Americans believe the MIAs from the Korean War were taken to the Soviet Union, and think some may still be alive in Russia. There is no evidence of any live Americans.

DECLASSIFIED GOVERNMENT MEMOS AFTER FORTY-THREE YEARS in the governments secret files show that top U.S. officials, including President Eisenhower, knew about the verified reports that POWs were still being held in the North Korea. But the officials, the government, our government who my comrade's had gone to war to defend, fearful of touching off a nuclear holocaust in the tense Cold War of the early 1950s, decided against pressing the issue. Fear of nuclear war was the reasoning.

The following poem is for the minimum of nine and ten hundred American "POW's" who were "abandoned by our politicians" on July 27th. 1953 at a North Korean POW camp less than ten miles from the peace talks at Panmunjon Korea.

James Woods

Flag Country Honor?

Eisenhower papers, were released in 1996. via freedom of information act.

For fifty years now more or less
you've hid dishonor from the press.
American people must not know
that politicians stoop this low.

One more fact that I must note
politicians need your vote.
So they sacrificed our men
they promised us the war would end.

The war did end just like they said.
It's tough to deal with commie red.
They were elected once again
all because the war did end.

They don't think they're full of shit
cause they really put an end to it.
They ended honor, ended pride,
deep within their graves they hide.

The maggots in their carcass gorge
upon dishonor. --- hell's their forge.

Jimmie Joe
fishhook junction, Alaska

A Healing

Flower Children, Vietnam to Kosovo & Serbia

It's something that needs asking my friends;

IN THE KOREAN WAR THE LAST TWENTY-SIX MONTHS WERE SPENT taking, losing, retaking the same hills and ridges over and over. The battle lines moved very little after July of nineteen fifty-one from where they were at the Armistice but the fighting and killing remained. Our Country let us down in Korea, before, during and after the battles ended. For over Two years Congress left young Men dying on hills and ridges for no gain, for absolutely nothing, because they did absolutely nothing to stop it. Congress let the Vietnam War continue for ten years after the Gulf of Tonkin, it took an eruption of Civilians against the War before Congress would intercede, all those dead young Men, all the dead Vietnamese numbering in millions. Congress's shame not the Grunts.

There will be times when the president should be allowed the kind of power to commit our country to war but Congress must decide if said war is justified and whether to supply the funding. In a war deemed not justified then congress should get the gonads to stop it as dictated by our Constitution. The way congress lets Warriors down is by sending our young people to die in a war which they consider an unjust cause and still allowing our missiles and bombs to kill the innocent. Year after year congress has funded wars many thought morally wrong, their courage is quite lacking. They should resign in protest, instead they rant against the Commander-and-Chief to the media to receive maximum national public coverage for political purposes, the enemy picks up on it, their killing and resolve is strengthened, their cause is enabled and more warriors' die.

Even tho I wrote the poem, which follows this dissertation, I had decided not to publish. I had mostly come to terms with the thought, maybe, just maybe, the ones who ran and the young who protested the war in Vietnam did so out of true caring about the civilians being killed and the deceptiveness and/or righteousness of the cause.

James Woods

With the war in Serbia (A small country the size of Ohio) I must reconsider which I had nearly come to accept. You flower children of the mid-sixties to the mid-seventies are nowhere to be found thirty years later with our massive seventy-eight days of bombing in Yugoslavia, why is this?

1 -- You're way past Draft age?
2 -- There is no Draft?
3 -- It's not the" in thing" anymore?
4 --War and killing is now acceptable since you've matured?

You helped stopped one War that needed stopping or winning (one of the two) and claimed your reasons were Honourable, I'm not sure about your hearts. (Your treatment of our returning Veterans had no honour), How much did you "flower children" contribute to their inability to adjust and how many suicides, which still go on, have you "compassionate flower children" donated to thru your actions in the late Sixties and early seventies and continued even after our Troops returned?

In Serbia we have flown about thirty thousand sorties at altitudes above twelve to fifteen thousand feet so as not to lose aircraft. This is not normal to a pilot when attacking troops or a convoy. The target (with the angle of attack) can't be identified from four miles away. So we have Civilians trying to flee the war zone being killed. We (in Korea) have been strafed by our own aircraft, the pilots couldn't identify us from about one half mile away. To begin firing four miles away from target of unknown humans is a political tactic! It is wrong. It is criminal.

NATO has lost no pilots but a hell of a lot of innocents have died because of political pressure not to lose pilots, the hell with civilians lives lost thru not being able to identify innocent from foe. Laws of land warfare are now antiquated. There is no question these tactics are something our pilots should (hopefully) hate, being aware it is wrong to put the innocent at risk when this can be mostly avoided by closer observation of the targets.

A Healing

A well thought plan by our commander-in-chief. (Stay high—Don't die) ** Hell man, I fought a war and killed about??? Thousand humans and never lost a man! What a guy! Could we have used Willie in Vietnam leading a line platoon? ** He could have been, he should have been. He should have seen the horror as a result of decisions made ten thousand miles away in the safety of an office in Washington D.C. Let him feel their pain, let him taste their fear, let him view the dead and dying Children and let him live with it for his lifetime.

Any excuse will be willingly accepted by a booming economy, any spin the Liberal Oval Office wishes to use will by faithfully reported by you of Americas fourth estate with no investigative reporting, no probing questions and no honour for your profession. It's all right if political parties of your bent piss on your open toed shoes while spinning. You are clones of liberal professors to whom truth is irrelevant and honour a misspelled word. The bias of your reporting is astoundingly different depending which party is in power in the executive office.

Collateral damage is such a sterile word, which for some reason is accepted as not a very big deal and a necessary part of war. The greater questions are; is the war necessary? Or where the hell have the brilliant diplomats and State Department been in the years preceding a decision to go to war? And where is/was Congress, why, I sometimes wonder, the hell do we have a Constitution?

Who made the decision to use cluster bombs at random on the wooded areas? They couldn't find the enemy in the open and decided they must be hiding in the woods, lets bomb the crap out of the woods, the hell with the civilians who were also hiding in the woods to get away from the bombing of the cities. Some questions should be asked about the whole conduct of NATO and our political leaders, it wasn't and won't be.

Any questions Flower Children? I thought not. You don't hear what I hear or see what I see. I hear the sound of bombers in the night, I see Mothers huddled with their Children in a cold dark basement, their frightened eyes looking up thru the dark ceiling when they hear the sound of jets, Mama pulls them close

James Woods

and says it will be all right. I feel fear you can cut with a knife in the Mothers heart, fear her Children won't live to see the sunrise tomorrow, or the day after, or the day after that. She must live thru seventy-eight nights of terror wondering each night if her Children will see that special sunrise, the one bringing peace and no death from the sky. Did you hear the bombers flower children? Did you feel the concussion shake the house from a nearby hit? Did you feel the Mothers fear? Did you feel the Children's fear in that cold dank basement?

We were wrong in our approach and method of solving a problem that has existed in the Balkans for centuries. We kill thousands of innocents rather than assassinate one man and there are no outcries from the old flower children of nearly forty years ago. May God forgive us!

PS: You are of course aware of bombs we tested filled with some kind of carbon fiber that temporarily shut down all the power in Belgrade, it worked quite well. It temporally shut down all the little Babies incubators and all life support machines of others. It permanently shut down the little babies along with others. Why would we even consider such tactics? Still no outrage from our fat, safe, aging, balding, gray-haired, paunchy bellied flower children. Go figure!

Ethnic cleansing is the lowest of the low in any country's conduct against Humanity.

Damn the worlds politicians, the safe, fat, contemptuous, flag waving bastards who consider a crime against Humanity as something only the loser can commit and be prosecuted for. The egotistical asses never even consider that "war itself is a crime against Humanity".

On the other side of this coin is a statement that is equally true, but the cases are more rare than the world seems to believe. "A crime against Humanity" is abstention from intervening and preventing "Crimes against Humanity" by the power of governments against their own peoples.

We generally have not reached this stage of civilized wisdom to discern the timely intervention into the internal affairs of

A Healing

another country. World politics must, and it is critical they do, play a large part in any decision of intervention.

The collective wisdom of the world's leaders must evolve far beyond its present degree if we are to be free of pure politics in our evaluation, than prevention, of the continued massacring of a people within a sovereign nation by said sovereign nation.

I agree the massacring of a nations own citizens is a cause for intervention, however the scales must be balanced with fairness of that which has actually occurred without using political rhetoric as proof or innocence in deciding a massacre is or is not a reality. Whether the time has come for some legally commissioned force to intervene, and the methods of warring we will use to stop it is where wisdom is paramount.

Many countries, including some members of NATO considered our conduct against Serbia to be acts of war crimes. Because America, with or without NATO, is extremely powerful we must accept the fact power does not give us wisdom. Power does not give us special rights we would deny other countries and power in the tactics we use in our conduct of warfare will not assuage our culpability of the innocent deaths we cause.

Very few hard facts were presented by any media source on Kosovo and Serbia prior to our intervention. Due to the massive amount of propaganda spewed forth from the Clinton administration, immediately after we began the bombing, I must question the basic premise of not only the legality but also the timing and it's validity.

For several years the Albanian Liberation forces had made forays into Kosovo attacking police stations, assassinating mayors, sometime their families, and various other public officials. [We must remember Serbia and Kosovo are what is left of Yugoslavia; they are the same sovereign country.] This went on for years and was to that degree covered on slow news days by the media, I can recall very little coverage of the Serbians committing mass killings of Albanians in Kosovo prior to Clintons committing our air war. Earlier in Bosnia, Croatia, and other areas of the Balkans all of the countries were engaged in ethnic cleansing with mass executions of innocent defenseless peoples and Serbia was probably the guiltiest.

Former Yugoslav President Slobodan Milosevic was and is a murderous bastard who must face the court at The Hague; there are many others in the Balkans including the Albanian terrorists who have been equally as guilty of crimes against Humanity. In my mind NATO also must answer for their methods of solving the Kosovo/Serbian crises.

Macedonia is now, in 2001, the country facing the problem of Albanian Liberation forces to impose their demands using methods much the same as those that were successful in Kosovo. When Macedonia attempts to squash this Guerrilla type warfare will NATO again step in on the side of the terrorists?

We send our Warriors into harms way in the Balkans while at the same time many nations in Africa are committing mass ethnic cleansing to a much greater degree. Slavery along with ethnic cleansing against the Christians by the Muslims in the Sudan has been and still is taking place. The media gives very little coverage to most horrors taking place in Africa; I'll let you ascertain the reason.

"Little, Children—Grown-ups War"

Ask about the little Children,
the ones you will never see.
The unnumbered maimed and dying Children,
the ones so far from you or me.

Some of them are Chinks you know,
or Japs, Ragheads or Gooks.
There's Ni**ers there in Africa
and Spearchuckers and Spooks.

There's Infidels and Sloops and Kikes
and names not known by me.
Worlds' drums of war will always claim
they're subhuman enemies.

A Healing

> Well, I've held collateral damage,
> my little Leaha and my Kim.
> Multiply these deaths by millions.
> Politicians' genocidal Sin.

The above lines are from a poem about two little Children dying in the Korea war where millions of innocent lives were lost. The causing of deaths among any helpless Humans; Men, Women or Children is deplorable, dead innocent adults only seem less appalling in our minds than the death of Children. Our innocent casualties of war be they maimed or killed, have no age that changes neither the righteousness nor the wrongfulness of a death or a cause. Before we go to war it is absolutely essential we use all pathways of diplomacy available to settle the problem. At times there is no recourse, war is forced upon us and that is usually where we like to believe we are coming from. In every case it's the lack of wisdom in the past as we observed the enemy arming well beyond his defensive mode and do not intercede early.

Dumb bombs? Smart bombs? Some ridicule smart bombs and use semantics' for their cause; they see no real difference between the two, as both will kill innocents. The smart bombs take lives but one hell of lot fewer then the dumb ones. I much prefer we have no war but when we do I greatly prefer any weapons system that kills the least innocents.

Peacenik types who consider war so terrible would condemn humanity to live under any oppressive government in lieu of war should realize the total population of this world would in time become enslaved to one tyrannical ruler, the leader believing in war would rule. There comes a time to get your head out of your ass and send prayers to God for the Warriors down thru the ages who have given their lives for all our freedoms. War is not a job anyone desires, is not pleasant and it stays in a Warriors mind throughout a lifetime.

Jimmie Joe
fishhook junction, Alaska

James Woods

Reality
(one of the first poems written)

"Reality" might not be real
it's as close as I can get.
It kind of shows the way I feel.
sadness is part of it.

Sadness for some friends who died
buried I don't know where.
Sadness for the ones who cried
for loss of loved ones there.

Sadness for some friends that lived,
for the cross that they will bear.
I hope somehow they all forgive,
"this land that didn't care".

Anger plays a larger part.
at the time we didn't know,
homeland ignored us from the start.
What's real was TV shows.

There's anger, hurt hid deep inside,
didn't know 'til I wrote these rhymes.
You've spurned us, smothered up the pride,
we should feel from warring times.

"Forgotten War" the name fits well
that bloody first damn year.
Forgotten too was frozen hell
and Pusan Perimeter.

Five to six million people died
on that small Korean ground.
While most Americans would hide.

A Healing

They heard no battle sounds,
as canasta made its rounds.

They didn't see the massacred civilians
or P.O.W.s murdered there.
They didn't see the dying children.
I have to wonder, would they care?

There was not the media coverage
we later had on TV screen.
Maybe it would have been different
if they'd shared the sights we'd seen.

Thru rhymes my anger will have to show,
love, sadness and compassion too.
The politicians I've placed below
what pig farmers get on shoes.

I can't believe how people were
in those times so long ago.
Can't believe they didn't care
about young men dying over there.

July and August have been months' of hell,
I hope September won't be worse.
Artillery, tank and mortar rounds
keep falling like God's curse.

Hot jagged shrapnel rips away
some arms, legs, heads or guts.
it's more than some men's minds can take,
today one went quite nuts.

Panic thrashing, legs, arms and knees,
his "screaming soul" could take no more.
Just trying to hide 'neath fallen leaves,
he'd left this godless place of war.

James Woods

Was the only one I've seen this bad,
it's worse then death; it's worse than sad.

Was an awful scene for men to see,
could it be curse or grace of God?
Well why not you? or why not me?
Sad abhorrent memory.

Next to hell, which is a dread,
that scene caused my greatest fear.
I don't want my mind to leave my head
and lose all thoughts that I hold dear.

Flat dull eyes can cope with death,
can cope with other sights and pain.
I think we never cope with this,
when Buddies mind escapes his brain.

Jimmie Joe
fishhook junction, Alaska

A Healing

"They are killing us again"
American Election of 2004

AS THE DEMOCRATIC PRESIDENTIAL HOPEFULS BEGAN THEIR CAMPAIGNS attempting to exceed each other in their public abuse of President Bush and **his** war in Iraq, the enemies use of IEDs (improvised explosive devices) began and increased in direct proportion to the amount of dissension our politicians and media showered upon **our** President. This vicious dissention by politicians against **our** President and **his** war has given aid and comfort to the enemy.

Politicians of Liberal ilk are again killing and maiming young American Warriors, again killing and maiming the innocent civilians. "They" do this from the safety of ten thousand miles separation; "They" do this with words. Speech is one of our freedoms, in addition speech may be a twisted killer used to meet political ends.

The generation now in power is made of the same liberals who gave Cambodia to the killing fields; sent unknown hundreds of thousands South Vietnamese to deaths in watery graves as they sought refuge from the North Vietnam victors and in following decades caused the death of thousands of OUR Veterans by their own hand. The young liberals from the Vietnam era are still with us, "they" have not changed, "they" will not change and their **old** voices are again killing and maiming **our** young Warriors we send into harms way.

I pray these "future Veterans" will be treated with honour and death will not arrive buy their own hand. May we help in their healing and may our Lord bless them.

James Woods,
Fishhook Junction, Alaska
Oakland, Arkansas

James Woods

Wahhabis' of a future time?
"Iraq"

OUR RESPONSE TO ACTS OF TERRORISM WILL NEVER BE ADEQUATE nor successful until terrorism becomes isolated acts performed without international sponsors. Terror will not be defeated until:

The Wahhabis' Sect is either eliminated or controlled by the Islamic religion itself.

The Madras's (schools) teach young male children that hate and killing of their fellow human beings is a sin against God.

A final knowledge that their death is not in compliance of Glory to God.

Until teaching hate is prohibited in Madras's world wide the Islamic mothers will continue to birth sons whose life must be taken in defense of our children and our culture, these sons will die in much greater numbers then our sons and we will prevail. Only the Islamic people can prevent the future annihilation of their sons, only the Islamic people can cause the reformation of fundamentalists' Islamic sects' and stop the teachings of hate and glorification for the death of sons as yet unborn.

I see no attempt by the Islamic masses to rectify acts of terrorism, nor even publicly condemn them. Their claim of Islam being a religion of peace and compassion does not fit the projection much of the world perceives or the acts of terrorism carried out by Islamic fundamentalists. The Islamic people can unravel this enigma thru the Islamic religion but never by their dead sons who may or may not be with God, or by the mothers who glorify their deaths.

James Woods,
Fishhook Junction, Alaska
Oakland, Arkansas

A Healing

"Johnson's List"
Johnnie died in 2005

WAYNE ARCHER "JOHNNIE" JOHNSON, L COMPANY, 21ST INFANTRY Regiment, 24th Infantry Division, U. S. Army, was captured on July 11, 1950. Johnson became part of the Tiger Survivors group and was held for nearly 38 months by the North Koreans and the Chinese Army. He is from Lima, Ohio.

Johnson started keeping a record of the men who died in his camp so that the families back home would know what happened to their loved ones. The fact that he could have been punished or even shot for keeping such a list did not stop him. Along the way, buddies would tell him about someone dying and others would stand guard while Johnson recorded the deaths.

See URL http://www.tigersurvivors.org/"

I wanted Johnny's list to be
included here within my rhymes.
I wanted to let my Children see
some men that died near Boyhood time.

The names are people young and real,
Dad was their age back then.
I would like them in their hearts to feel
gratitude and thank these Warrior men.

They did await an awful fate
at the hands of North Korean Reds.
They struggled forth on death march north
before their saga ended most were dead.

Records now tell of Suffering hell,
their torturous pain of long ago.
By luck not prayer, Dad wasn't there,
their awful fate he wouldn't know.

Jim Woods, 34th./21st. inf. RCT,24TH. Inf. Division

James Woods

On July 11, 1950, "Johnnie Johnson was captured, the following night American planes strafed a building where he and other POWs were interned killing several men. Somebody might forget these guys, Johnnie thought and their families should know where and when they died. Using a pencil stub, he wrote on a scrap of paper their names, units and date of death. By late October, most of Johnson's POW groups were sick and malnourished; 70 were already dead, including seven executed. Johnson listed each name on bits of discarded cigarette packages and a strip of wallpaper.

In October 1950, a extremely cruel, sadistic, murderous North Korean Army major referred to as "The Tiger" took command of more than 758 American service men, a few British Marines, Priests, Nuns and other civilians who had been captured and interned as prisoners of war.

During a 120-mile march across snowy mountain terrain, Johnson managed to jot down the names of over 100 men who died en route. That winter, in a camp on the Yalu River, almost 300 more prisoners died. Johnson added their names to his secret list.

In October 1951 after being transferred to Chinese control, Johnson made two identical lists and hid one in the mud-hut wall, the other in the dirt floor. When guards discovered the list hidden in the wall, the commandant beat Johnson, accusing him of maintaining "criminal propaganda" for his government. *"It's not propaganda," Johnson replied. "It's for the families."*

In August 1953, the 262 Tiger survivors were ordered to prepare for repatriation. Johnnie dug up his list and sealed it inside a toothpaste tube. Not until he was safely on a troopship home did he bring it out. "What have you got there?" an officer asked. "It's my list, sir," Johnnie explained. The officer held up the thin sheets crammed with tight columns. There were 496 names.

A lieutenant made a note of "the list" in Johnnie's debriefing report. But as America tried to forget the tragedy of Korea, the record of Johnson's list slipped into limbo, it was neither recorded nor recovered from "Johnnie" but "Johnnie"" saved the

241

A Healing

"list" for the next 43 years until "The List," as Johnson's tattered tabulation of tragedy has been dubbed, came to light in the Defense Department after Sgt. Victoria Bingham, an Army researcher dealing with Korean War POWs, got wind of what Johnson did. She caught up with him in 1995 at a reunion of former POWs in Sacramento, Calif. Johnson had shared his list with Army debriefers after the war, but some of the information fell through the cracks and was not passed to victims' families."

"Officials at Bingham's office, which is in charge of accounting for servicemen missing from the Korean and other wars, are using Johnson's list to cross-check their incomplete database. Larry Greer, spokesman for the Defense POW-MIA Office, said it has enabled the Pentagon to determine for the first time that some men listed as missing had been prisoners of war."

On the next page, 40 years later, published for the first time for families and friends of America's lost heroes, is the list.

Tiger Survivors List

A document examiner recovered nearly all the names from Johnson's original list. Some entries, however, could not be saved. Thus, there are fewer than 496 names on the list below. Entries are presented in the following form:
LAST NAME, First and Middle Names, Rank—Date Deceased -- (Unit,) Regiment (, Division) -- Hometown City, State/Country
Notes: Date Deceased is given as YYMMDD and is actual date deceased as recorded by PFC Johnnie Johnson. *Unit is only given where applicable, and Division is only given if other than the 24th. Infantry Division.*

James Woods

A----

ADAMS, Daryl Tine, PVT—NA -- 19 Inf—Los Angeles, CA
ADAMS, Robert Irving, 1LT -- 501115 -- 34 Inf—MA
AHERN, Gerald, MNE -- 510507 -- British, 41 R. **Marine Commando**— London, England UK
AKINS, Willis L., PVT—NA -- 21 Inf—Milwaukee, WI
ALBRECHT, John A., PFC -- 510131 -- I Co, 21 Inf—Pittsburg, PA
ALEXANDER, Jack Duane, PFC -- 501119 -- 21 Inf—Eildeaur, WI
ALFORD, Raymond K., PVT -- 510227 -- L Co, 21 Inf—Atlanta, GA
AMBEAU, Donald F., PVT -- 501101 -- L Co, 21 Inf—Escanaba, CA
AMPON, Joseph Obonon, CPL -- 520120 -- L Co, 21 Inf—Chicago, IL
ANDERSON, Douglas R., CPT -- 510814 -- Med Co, 21 Inf— Rockford, IL
ANDERSON, Larry Joe, PVT -- 501225 -- 19 Inf—Battle Creek, MI
ANDERSON, Omer Lee, CPL -- 510205 -- 21 Inf—Floyd, TX
ANGELL, Eugene Leroy, CPL -- 500925 -- C Co, 19 Inf—WI
ANZALDUA, Baldomero, SGT -- 510417 -- 21 Inf—Raymondville, TX
ATEN, Fred William, PFC -- 501024 -- 34 Inf—NJ
AYO, Albert James, PFC -- 510110 -- 19 Inf—Bronx, NY

B ---

BAER, Donald L., PFC -- 501203 -- 34 Inf—WI
BAILEY, Charles V., CPL -- 510122 -- L Co, 21 Inf—Holly, MI
BAKER, Walter R., PFC -- 510112 -- 21 Inf—Rockbridge, IL
BAMFORD, Charles M., SFC - --510724 --- D Btry, 15 AAA Bn, 7 **Div**—Ontario, CA
BARNES, Herbert R., PFC -- 510503 -- 19 Inf—Lonaconing, MD
BARNETT, Raymond E., PFC -- 500800 -- 21 Inf—Seattle, WA
BARON, John, PFC -- 510125 -- 21 Inf—Pawtucket, RI
BARRICK, George M., 1LT -- 501107 -- L Co, 21 Inf—WV
BARTER, Charles Tracy, MAJ -- 510503 -- Hq Btry, 63 FA Bn—Mt Vernon, IN
BASTIN, Sr. Therese, CIV -- 501130 -- Belgian, R. **Catholic nun** –
BAULK, Richard E., PVT -- 510111 -- C Co, 19 Inf—Detroit, MI

A Healing

BEAHM, Thomas J., PVT -- 510116 -- 21 Inf—Bethleham, PA
BECKHAM, Larry E., PVT -- 510224 -- C Co, 19 Inf—Lutherville, AR
BEECHER, Wilbert C., PVT -- 510122 -- 34 Inf—S. Miami, FL
BENNER, Warren W., PFC -- 510108 -- 21 Inf—Chester, PA
BERARDI, Thomas Henry, PFC -- 510711 -- 21 Inf—N. Bellingham, MA
BERGE, Ralph O., PVT -- 501226 -- 21 Inf—Clearwater, TX
BERGERON, Joseph E., PFC -- 510116 -- Med Co, 34 Inf—Waterbury, CT
BERGMAN, William J., 1LT -- 510618 -- 34 Inf—Little Rock, AR
BERRIER, Jackie G., PVT -- 510105 -- L Co, 21 Inf—Kansas City, MO
BEVELS, Charles M., CPL -- 501224 -- I Co, 21 Inf—Houston, MS
BILYEU, Michael G., PVT -- 500926 -- 21 Inf—OR
BISHOP, Arthur L., PVT -- 501122 -- 21 Inf—San Angelo, TX
BISSELL, James R., SGT -- 510602 -- 57 FA Bn, **7 Div**—Barton, OH
BLOCK, Robert S., PVT -- 501104 -- 19 Inf—Lyle, MN
BLUE, Adelbert, PFC—NA -- 34 Inf—Dayton, OH
BOLLES, Lloyd J. Jr, PVT -- 520413 -- 34 Inf—MI
BOOKS, Arthur Howard, 2LT -- 501101 -- 52 FA Bn—Norwood, OH
BOONE, James L., PVT -- 501103 -- 63 FA Bn—AR
BOR, Felix V., PFC -- 501112 -- 21 Inf—Detroit, MI
BORDEAU, Alfred C., PFC -- 510429 -- 21 Inf—Bay City, MI
BOTSFORD, Philip A., PFC -- 501029 -- 34 Inf—Manchester, NH
BOWSER, Lemuel R., PFC -- 510222 -- 21 Inf—Elmbank, PA
BOYER, Charles Edwin, CPL -- 510128 -- L Co, 21 Inf—Benton Harbor, MI
BOYIDDLE, Silas W., PVT -- 501027 -- L Co, 21 Inf—OK
BRADLEY, Edgar N., PFC -- 501115 -- 21 Inf—Honar, AR
BRANDENBURG, Kenneth, CPL -- 501030 -- 21 Inf—Norwood, OH
BRINGE, Donald P., PFC -- 510318 -- 63 FA Bn—Milwaukee, WI
BROCKMAN, John Joseph, 1LT -- 501212 -- I Co, 21 Inf—Tarpon Springs, FL
BROWN, Arthur Leroy, PFC -- 510119 -- 21 Inf—Cincinnati, OH
BROWN, David O., PFC -- 501113 -- H Co, 19 Inf—Farmington, MI
BROWN, Joseph C., CPL -- 510700 -- M Co, 21 Inf—Briggsdale, OH
BROWN, William E. Jr, PFC -- 501125 -- 34 Inf—Weissport, PA
BUFF, Jack Y., MSG -- 501028 -- 19 Inf—McAlester, OK
BULTEAU, Fr. Joseph, CIV -- 510106 -- French, **R. Catholic priest** –
BUNTING, Worth L., CPL -- 510108 -- 21 Inf—Ahan, NC

James Woods

BURFORD, Bobby L., PFC -- 501104 -- A Btry, 11 FA Bn—Lynchburg, VA
BURNS, Francis T., CPL -- 500902 -- 34 Inf—Santa Monica, CA
BURROUGHS, SGT—N/L -- -- CA
BUSICO, Ernest, PFC -- 510303 -- 19 Inf—NY
BUSKIRK, George E., PVT -- 510128 -- 21 Inf—Topeka, KS
BYERS, Charles E., PVT -- 501227 -- 21 Inf—Fort Plain, NY
BYRNES, Bishop Patrick, CIV -- 501125 -- USA, **R. Cath bishop** –

C ---

CADARS, Fr. Joseph, CIV -- 501218 -- French, **R. Cath priest** –
CALAWAY, William E., PFC -- 501024 -- C Co, 19 Inf—Quincy, IL
CAMMARANO, Thomas A., PVT -- 501102 -- 34 Inf—Brooklyn, NY
CANAVAN, Fr. Francis, CIV -- 501206 -- Irish, R. Cath priest –
CARMAN, Lyle Harvey, PFC -- 501207 -- 21 Inf—Marietta, OK
CARNES, Harry Zane, PFC -- 501122 -- 63 FA Bn—Detroit, MI
CASPER, Charles D., PFC -- 510109 -- 21 Inf—Eure, NC
CHARLES, Madison F., CPL -- 501103 -- 21 Inf—North Chatham, MA
CHARLES, Raymond N., PFC—NA -- 19 Inf—OH
CHEFF, Louis, PVT -- 501228 -- 34 Inf—Niagara Falls, NY
CHERRY, Richard F., PFC—NA -- 19 Inf—TX
CHOAT, Loyd L., PVT -- 501101 -- A Co, 19 Inf—Lonoke, AR
CHRISTENSEN, Jerry C., SFC -- 501210 -- Hq Co, 34 Inf—Dalton, MN
CHRISTIAN, Stuart B., PFC -- 510321 -- M Co, 21 Inf—Richmond, VA
CHRISTOPULOS, Clayton, PVT -- 501201 -- 34 Inf—Salida, CO
CLARE, Sr. Mary, CIV -- 501106 -- Irish, **Anglican nun** –
CLARK, Glenn M., PVT -- 501116 -- 21 Inf—Springfield, WV
CLARK, O C Jr, PVT—NA -- 21 Inf—Andalusia, AL
CLARKE, Harry Bernard, PFC -- 510427 -- 19 Inf—Dunnellen, NY
CLOSSON, Archie J., PVT—NA -- 21 Inf—RI
COLFORD, Wilber B., PVT -- 501031 -- 21 Inf—Fairfield, ME
CONNICK, Karl F., PFC -- 510618 -- 21 Inf—West Chazy, NY
CORONA, Jamie, PVT -- 510424 -- HvyMtrCo, 19 Inf—El Paso, TX
COSKEY, John H., PFC—NA -- 21 Inf—Philadelphia, PA
COUNCIL, William E., PFC -- 501104 -- 63 FA Bn—Pittsboro, NC
COX, Jansen Calvin, 2LT -- 501228 -- L Co, 21 Inf—Woodlawn, VA

A Healing

COX, Lester A., CPL -- 501031 -- 21 Inf—Lincoln, NE

COX, Robert C., CPL -- 510108 -- L Co, 21 Inf—Richmond, VA

CROGHAN, Varnold Gene, PFC -- 501213 -- Med Co, 19 Inf—Batelian, OH

CUMMING, Zolton, PFC -- 511031 -- C Co, 19 Inf—New York, NY

D ---

DAGGETT, Calvin A., PVT -- 501109 -- 63 FA Bn—Stamford, NY

DANIEL, Richard A., PVT—NA -- 21 Inf—WA

DANOWSKI, Alex, SFC -- 510317 -- L Co, 21 Inf—Ashley, PA

DAVIS, George Parker, PFC -- 510615 -- 21 Inf—Pawhuska, OK

DAVIS, Leo Clifford, PFC -- 501114 -- 19 Inf—NY

DAY, Donald, PVT -- 501030 -- 21 Inf—Cincinnati, OH

DE CICCO, Leo N., PFC -- 500902 -- 34 Inf—Hoboken, NJ

DE LUCA, Leslie J., PFC -- 501203 -- A Co, 19 Inf—WI

DE VRIESE, Sr. Mechtilde, CIV -- 501118 -- Belgian, **R. Cath nun** –

DEAN, Alvin Clinton, PFC -- 510518 -- 21 Inf—New Orleans, LA

DEMMIN, Dale Allen, PFC -- 510111 -- 34 Inf—Peoria, IL

DETAMORE, Robert Gail, PFC -- 501030 -- 34 Inf—WV

DIEKMAN, Lester H., CPL -- 501129 -- 52 FA Bn—Readlyn, IA

DIRKSEN, Abraham Jr, CPL -- 510508 -- 34 Inf—Blackwell, OK

DITMER, Elwood Lewis, CPL -- 501102 -- 63 FA Bn—Kansas City, MO

DOBBS, J.B., PFC -- 501105 -- 34 Inf—Mellette, OK

DOWLING, James Robert, PVT -- 501015 -- Med Co, 21 Inf—GA

DOXIE, Paul, SGT -- 501101 -- 34 Inf—Ontario, CA

DOYLE, Lawrence A., PFC -- 501028 -- D Co, 19 Inf—Baltimore, MD

DRISKELL, Herman L., 2LT -- 500907 -- A Co, 34 Inf—LA

DU BOSE, Clyatt R., PFC -- 510527 -- 21 Inf—Tampa, FL

DUNCAN, Lester A., PFC -- 510408 -- 34 Inf—Frederick, OK

DUNHAM, Leland R., MAJ -- 510807 -- Hq,1Bn, 34 Inf—Littleton, NH

DUNN, Francis, PFC -- 501027 -- A Co, 19 Inf—Troy, NY

E ---

EASTERDAY, Charles W., PFC -- 501116 -- L Co, 21 Inf—Ann Arbor, MI

EATON, Edward Drew, CPL -- 501125 -- 63 FA Bn—AR

EATON, John Omer, PFC -- 510508 -- C Co, 19 Inf—Sulphur, IN

EBENSPERGER, Clarence W., CPL -- 501102 -- G Co, 34 Inf—Utica, NY

EDGE, Edward C., PFC -- 501120 -- A Co, 19 Inf—Seaside Park, NJ

EDOUARD, Sr. Beatrix, CIV -- 501103 -- French, **R. Cath nun** –

ELTRINGHAM, Walter, CIV -- 501117 -- USA, ECA Engineer –

EMMOTT, Robert P., CPL -- 500700 -- 63 FA Bn—NY

ESTES, Edward Eugene, PFC -- 510207 -- 34 Inf—Cane Hill, AR

EVANS, Joseph Kenneth, SGT -- 510102 -- 21 Inf—Macon, GA

EVANS, William H. Sr., CIV -- 501212 -- USA, **Mining engineer** –

F ---

FABBI, Ernest, PVT -- 501220 -- 21 Inf—Carthage, NY

FAHRMEYER, Kermit C., PVT -- 500929 -- 34 Inf—KS

FALLON, Richard Lee, PVT -- 510202 -- F Co, 35 Inf, 25 Div—Fort Dodge, IA

FANCHER, Harold S., PFC -- 510507 -- Med Co, 34 Inf—Johnstown, NY

FANNIN, Clyde A., CPL -- 511100 -- 24 QM Co—Tyler, TX

FARONE, William M., CPL -- 501031 -- 21 Inf—Watertown, NY

FILLER, Donald L., PFC -- 510108 -- 34 Inf—Stockton, CA

FINE, John, PFC -- 510122 -- 21 Inf—Pittsburg, PA

FINE, Richard Melvin, PFC -- 510209 -- 21 Inf—Monongahela, PA

FITZGERALD, Edward, PFC -- 501212 -- 34 Inf—Syracuse, NY

FLEMING, John, PVT -- 510112 -- 63 FA Bn—Philadelphia, PA

FLETCHER, Robert S., CPL -- 510109 -- A Co, 19 Inf—Manchester, NH

FLOOK, Grady Harold, CPL -- 501114 -- Hq Btry, 52 FA Bn—Alhambra, CA

FLORCZYK, Edward S., PVT -- 501026 -- 34 Inf—NY

FRANKLIN, John D. Jr, PFC -- 510606 -- 19 Inf—Salem, NJ

FRANTZ, George Arthur, PFC -- 501205 -- L Co, 21 Inf—Indianapolis, IN

A Healing

FRECHETTE, Charles J., PFC -- 501021 -- 21 Inf—MI
FREUND, Aloysius J., SGT -- 510105 -- Hq,1 Bn, 19 Inf—Fond Du Lac, WI
FREYTAG, Reuben W., SGT -- 510120 -- 34 Inf—Wartburg, TN
FULLER, Donald A., PVT -- 510108 -- 34 Inf—Stockton, CA
FULLERTON, Harold O., PFC -- 501001 -- L Co, 21 Inf—Butler, PA
FUNA, John Francis, PFC -- 510105 -- 21 Inf—Pittsburgh, PA
FUNDERAT, Mrs., CIV -- 501103 -- **W. Russian, Widow** –
FURLOW, Robert Daniel, PFC -- 510503 -- 21 Inf—Mechanicville, NY

G ---

GAILEY, Robert George, CPL -- 510212 -- 63 FA Bn—Smiths Ferry, PA
GARCIA, Roger B., PFC -- 510320 -- 34 Inf—Los Angeles, CA
GARZA, Nicolas C., PVT -- 501220 -- 21 Inf—Rockdale, TX
GEARHART, William R., PVT -- 510103 -- M Co, 21 Inf—Ft Indiantown Gap, PA
GEDNEY, Robert Earl, PVT -- 501209 -- 34 Inf—Cleveland, OH
GENDILO, James F., PFC -- 501104 -- 21 Inf—Santa Clara, NY
GEORGE, Edward, PVT -- 501122 -- 34 Inf—Dallas, PA
GEORGE, Edwin, PVT—N/L -- 21 Inf—IL
GIBSON, Charles V., PVT -- 501200 -- 21 Inf—KS
GILLETTE, Robert Lee, PVT -- 510111 -- 34 Inf—Alanson, MI
GIRONA, Emil J., SFC -- 500906 -- 34 Inf—Los Angeles, CA
GLASS, Cecil Robert, PVT -- 510331 -- 34 Inf—Louisburg, MO
GOHL, Lavern P., PVT -- 501021 -- 19 Inf—Wiliston, ND
GOMBERT, Fr. Antoine, CIV -- 501112 -- French, **R. Cath priest** –
GOMBERT, Fr. Julien, CIV -- 501113 -- French, **R. Cath priest** –
GONZALEZ, Joe, PVT -- 501229 -- C Co, 3 EngrC Bn—Montebello, CA
GRAFF, Herman L. Jr, CPL -- 501117 -- 34 Inf—Knox City, MO
GRAHAM, William M., CPL -- 511127 -- 21 Inf—Bordentown, NJ
GRAMBERG, Bernard M. Jr, 1LT -- 501210 -- B Co, 27 Inf, **25 Div**— Glendale, CA
GRESSENS, Norman J., CPL -- 500928 -- 34 Inf—Ashland, PA
GRIFFITH, William G., PVT -- 501101 -- 34 Inf—Pittsburg, PA
GROSS, Myron E., PVT -- 510114 -- 21 Inf—Sundale, PA
GUIDRY, Joseph, CPL -- 510703 -- 21 Inf—Marrero, LA
GUSTAFSON, Harold W., PVT -- 501221 -- 34 Inf—Madisonville, TN

James Woods

H ---

HAGGARD, Billy M., PFC -- 510626 -- L Co, 21 Inf—Savano, TN
HALBURT, George R. Jr, PFC -- 510601 -- 21 Inf—Hermosa Beach, CA
HALE, George, CIV -- 500000 Autumn—USA, **Elect Engineer** –
HALEY, Richard A., 1SG -- 500811 -- I Co, 21 Inf—Auburndale, MA
HALLUM, Leonard David, PVT -- 510609 -- 34 Inf—Cookeville, TN
HAMILTON, Merlin Jack, SGT -- 520205 -- 34 Inf—Beloit, KS
HAMMOND, Robert T., PFC -- 501102 -- 34 Inf—Ilion, NY
HANNON, Arthur Thomas, PFC -- 501123 -- B Co, 27 Inf, 25 Div—Gardner, IL
HANSEN, Dan H., PVT -- 501210 -- 21 Inf—Correctionville, IA
HANSINGER, Nicholas J., PVT -- 501028 -- Med Co, 21 Inf—Los Angeles, CA
HARBOUR, Ronald E., PFC -- 501209 -- 34 Inf—Colfax, IA
HARDY, Edgar Warren, SFC -- 510511 -- 21 Inf—Nowata, OK
HARRINGTON, James A., PVT -- 501004 -- C Co, 19 Inf—Brooklyn, NY
HARRIS, Howard K., CPL -- 501104 -- 34 Inf—Providence, RI
HARRIS, Thomas W., PVT—NA -- 21 Inf—GA
HART, Michael J. Jr, PFC -- 500912 -- 24 QM Co—IL
HARTMAN, David R., PVT -- 500700 -- 34 Inf—MI
HARTMAN, Roger W., 1LT -- 510308 -- 52 FA Bn—Santa Fe, NM
HAYMAN, James R., PFC -- 501028 -- 21 Inf—Tampa, FL
HEATH, Richard C., SFC -- 510318 -- 21 Inf—Richfield Springs, NY
HEFFLEY, Edgar S., PVT -- 501114 -- 21 Inf—Chicago, IL
HELMES, Eugene, PFC -- 501029 -- E Co, 19 Inf—Pittman, OH
HENNESS, Jimmy E., PVT -- 501211 -- 63 FA Bn—Wichita, KS
HENSLEY, Bird Jr, SGT -- 501031 -- 620 AWS, USAF—Caywood, KY
HENSLEY, Eldred J., PFC -- 501105 -- 21 Inf—Hullinus, WV
HESS, Kenneth Leland, PVT -- 510207 -- C Co, 19 Inf—Concordia, KS
HICKS, Chester S., PFC -- 501223 -- 63 FA Bn—Madisonville, TN
HIGGS, William O. Jr, PFC -- 501102 -- 34 Inf—KS
HILL, Donald G., PVT -- 510124 -- 21 Inf—Riverton, WY
HILL, James C., PFC -- 510114 -- 29 RCT—MD
HILL, Melvin Jalmer, PVT -- 501118 -- 52 FA Bn—Negaunee, MI
HILLEN, James W., PVT -- 510114 -- 19 Inf—Detroit, MI

A Healing

HOAK, Charles R., PFC—NA -- 21 Inf—PA
HOLENCIK, Joseph P., PFC -- 510316 -- C Co, 19 Inf—Egypt, PA
HOLLAND, William K., PFC -- 510611 -- M Co, 21 Inf—Cincinnati, OH
HOLMAN, Albert C. Jr, PFC -- 510606 -- 34 Inf—Statesville, NC
HOULIHAN, Patrick J., SGT -- 501223 -- 34 Inf—Lawrence, MA
HOWARD, Ralph A., PFC -- 501120 -- 63 FA Bn—Lacona, NY
HUDSON, William J., PVT -- 501218 -- F Co, 35 Inf, 25 Div—Niles, MI
HUNT, Rev. Charles, CIV -- 501126 -- British, **Anglican priest** –
HUTTON, Donald J., CPL -- 501104 -- 63 FA Bn—St Louis, MO

I ---

IZU, Isamu, PFC -- 510712 -- Hq,3 Bn, 21 Inf—Kaalalila, HI

J ---

JESTER, William F., 1LT -- 510526 -- Hq,3 Bn, 21 Inf—Indianapolis, IN
JESTER, William R., PFC -- 510616 -- L Co, 21 Inf—Vevay, IN
JIMENEZ, Victor P., PFC -- 510416 -- C Co, 19 Inf—San Antonio, TX
JOHNNY (Korean Boy), CIV -- 501103 -- S. Korean, **US Army
 employee** ? –
JOHNSON, De Witt W., PFC -- 501230 -- 34 Inf—Doniphan, MO
JOHNSON, Harry W. Jr, PVT -- 501122 -- 21 Inf—Cleveland, OH
JOHNSON, John E., SGT -- 510109 -- 21 Inf—Council Hill, OK
JONES, Arthur Macon, CPL -- 501031 -- 21 Inf—Baltimore, MD
JONES, Dale Royce, PFC -- 510712 -- Med Co, 21 Inf—Piqua, OH
JONES, Thomas Dale, PFC -- 510101 -- 52 FA Bn—Colliers, WV

K ---

KACAR, Stanley J., PVT -- 500705 -- 34 Inf—Youngstown, OH
KAILIANU, Robert W., PFC -- 501223 -- 19 Inf—Honolulu, HI
KEKOA, Joseph K., PVT -- 500926 -- 21 Inf—HI
KELLY, Ernest M., SFC -- 500906 -- 21 Inf—Washington, PA
KELLY, Robert Thomas, PFC -- 510116 -- I/Med Co, 21 Inf—
 Pittsburg, PA

James Woods

KENDALL, Richard, PVT—NA -- 21 Inf—Indianapolis, IN
KENDIG, John Philip, PFC -- 501120 -- 63 FA Bn—York, PA
KIJIKOFF, Ilian, CIV -- 521217 -- **W. Russian** –
KIM, Chan JP Jr (George), PVT -- 501214 -- 34 Inf—Honolulu, HI
KING, Ralph E., PFC -- 520206 -- 21 Inf—New Albany, IN
KINGSLEY, Willie L., MSG -- 501117 -- 34 Inf—Birmingham, AL
KISCH, Dr. Ernst, CIV -- 510629 -- Austrian, **Methodist Hosp** –
KISER, Henry Gaines, SGT -- 510625 -- 21 Inf—Paris, KY
KIVLEHAN, Allen F., PFC -- 501103 -- Hq Co, 34 Inf—NY
KLIMSEY, Joseph W. Jr, PVT -- 510102 -- A Co, 21 Inf—Cleveland, OH
KNAPKE, Anthony L., CPL -- 501104 -- A Co, 19 Inf—Minster, OH
KOCH, Kermit K., PVT -- 510503 -- Med Co, 21 Inf—Frederickburg, TX
KOLBERG, William V., PFC -- 501228 -- 21 Inf—Keyser, WV
KRISTANOFF, George W., 1LT -- 510429 -- 24 Rcn Co—Pengilly, MN

L ---

LA-----Y, John, PFC -- 501114 -- 21 Inf—Philadelphia, PA
LAESSIG, Kenneth F., PVT -- 501122 -- 21 Inf—Whitefield, MI
LASSITER, Donald T., PFC -- 501120 -- 34 Inf—Ripley, TN
LAYTON, Robert Hollace, 1LT -- 510400 -- 28 BS, 19 BG, **USAF**—Tulsa, OK
LE MATTY, Donald Gene, PFC -- 501101 -- 63 FA Bn—Keokuk, IA
LEBIEDZ, Joseph, CPL -- 501103 -- 19 Inf—E. Cambridge, MA
LEE, Charles S.A., PFC -- 510106 -- 34 Inf—Honolulu, HI
LENZ, Robert G., PFC -- 501225 -- C Co, 19 Inf—Beloit, WI
LEONOFF, CIV -- 501209 -- **W. Russian** –
LEWIS, Warren Gunn, 2LT -- 501206 -- M Co, 21 Inf—Cartersville, GA
LIEBEG, Robert W., PFC -- 510301 -- 19 Inf—Brainerd, MN
LINGLE, Keith Le Velle, CPL -- 510101 -- 63 FA Bn—Coalwood, WV
LIPES, Richard Ray, PFC -- 501223 -- 19 Inf—Lewisburg, WV
LOGSTON, Edward R., A2C -- 501104 -- 620 AWS, **USAF**—
    Richmond, CA
LOOMIS, Otis Wayne, CPL -- 501225 -- C Co, 19 Inf—Caledonia, NY
LORENZ, Robert Edward, PFC -- 501028 -- 63 FA Bn—Chicago, IL
LOVE, Robert James, PVT -- 501114 -- 21 Inf—Mansfield, OH
LUKITSCH, John Joseph, PFC -- 501027 -- C Co, 19 Inf—Allentown, PA
LYCAN, John Smith Jr, PFC -- 501205 -- 21 Inf—Sun Valley, CA

251

A Healing

M ---

MAC GILL,Henry Tomlinson, 1LT -- 500716 -- C Co, 21 Inf—NC
MAC NAIR-RAGA, Hector, PVT -- 510116 -- 34 Inf—New York, NY
MACHEN, William Allen, PFC -- 501104 -- 21 Inf—WA
MACOMBER, Wayne B., CPT -- 510719 -- Hq,1 Bn, 19 Inf—Oakland, CA
MAGNUS, Donald F., PFC -- 510104 -- 21 Inf—Evansville, IN
MAHER, Frank X., SGT—NA -- 34 Inf—Philadelphia, PA
MAHONEY, Kenneth R., PVT -- 500803 -- 21 Inf—MA
MAJESKE, Arthur Jr, PVT -- 510101 -- 21 Inf—West Allis, WI
MALDONADO, Victor S., PVT -- 501127 -- 34 Inf—New York, NY
MALONE, Francis P. Jr, CPL -- 510129 -- 19 Inf—FL
MANN, William Cornett, PFC -- 510303 -- Hq Btry, 52 FA Bn—Indian Mound, TN
MANROSS, Thomas M., PFC -- 501114 -- 19 Inf—Titusville, PA
MARSH, Harold L., SFC -- 500800 -- 34 Inf—Oshkosh, WI
MARTIN, Elwin C Jr., CPL—NA -- 21 Inf—Leaksville, NC
MARTIN, John A., CPL -- 510502 -- D Co, 21 Inf—Ridgeway, TX
MARTY, Albert E., PFC -- 500717 -- C Co, 19 Inf—OH
MARZLITSKY, Andre, CIV—Disappeared Pyong-yang—**W. Russian**, ECA Diver –
MATHEWSON, Ward F., SFC -- 500716 -- 21 Inf—NY
MATTHEWS, Richard F., SFC -- 501031 -- 34 Inf—Sacramento, CA
MATTI, Alfred, CIV -- 501130 -- Swiss, **Chosen Hotel Manager** – *
MAYNARD, Edward Wiley, 1LT -- 510620 -- Hq Btry, 63 FA Bn—Baltimore, MD
MC CABE, Donald John, PVT -- 501104 -- A Co, 19 Inf—Brooklyn, NY
MC CLAIN, Frederick F., SGT -- 501102 -- 34 Inf—OH
MC CORMICK, Billy Gene, PVT -- 501106 -- **5 RCT**—Santa Paula, CA
MC DONNELL, John James, PVT -- 501114 -- 34 Inf—Philadelphia, PA
MC ELROY, Joseph A., CPL -- 501213 -- 34 Inf—W----port, PA
MC GILL, William R., PVT -- 501218 -- 21 Inf—Lock Haven, PA
MC GRATH, Ross Robert, PVT -- 501102 -- 63 FA Bn—MA
MC INTYRE, James T., PFC -- 501228 -- 21 Inf—New Albany, IN
MC KINLEY, Ralph H., PVT -- 510505 -- 21 Inf—Atlanta, GA
MC NARY, Walter David, PVT -- 501122 -- 34 Inf—East Detroit, MI

James Woods

MC QUEEN, Norman, SFC -- 510116 -- 63 FA Bn—OK
MC SHANE, Edward P., PFC -- 501214 -- C Co, 19 Inf—Pittsburg, PA
MELCHIORRE, Joseph D., PFC -- 510319 -- 21 Inf—Utica, NY
MELLINGER, James R., PFC -- 501102 -- 34 Inf—Billingdale, OH
MENTZOS, Paul Gust, SGT -- 510703 -- 21 Inf—St Louis, MO
MERSHON, David F., PVT -- 501104 -- A Co, 19 Inf—Portsmouth, OH
MERTH, Philip F., CPL -- 500700 -- 63 FA Bn—IN
MIELKE, Robert C., PVT -- 501031 -- C Co, 34 Inf—Kenosha, WI
MILLER, Paul Luther, A1C -- 501115 -- 28 BS, 19 BG, **USAF**—Flat Rock, MI
MINER, Donald W., PVT—NA -- 21 Inf—Hudson Falls, NY
MITCHELL, Rudus Jr, PFC -- 501104 -- Hq Co, 19 Inf—New Orleans, LA
MITCHELL, William B. Jr, PVT -- 500729 -- A Co, 19 Inf—Jackson, MS
MITCHELSON, Thomas P., PFC -- 500924 -- 34 Inf—WY
MOMPHER, David P., PFC -- 501029 -- 24 Rcn Co—Fostoria, OH
MONROE, James H., PFC -- 501102 -- C Co, 19 Inf—Meridian, ID
MONTGOMERY, Harold W., SGT -- 510103 -- 21 Inf—Madera, CA
MORALES, Joseph S., PVT -- 501126 -- 34 Inf—Johnstown, PA
MORENO, Raymond M., PFC -- 510517 -- 21 Inf—Los Angeles, CA
MORGAN, Melvin H., PFC -- 501206 -- L Co, 21 Inf—Stanfield, NC
MOSS, William R., CPL -- 510118 -- 21 Inf—MA
MULOCK, Arthur F., 1LT—NA -- 34 Inf—Waltham, MA
MURDOCK, Jackie Lee, PVT -- 501029 -- 34 Inf—Crawfordsville, IN
MURPHY, Michael D., CPL -- 501114 -- Med Co, 34 Inf—Oklahoma City, OK
MURPHY, Robert Mervin, PFC -- 510527 -- 34 Inf—Fairchance, PA
MYERS, Guy K., PVT -- 501031 -- 34 Inf—Boston, VA

N ---

NAZELROD, Earl C., PFC -- 510414 -- 34 Inf—Oakland, MD
NELSON, Oscar R., PVT -- 501026 -- C Co, 19 Inf—Detroit, MI
NELSON, Woodrow W., PFC -- 501019 -- L Co, 21 Inf—New Biochices, OH
NICHOLS, Robert A., PFC -- 510103 -- L Co, 21 Inf—Toledo, OH
NIEMANN, Robert C., 2LT -- 500800 -- Hq,1 Bn, 21 Inf – IA

A Healing

O ---

O HARA, William T., PFC -- 501121 -- 19 Inf—Milwaukee, WI
OAKS, Joseph Stephen, PFC -- 500928 -- 34 Inf—Philadelphia, PA
OLES, Peter, PVT -- 501208 -- C Co, 19 Inf—Batavia, NY
OLLERO, Luciano F., PFC -- 510523 -- C Co, 19 Inf—PI
OLSON, Sigurd Carl, PVT -- 510205 -- 21 Inf—Bethel, ME
OLTMAN, Charles R.L., PVT -- 510128 -- Hq Btry, 63 FA Bn—
    Springfield, MO
ONION, Vernon James, PFC -- 501225 -- 34 Inf—Foreston, MD
ORCHESTRAIA, Helena, CIV—Disappeared Pyong-yang—**Polish-
    Korean, US Civ Commissary** –
OSTROWSKI, Chester, PFC -- 501120 -- 21 Inf—Onamia, MN
OXNER, Harvey, PVT -- 500728 -- 19 Inf—Bri----, AR

P ---

PALLESEN, Robert Gene, PFC -- 501030 -- Divarty—Racine, WI
PARKS, Ralph Leonard, CPL -- 510315 -- 19 Inf—Carlyle, IL
PASTUSZEK, Walter J., PVT -- 501217 -- 21 Inf—Philadelphia, PA
PEARSON, Raymond E., 2LT -- 510124 -- SvcBtry, 63 FA Bn—
    Crawfordsville, IN
PEETERS, Marcel C., PVT -- 510121 -- 19 Inf—Alanson, MI
PERRY, Fletcher F., CPL -- 500907 -- 19 Inf—Hilton, GA
PETERSON, Donwin Ross, PFC -- 510805 -- C Co, 19 Inf—Osakis, OK
PETTIS, Gilbert L., PFC -- 501031 -- C Co, 19 Inf—Smithville Flats, NY
PHILLIPS. Elda Jr, PFC -- 501030 -- 34 Inf—Grandview, TX
PIERCE, Frederick E., PFC -- 501104 -- 34 Inf—Edgerton, WI
PIERCE, Leonard L. Jr, PVT—NA -- 34 Inf—Dubois, PA
PITRE, Charles D. Jr, PVT -- 501130 -- 34 Inf—Alexandria, LA
PITTMAN, Irvin Wilbur, CPL -- 501107 -- 21 Inf—Burlington, NJ
PLOTNER, Gerald R., PVT -- 510306 -- L Co, 21 Inf—Prospect, OH
POLKA, Francis, SGT -- 510111 -- C Co, 19 Inf—Melvindale, MI
POSEY, Harold T., PVT -- 501108 -- 21 Inf—Cleveland, OH
POSIVAK, Michael J. Jr, CPL -- 510101 -- 21 Inf—Philadelphia, PA
PRATT, Glen Leroy, PFC -- 501104 -- 34 Inf—Lowell, WA
PROVOST, Leonard E., PVT -- 510214 -- 21 Inf—Piercefield, NY

James Woods

R ---

RABORN, Cleon, SFC -- 501226 -- L Co, 21 Inf—Baconton, GA
RABOYE, Ronald, PVT -- 510101 -- 21 Inf—Alexandria, VA
RADANOVICH, Harry J., PFC -- 501120 -- 21 Inf—Rockford, IL
RAILLING, Thomas Earl, CPL -- 510114 -- 63 FA Bn—OH
RAINEY, William J., CPL -- 501100 -- -- Minden, WV
RANDALL, Elgin Vogala, CPL -- 510705 -- 21 Inf—Anniston, AL
RARICK, Rolan Deane, SGT -- 501101 -- 34 Inf—Hudson, MI
REED, Lee Bright, PFC -- 501130 -- 34 Inf—Organ Cave, WV
REED, Ray W., PVT -- 501126 -- 34 Inf—Detroit, MI
RHODES, Edward W., PFC -- 520100 -- G Co, 19 Inf—Tucson, AZ
RICKENBACH, Adam L., PFC -- 501104 -- 34 Inf—Reading, PA
RIVERA, Fernando Jr, PVT -- 501102 -- 34 Inf—Hilo, HI
RIVRI---, Dick, PFC -- 501105 -- 21 Inf–
ROBINSON, George, PVT -- 500912 -- 63 FA Bn—Pittsburg, PA
ROCKWELL, Clyde T., PFC -- 501122 -- 21 Inf—Hayden Lake, ID
ROGERS, Raymond Jr, PFC -- 500900 -- M Co, 34 Inf—Yalesville, CT
ROMO, Angel Peter, PVT -- 501104 -- I Co, 21 Inf—Whittier, CA
ROSE, Albert Eugene, PFC -- 501215 -- 21 Inf—West Frankfort, IL
ROTH, Bernard F., 1LT -- 511026 -- 11 FA Bn—Dayton, OH
ROY, Floyd Alexander, SGT -- 510703 -- 21 Inf—Cloquet, MN
RUDDELL, James C. Jr, 1LT -- 510121 -- Hq,1 Bn, 19 Inf—Ft
    Hamilton, WV
RUFENER, John F., PFC -- 501121 -- 34 Inf—South Gate, CA
RUSSELL, Gordon C., SGT -- 501230 -- 63 FA Bn—Caniesville, IL
RUSSELL, John W., SFC -- 501028 -- 34 Inf—Lawton, OK

S ---

SADDER, William, PFC -- 501110 -- 34 Inf—Altoona, PA
SALMON, Donald W., PVT -- 501022 -- 21 Inf—Maplewood, NJ
SAMMS, Jack Clinton, PFC -- 501113 -- G Co, 19 Inf—Ashland, KY
SANDERS, Gene A., PFC -- 501101 -- 34 Inf—Greenville, CA
SCHMOLLINGER, James E., PFC -- 501102 -- 21 Inf—Platte City, MO
SCHOULTHIES, George L., PVT -- 501130 -- 21 Inf—California, KY
SCHRECENGOST, Paul M., PVT -- 501104 -- 26 AAA Bn—
Mayport, PA

A Healing

SCHUMAN, John Henry, CPL -- 510301 -- C Co, 3 EngrC Bn—Ridgefield, NJ

SCOTT, Amos L., PFC -- 520100 -- 19 Inf—Rose Hill, VA

SCOTT, Floyd Edward, PFC -- 501111 -- A Co, 19 Inf—MO

SCOTT, Neil Roger, PVT -- 510105 -- Med Co, 34 Inf—Hillsboro, OH

SESLER, Philip K., PFC -- 501117 -- C Co, 3 EngrC Bn—Smock, PA

SEXTON, Talmage J., PFC -- 501103 -- 21 Inf—VA

SHACKELFORD, Howard J., PFC -- 501102 – 63 FA Bn—Oklahoma City, OK

SHARP, Raleigh T., CPL -- 501205 -- 63 FA Bn—Guthrie, OK

SHORTER, James W., PFC -- 501031 -- 63 FA Bn—Davis, SC

SIEGMUND, Earl V., CPL -- 501103 -- 21 Inf—Newark, OH

SIMS, Holly B., PVT -- 510202 -- 21 Inf—Wichita, KS

SIRMAN, Donald S., 1LT -- 510707 -- 35 FBS, **USAF**—Hartford, CT

SKEENS, Irvin K., PVT -- 510320 -- 34 Inf—Goldvein, VA

SKERO, Charles M., PFC -- 510622 -- B Co, 34 Inf—Mt Pleasant, PA

SKINNER, Kenneth L., PVT -- 510109 -- 34 Inf—Abingdon, IL

SMIRNOFF, CIV -- 500601 -- **W. Russian** –

SMITH, Billy E., PVT -- 501104 -- I Co, 21 Inf—AL

SMITH, George R., PFC -- 501212 -- L Co, 21 Inf—Whitehall, MT

SMITH, John D., MSG -- 510111 -- 34 Inf—Gastonia, GA

SMITH, Leonard J. Jr, CPL -- 510203 -- 7 Med Bn, 7 Div—Tampa, FL

SMITH, William L., PFC -- 510220 -- 21 Inf—York, PA

SMITHSON, Donald, CPL -- 501122 -- 21 Inf—Gaywood, MD

SPARKS, Donald D. Jr, CPL -- 501104 -- 52 FA Bn—Hawthorne, CA

SPECHT, Wilfred G., CPL -- 501204 -- 21 Inf—Saginaw, MI

SROGONCIK, George J., PFC -- 510108 -- 21 Inf—Mt Pleasant, PA

STALLINGS, Vernon D., PVT -- 501101 -- 21 Inf—Mooreston, NC

STANSBURY, William H. Jr, PFC -- 501102 -- 34 Inf—Kansas City, MO

STEELE, Clyde D., CPL -- 501210 -- 24 Rcn Co—Charles City, IA

STEPHENS, Robert D., PFC -- 510114 -- 52 FA Bn—Clayton, KS

STEWART, Robert Edwin, PFC -- 501226 -- L Co, 21 Inf—Detroit, MI

STOUT, Johnnie Oval, PFC -- 501114 -- F Co, 19 Inf—Old Hickory, TN

STRAWSER, Paul P., PFC -- 501122 -- 34 Inf—Ashley, IN

SUMNER, William G., CPL -- 501212 -- 21 Inf—Greer, SC

SUMPTER, Bill S., CPL -- 501107 -- C Co, 19 Inf—Kanokatto, MO

SUNSDAHL, Roy L., PVT -- 501204 -- C Co, 19 Inf—Cambridge, MN

SWANSON, Richard P., PVT -- 510212 -- 34 Inf—Enfield, MN

James Woods

SWEET, Richard L., PFC -- 501219 -- C Co, 19 Inf—Huntsville, TX
SWEITZER, William C., PFC -- 501111 -- 34 Inf—Altoona, PA
SZCZEPANSKI, Anthony A., PFC -- 501104 -- L Co, 21 Inf—McKees Rocks, PA

T ---

TATE, Hershel Leon, SGT -- 510112 -- 34 Inf—Beersheba Springs, TN
TAYLOR, William E., PVT -- 501122 -- 34 Inf—Greencastle, IN
TEIXEIRA, James Cunha, SFC -- 501121 -- 63 FA Bn—Los Angeles, CA
THOMPSON, Ronald L., PFC -- 500000 -- 21 Inf—IA
THOMSON, Keith Edward, ENS -- 510103 -- , **USNAF**—Macomb, IL
THORNTON, Cordus H., 1LT -- 501101 -- L Co, 34 Inf—Dallas, TX
TIERNAN, John J., PVT -- 500729 -- L Co, 21 Inf—New York, NY
TITUS, Robert Eli, PFC -- 501123 -- C Co, 19 Inf—Fairland, IN
TODD, Blanton, SGT -- 510203 -- 21 Inf—Orlando, FL
TOMASZEWSKI, Waclaw A., 2LT -- 510102 -- 34 Inf—MI
TORHAN, George, PVT -- 510527 -- 34 Inf—Ambridge, PA
TOTLAND, Mical M., PVT -- 501031 -- 34 Inf—Bronx, NY
TREXLER, Rayfield A., PFC -- 501102 -- 34 Inf—Breinigsville, PA
TROSS, Eugene F., PFC -- 501223 -- 21 Inf—St Louis, MO
TUGMAN, Richard J., PVT—NA -- 63 FA Bn—Chicago, IL
TYLER, Charles R., PFC -- 510614 -- L Co, 34 Inf—Reyno, AR

U ---

UNDERHILL, Virgil E., CPL -- 510805 -- 57 FA Bn, **7 Div**—Tampa, FL

V ---

VAN DEWERKER, Patrick W., PFC -- 501104 -- 34 Inf—Bryce Canyon, UT
VAN WINKLE, Calvin A., PVT -- 510216 -- 21 Inf—Ft Calhoun, NE
VANN, Harvey Thomas, MSG -- 510106 -- 21 Inf—Portland, OR
VANNOSDALL, Gilbert A., CPL -- 501121 -- , 1 Mar—Bronx, NY

A Healing

VARNER, Edmund Stanley, PVT -- 510205 -- 34 Inf—Summit, NJ
VARNEY, Basil Jr, PFC -- 500925 -- 34 Inf—Hardy, KY
VERCOLEN, Albert L., SGT -- 500720 -- 34 Inf—Rochester, NY
VIARS, James E., PFC -- 501127 -- 21 Inf—Baymeadow, VA
VILLEMONT, Fr. Paul, CIV -- 501111 -- French, **R. Cath priest** –
VINCENT, Albert A., PFC -- 501104 -- 21 Inf—Kearney, MO
VINCENT, William E.R., PFC -- 501220 -- 21 Inf—St Louis, MO

W ---

WAGONER, James C., PFC -- 501217 -- 34 Inf—Kannopolis, NC
WALTEN, Thomas, PFC -- 501104 -- 34 Inf—Bainbridge, NY
WANCOSKI, Frank P., PFC—NA -- 21 Inf—Dunmore, PA
WARD, Delmer R., PFC -- 501116 -- Hq,1 Bn, 19 Inf—Greenville, TN
WARREN, Everett, PFC -- 501028 -- Hq Co, 19 Inf—Meigs, GA
WARRICK, John E., CPL—NA—C Co, 19 Inf—PA
WENDLING, Ernest A., PVT -- 501104 -- 21 Inf—Chicago, IL
WILLIAMSON, Claud H., PVT -- 501112 -- L Co, 21 Inf—Weissport, PA
WILNER, William H., PFC -- 510601 -- 21 Inf—CA
WILSON, David H., PFC -- 501126 -- L Co, 21 Inf -- ------oha, IA
WILSON, Earl T., PVT -- 501212 -- 21 Inf—Cromwell, KY
WINTER, Gerald A., PFC -- 501103 -- A Co, 19 Inf—Berwick, PA
WISE, Arthur F., PVT -- 501122 -- C Co, 3 EngrC Bn—Pomeroy, OH
WOODRING, Raymond L., PFC -- 501102 -- 21 Inf—Waynesboro, PA
WRIGHT, Chester A., PFC -- 510113 -- L Co, 21 Inf—Battle Creek, MI

Y ---

YOST, Edward F., PFC -- 501102 -- A Co, 19 Inf -- -------ville, PA
YUHASZ, Tony F., PFC -- 501102 -- 19 Inf -- -------ville, MI

Z ---

ZAMORA, Anselmo, PFC -- 510224 -- 21 Inf—New Braunfels, TX
ZUVER, Robert L., PFC -- 501210 -- 21 Inf—Whittier, CA

James Woods

"Johnnie Johnson"

For the extreme danger involved in the three years of keeping the "**list**"; **Wayne "Johnnie" Johnson** was awarded the nations third highest award for valor, the Silver Star medal. He was once caught with the list and was nearly executed for keeping it, despite the danger to his life "Johnnie" continued keeping and adding to his list because "their parents or someone would want to know when they died". This very brave young Soldier left us in 2005, God bless you Johnnie.

James Woods

A Healing

"A Boy and His Journey" ******

Jimmie Joe is a natural born author.

Granted I have a special interest in the subject of this book, my father was killed in action in Korea, so being a child of a man who died before seeing him, this book makes it easier for me to understand what happened and why, and I thank Jimmie Joe so very much for giving me this gift. Unless you don't have a heart, you will be crying when you read this book, but it's so worth it. Awesome book, great work Jimmie Joe.

<u>**Cilia**</u> (ms.gulf coast usa)

"A Boy and His Journey"
"e-mail"

Jim,
I got your book in the mail this week and I couldn't put it down. You started at Taejon and that's where my war ended. I too, was able to suppress my feelings long enough to raise a family. After retirement, with time on my hands, they came back. I went to a few reunions and renewed some old friendships, however, I learned that large crowds annoy me. I started writing to several buddies after I learned about e-mail. You and I kept in touch for a long time but I've lost your address. I thought the earthquake you had may have put you out of business. Anyway, I hope you get this note. I got this address out of your book. Thanks again for sending it to me. I can relate to that time in our history. Please keep in touch *The 34th still lives in the hearts of those who served!* Stay well, Charlie

(Charlie my internet friend was severely wounded in July, 1950 at Taejon, Korea.) jimmie joe.

James Woods

"A Boy and His Journey"
"e-mail"

Dear Jim:

Thanks for the paper back version of your book. Mike brought it by the other night. I have started reading it. You write very well and, I can tell it comes from the heart and the gut. I know many of the combat veterans and other service men appreciate what effort you put out doing this book.

You've spent a lot of time on research and gut-wrenching thought to put all the poems together. We're proud of Jimmy Joe out here at Fishhook Junction. I still have my order in for the signed hardback copy, ok!

Ted,
fishhook junction, Alaska

"A Boy and His Journey" *****
A True Picture of War, and the real victims: June 16, 2002

Jimmie Joe does not write to entertain, he writes to tell exactly what War does to young men, and to those who live in War's path. If you can read this without tears, you must be from another planet! Every Vet who has seen action has vivid memories, this Vet not only describes the horror of war, but the rage and frustration that comes later when he learns of decisions that reveal betrayal and "ego-trips" that cause many deaths. I pray Jimmie Joe has finally obtained some peace with the memories.

joe-byrd,
Joe served in Korea as a Marine. Pennsylvania

A Healing

"love, War and Little Children" *****

Jim has written a fine book that will give anyone reading it a sense of what war means to each that answered the call to duty., it is a call that will last a lifetime! I salute Jim for having given his time again for us to learn about a world we are ignorant of. This book brings up front and center the effect of war on the ones we love. Thank you Jim.

cy st-amand
Homer, Alaska

"Love, War and Little Children" *****
Recommended Reading, January 7, 2002

"Shirljo" (OK USA)

Jimmie Joe's book of stories and poems is a must read for anyone who has friends or family that have gone to war. A very moving experience as told through the eyes of someone who was there. I feel that reading these stories helps me to better understand PTSD and the nightmares of war. I have not finished but will continue to read some as I can, it's hard to see through the tears. Welcome Home Jimmie!!

James Woods

"love, War and Little Children" *****
awakening

Don't look for a 'feel good' holly-wood script here. This is an emotional, gut level awakening of a man trying to come to terms with events thrust on him as a young man in the Korean War. The poetry is REAL, based on true hardship from overwhelming situations that can only be experienced when men and governments are on the 'killing fields'. Reading this book moves you a big step futher from innocence.

Bob (nwtrim@pobox.alaska.net), A reviewer, December 19

A Healing

TEXT OF THE KOREAN WAR ARMISTICE AGREEMENT
July 27, 1953

http://news.findlaw.com/hdocs/docs/korea/kwarmagr072753.html

Article III Arrangement Relating to Prisoners of War

51. The release and repatriation of all prisoners of war held in the custody of each side at the time this armistice agreement becomes effective shall be effected in conformity with the following provisions agreed upon by both sides prior to the signing of this armistice agreement.

(a) Within sixty (60) days after this agreement becomes effective each side shall, without offering any hindrance, directly repatriate and handed over in groups all those prisoners of war in its custody who insist on repatriation to the side to which they belonged at the time of capture. Repatriation shall be accomplished in accordance with the related provisions of this Article. In order to expedite the repatriation process of such personnel, each side shall, prior to the signing of the Armistice Agreement, exchange the total numbers, by nationalities, or personnel to be directly repatriated. Each group of prisoners of war delivered to the other side shall be accompanied by rosters, prepared by nationality, to include name, rank (if any) and internment or military serial number.

(b) Each side shall release all those remaining prisoners of war, who are not directly repatriated, from its military control and from its custody and hand them over to the Neutral Nations Repatriation Commission for disposition in accordance with the provisions in the

Annex hereto, "Terms of Reference for Neutral Nations Repatriation Commission."

(c) So that there may be no misunderstanding owing to the equal use of three languages, the act of delivery of a prisoner of war by one side to other side shall, for the purposes of the Armistice Agreement, be called "repatriation" in English, ( ) "Song Hwan" in Korean and ( ) "Ch'ien Fan" in Chinese, notwithstanding the nationality or place of residence of such prisoner of war.

52. Each side insures that it will not employ in acts of war in the Korean conflict any prisoner of war released and repatriated incident to the coming into effect of this armistice agreement.

53. All the sick and injured prisoners of was who insist upon repatriation shall be repatriated with priority. Insofar as possible, there shall be captured medical personnel repatriated concurrently with the sick and injured prisoners of war, so as to provide medical care and attendance enroute.

54. The repatriation of all of the prisoners of war required by Sub-paragraph 51 (a) hereof shall be completed within a time limit of sixty (60) days after this Armistice Agreement becomes effective. Within this time limit each side undertakes to complete repatriation of the above- mentioned prisoners of war in its custody at the earliest practicable time.

55. PANMUNJOM is designated as the place where prisoners of war will be delivered and received by both sides. Additional place(s) of delivery and reception of prisoners of war in the Demilitarized Zone may be designated, if necessary, by the Committee for Repatriation of Prisoners of War.

56.

(a) A committee for Repatriation of Prisoners of War is hereby established. It shall be composed of six (6) officers of field grade, three (3) of whom shall be appointed by the Commander-in-Chief, United Nations Command, and three (3) of whom shall be appointed jointly by the Supreme Commander of the Korean People's Army and the Commander of the Chinese

A Healing

People's Volunteers. This Committee shall, under the general supervision and direction of the Military Armistice Commission, be responsible for co-ordinating the specific plans of both sides for the repatriation of prisoners of war and for supervision the execution by both sides of all of the provisions of this Armistice Agreement relating to the repatriation of prisoners of war. It shall be the duty of this Committee to co-ordinate the timing of the arrival of prisoners of war at the place(s) of delivery and reception of prisoners of war from the prisoner of war camps of both sides; to make, when necessary, such special arrangements as may be required with regard to the transportation and welfare of sick and injured prisoners of war; to co-ordinate the work of the joint Red Cross teams, established in Paragraph 57 hereof, in assisting in the repatriation of prisoners of war; to supervise the implementation of the arrangements for the actual repatriation of prisoners of war stipulated in Paragraphs 53 and 54 hereof; to select, when necessary, additional place(s) of delivery and reception of prisoners of war; and to carry out such other related functions as are required for the repatriation of prisoners of war.

When unable to reach agreement on any matter relating to its responsibilities, the committee for Repatriation of Prisoners of War shall immediately refer such matter to the Military Armistice Commission for decision. The Committee for Repatriation of Prisoners of War shall maintain its headquarters in proximity to the headquarters of the Military Armistice Commission

(c) The Committee for Repatriation of Prisoners of War shall be dissolved by the Military Armistice Committee upon completion of the program of repatriation of prisoners of war.

57.

(a) Immediately after this Armistice Agreement becomes effective, joint Red Cross teams composed of representatives of the national Red Cross Societies of countries contributing forces to the United Nations Command on the one hand, and representatives of the of the Red Cross Society of the Democratic People's Republic of Korea and representatives of the Red Cross Society of the People's Republic of China on the other hand, shall be established. The joint Red Cross teams shall assist in the execution by both sides of those provisions of this Armistice Agreement relating to the repatriation of all the prisoners of war specified in Sub-paragraph 51 (a) hereof, who insist upon repatriation, by the performance of such humanitarian services as are necessary and desirable for the welfare of the prisoners of war. To accomplish this task, the joint Red Cross teams shall provide assistance in the delivering and receiving of prisoners of war by both sides at the place(s) of delivery and reception of prisoners of war, and shall visit the prisoner-of-war camps of both sides to comfort the prisoners of war.

(b) The joint Red Cross teams shall be organized as set forth below:

(1) One team shall be composed of twenty (20) members, namely, ten (10) representatives from the national Red Cross Societies of each side, to assist in the delivering and receiving of prisoners of war by both sides at the place(s) of delivery and reception of prisoners of war. The chairmanship of this team shall alternate daily between representative from the Red Cross Societies of the two sides. The work and services of this team shall be coordinated by the Committee for Repatriation of Prisoners of War.

2) One team shall be composed of sixty (60) members, namely, thirty (30) representatives from the national Red Cross Societies of each side, to visit the prisoner-of-war camps under

A Healing

the administration of the Korean People's Army and the Chinese People's Volunteers. This team may provide services to prisoners of war while en route from the prisoner of war camps to the place(s) of delivery and reception of prisoners of war. A representative of a Red Cross Society of the Democratic People's Republic of Korea or of the Red Cross Society of the People's Republic of China shall serve as chairman of this team.

(3) One team shall be composed of sixty (60) members, namely, thirty (30) representatives from the national Red Cross Societies of each side, to visit the prisoner of war camps under the administration of the United Nations Command. This team may provide services to prisoners of war while en route from the prisoner of war camps to the place(s) of delivery and reception of prisoners of war. A representative of a Red Cross Society of a nation contributing to forces to the United Nations Command shall serve as chairman of this team

(4) In order to facilitate the functioning of each joint Red Cross team, sub-teams composed of not less than two (2) members from this team, with an equal number of representatives from each side, may be formed as circumstances require.

(5) Additional personnel such as drivers, clerks, and interpreters, and such equipment as may be required by the joint Red Cross teams to perform their missions, shall be furnished by the Commander of each side to the team operating in the territory under his military control.

(6) Whenever jointly agreed upon by the representatives of both sides on any joint Red Cross team, the size of such team may be increased or decreased, subject to confirmation by the committee for Repatriation of Prisoners of War.

(c) The Commander of each side shall co-operate fully with the joint Red Cross teams in the performance of their functions, and undertakes to insure the security of the personnel of the Joint Red Cross team in the area under his military control. The Commander of each side shall provide such logistic, administrative, and communications facilities as may be required by the team operating in the territory under his military control.

(d) The joint Red Cross teams shall be dissolved upon completion of the program of repatriation of all of the prisoners of war specified in Sub-paragraph 51 (a) hereof, who insist upon repatriation.

58. (a) The Commander of each side shall furnish to the Commander of the other side as soon as practicable, but not later than ten (10) days after this Armistice Agreement becomes effective, the following information concerning prisoners of war:

(1) Complete data pertaining to the prisoners of war who escaped since the effective date of the data last exchanged.

(2) Insofar as practicable, information regarding name, nationality, rank, and other identification data, date and cause of death, and place of burial, of those prisoners of war who died while in his custody.

(b) If any prisoners of war escape or die after the effective date of the supplementary information specified above, the detaining side shall furnish to the other side, through the Committee for Repatriation of Prisoners of War, the data pertaining thereto in

A Healing

accordance with the provisions of Sub-paragraph 58 (a) hereof. Such data shall be furnished at ten-day intervals until the completion of the program of delivery and reception of prisoners of war.

(c) Any escaped prisoner of war who returns to the custody of the detaining side after the completion of the program of delivery and reception of prisoners of war shall be delivered to the Military Armistice Commission for disposition.

59.

(a) All civilians who, at the time this Armistice Agreement become effective, are in territory under the military control of the Commander-in-Chief, United Nations Command, and who, on 24 June 1950, resided north of the Military Demarcation Line established in this Armistice Agreement shall, if they desire to return home, be permitted and assisted by the Commander-in-Chief, United Nations Command, to return to the area north of the military Demarcation Line; and all civilians who, at the time this Armistice Agreement becomes effective, are in territory under the military control of the Supreme Commander of the Korean People's Army and the Commander of the Chinese People's Volunteers, and who on 24 June 1950, resided south of the Military Demarcation Line established in this Armistice Agreement shall, if they desire to return home, be permitted and assisted by the Supreme Commander of the Korean People's Army and the Commander of the Chinese People's Volunteers to return to the area south Military Demarcation Line. The Commander of each side shall e responsible for publicizing widely throughout the territory under his military control the contents of the provisions of this Sub-paragraph, and for calling upon the appropriate civil authorities to give necessary guidance and assistance to all such civilians who desire to return home.

James Woods

(b) All civilians of foreign nationality who, at the time this Armistice Agreement becomes effective, are in territory under the military control of the Supreme Commander of the Korean People's Army and the Commander of the Chinese People's Volunteers shall if they desire to proceed to territory under the military control of the Commander-in-Chief, United Nations command, be permitted and assisted to do so; all civilians of foreign nationality who, at the time this Armistice Agreement becomes effective, are in territory under the military control of the Commander-in- Chief, United Nations Command, shall, if they desire to proceed to territory under the military Control of the Supreme Commander of the Korean People's Army and the Commander of the Chinese People's Volunteers, be permitted and assisted to do so. The Commander of each side shall be responsible for publicizing widely throughout the territory under his military control of contents of the provisions of this sub-paragraph, and for calling upon the appropriate civil authorizes to give necessary guidance and assistance to all such civilians of foreign nationality who desire to proceed to territory under the military control of the Commander of the other side.

(c) Measures to assist in the return of civilians provided for in Sub-paragraph 59 (a) hereof and the movement of civilians provided for in Sub-paragraph 59 (b) hereof shall be commenced by both sides as soon as possible after this Armistice Agreement becomes effective.

(d)

> **(1)** A Committee for Assisting the Return of Displace Civilians is hereby established. It shall be composed of four (4) officers of field grade, two (2) of whom shall be appointed jointly by the Commander-in-Chief, United Nations Command, and two (2) of whom shall be appointed jointly by the Supreme Commander

A Healing

of the Korean People's Army and the Commander of the Chinese People's Volunteers. This committee shall, under the general supervision and direction of the Military Armistice Commission, be responsible for coordinating the specific plans of both sides for assistance to the return of the above-mentioned civilians. It shall be the duty of this Committee to make necessary arrangements, including those of transportation, for expediting and coordinating the movement of the above-mentioned civilians; to select the crossing point(s) through which the above-mentioned civilians will cross the Military Demarcation Line; to arrange for security at the crossing point(s); and to carry out such other functions as are required to accomplish the return of the above-mentioned civilians.

When unable to reach agreement on any matter relating to its responsibilities, the Committee for Assisting the return of Displaced Civilians shall immediately refer such matter to the Military Armistice Commission for decision. The Committee for assisting the Return of Displaced Civilians shall maintain its headquarters in proximity to the headquarters of the Military Armistice Commission.

(2) The Committee for Assisting the Return of Displaced Civilians shall be dissolved by the Military Armistice Commission upon fulfillment of its mission.

Credit—Coalition of Families of Korean & cold war
pow/mias

Background of Korean War POW/MIA Issue

The Korean War ended in July of 1953. The Chinese had controlled U.N. prisoners and were primarily responsible for accounting for them. POWs were returned throughout that summer during Operations Little and Big Switch. In the end, there were 8,217 Americans who did not come home and who were not accounted for. The U.S. government ("USG") was indignant at the time, citing various sources of information that indicated a grossly insufficient accounting by the Communists.

http://www.coalitionoffamilies.org/korean_issue.html

A Healing

About the author, James Joseph Woods,

JIMMY JOE --- "BOY", THE AUTHOR WHEN HE WAS YOUNG, A NAIVE farm "Boy", a skipper of schooling for fishing. Born October 11, 1930.

"Old Gent" --- A dog "Boy" loved throughout his childhood (and still does), a wondrous dog, a healing dog. I miss "Old Gent".

jimmy joe --- My first love Helen's nickname when she was a little tike, I have no idea why, she was a real woman (long deceased), who completely stole my heart.

jimmy joe --- My little Son who died in Nineteen fifty-four, a Dandy, happy "Boy".

I lost my Wife in 1966 and for the next sixteen years I raised our children. The late Sixties and Seventies were rough on a papa trying to raise six Daughters and a Son as times had definitely changed. I regret I never remarried; I should have given the Kids a loving Mother as a balance and an example of what a marriage should be. The observing of love between a husband and wife, the visual kindness, caring and understanding are vital to offspring picking the right mate.

My times of real contentment have been when my Children and Grandchildren were small, holding them as I sang, walking with them while they held my finger. Showing them the wonders of nature, hearing all their "whys" and not being able to answer most as it seemed to just bring another "why".

Now I have Great Grandchildren for sharing these treasured times. Catch those fish in places wild? My lord blessed me; Alaska has been a great place to live. I am thankful I moved here forty years ago. I love this land. I love her Oceans, Mountains, Wildness and the Peace I have found while fishing her waters. I've seen the Northern Lights rippling across the entire sky in displays of shimmering colors only God could mix, leaving me in awe I still recall, awe I still feel. Alaska, my Alaska is a wondrous land, a healing land in a way.

James Woods,
Fishhook junction, Alaska -- Oakland, Arkansas

James Woods

James Joseph Woods, Age 21, 1952

Printed in the United States
62149LVS00002B/85-111